MANAGING SOCIAL POLICY

edited by

John Clarke, Allan Cochrane and Eugene McLaughlin

SAGE Publications
London · Thousand Oaks · New Delhi

First published 1994

 SAGE Publications Ltd
6 Bonhill Street
London EC2A 4PU

SAGE Publications Inc
2455 Teller Road
Thousand Oaks, California 91320

SAGE Publications India Pvt Ltd
32, M-Block Market
Greater Kailash - I
New Delhi 110 048

British Library Cataloguing in Publication data

A catalogue record for this book is available from the British
Library.

ISBN 0 8039 7768 9
ISBN 0 8039 7769 7 (pbk)

Library of Congress catalog card number 94–065826

Typeset by Type Study, Scarborough
Printed in Great Britain by Redwood Books,
Trowbridge, Wiltshire

Contents

Notes on Contributors

Alan Clarke is Director of Research for the Business School and a member of the Centre for Leisure and Tourism Studies at the University of North London. He has researched and published extensively in the fields of leisure and tourism.

John Clarke is Senior Lecturer in Social Policy at the Open University. He is the author of *New Times and Old Enemies: Essays on Cultural Studies and America* (1991) and co-author, with Allan Cochrane and Carol Smart, of *Ideologies of Welfare* (1987). He is also the editor of *A Crisis in Care?* (Sage, 1993) and, with Allan Cochrane, of *Comparing Welfare States* (Sage, 1993).

Allan Cochrane is Senior Lecturer in Urban Studies and Dean of the Faculty of Social Sciences at the Open University. He is the author of *Whatever Happened to Local Government?* (1993) and co-editor, with James Anderson, of *Politics in Transition* and *A State of Crisis* (1989). He also edited, with John Clarke, *Comparing Welfare States* (Sage, 1993).

Ross Fergusson is a staff tutor in social science at the Open University. He was previously staff tutor in the school of education, working on courses in the sociology of education and initial teacher education. His current interests include developments in education policy in the context of public and social policy and school leavers' transitions at the age of sixteen.

Norman Flynn is a research fellow at the London School of Economics and Political Science, where he also runs the Public Sector Management Programme. He has been a lecturer at the London Business School and the University of Birmingham. He is the author of *Public Sector Management* (1993) and co-author, with R. Common and E. Mellon, of *Managing Public Service: Competition and Decentralisation* (1992).

June Greenwell is a registered nurse attached to both the University of Lancaster and the University of Bristol. She is co-editor, with Sylvia Walby, of *Medicine and Nursing: Professions in a Changing Health Service* (Sage, 1994).

Mary Langan is Lecturer in Social Policy at the Open University. She is general editor of the Routledge social policy series, *The State of Welfare*. She is also co-editor, with Phil Lee, of *Radical Social Work Today* (1989) and, with Lesley Day, of *Women, Oppression and Social Work* (1992).

Tom Ling is Senior Lecturer in Politics at Anglia Polytechnic University. He is also a director of the Centre for Citizenship Development and is currently working on the relationship between managerial styles and political strategies.

Eugene McLaughlin is Lecturer in Criminology and Social Policy at the Open University. His previous publications include, with E. Cashmore, *Out of Order: Policing Black People* (1991). He is the editor, with Rudi Dallos, of *Social Problems and the Family* (Sage, 1993).

John Muncie is Senior Lecturer in Criminology and Social Policy at the Open University. He is the author of *Systems of Justice* (1983), *The Trouble with Kids Today: Youth Crime in Post-War Britain* (1984) and co-editor, with Richard Sparks, of *Imprisonment: European Perspectives* (1991) as well as articles on juvenile justice and criminal justice reform.

Janet Newman is Lecturer in Public Policy and Strategy at the Institute of Local Government Studies, University of Birmingham. She is co-editor, with Kathy Itzin, of *Gender and Organizational Change*.

Sylvia Walby is Professor of Sociology at the University of Bristol. Her previous publications include *Restructuring: Place, Class and Gender; Patriarchy at Work* and *Theorizing Patriarchy*. She is co-editor, with June Greenwell, of *Medicine and Nursing: Professions in a Changing Health Service* (Sage, 1994).

Acknowledgements

We would like to thank all the contributors for the speed and enthusiasm with which they have worked on this project and particularly for taking part in the two workshops held at the Open University which helped to shape the final outcome. We are also grateful to the Applied Social Sciences discipline for funding the two workshops.

Both Juliette Cowan and Ann Boomer helped to prepare the final typescript and we are grateful to them for doing so. Sue Lacey provided both secretarial and organizational support throughout and also prevented the editors from engaging headless chicken mode too often. Our thanks are due to her and to everyone who helped to make the production of this book an unusually pleasant process. This includes Stephen Barr at Sage whose enthusiasm for the book has remained undimmed despite our best efforts.

John Clarke, Allan Cochrane, Eugene McLaughlin

Introduction: Why Management Matters

John Clarke, Allan Cochrane and Eugene McLaughlin

During the past decade the rationale, organizational infrastructure and delivery of social policy in Britain have undergone radical transformation. Academic analysis of the forms and processes of restructuring has also undergone notable shifts. In the beginning there was deep pessimism. During the 1980s an orthodoxy quickly emerged which claimed that the old welfare regime, what was commonly referred to as the Keynesian welfare state, was in terminal crisis. Some social policy commentators argued forcefully that Britain, under a hegemonic neo-conservative administration, was shifting rapidly and irreversibly towards a North American-style residual welfare regime, in which 'promises' of full employment and universalist welfare provision were being replaced by privatized arrangements and minimal public service provision (see Krieger, 1986; Johnson, 1990; Mishra, 1990). More recently rather different and more optimistic conclusions have been drawn. Pierson (1991) has argued that there was never really a crisis, at least in the sense of that the 1980s did not witness massive cuts in state social expenditure. While noting important shifts in patterns of spending and their differential impact on different groups, the comprehensive survey of British welfare undertaken by Hills and his colleagues also emphasizes the continued stability of levels of provision (Hills, 1990). Le Grand has suggested that the welfare system has proved itself to be remarkably resilient, paradoxically making the success of the main project of the neo-conservatives in restructuring British industry and freeing the labour market easier to achieve (Le Grand, 1990; Le Grand and Bartlett, 1993). According to these analysts, therefore, reports of the death of the old welfare regime have been much exaggerated.

And yet something has clearly happened. The 'welfare state' is not the same organizational entity that was developed in the immediate post-war decades, even if levels (and patterns) of welfare spending have changed less than one might have expected from party political rhetoric (to which, with hindsight, rather more credence was paid in the academic and critical literature than was ever justified). Not only may similar overall levels of expenditure mask quite distinctively separate experiences of different groups, particularly because of demographic shifts and the maintenance of high levels of unemployment since the late 1970s, but changes in the ways in which the welfare system functions may also imply changing power relations within it. Key themes in the emergent world(s) of welfare include:

1   a new emphasis on market approaches, as guiding principles, expressed in initiatives such as compulsory competitive tendering, contractualization, the construction of internal markets (with 'producers', 'providers' and 'choice') and a cultural shift to defining welfare services users as customers and citizen-consumers who have their 'rights' secured through citizen's charters (where competitive markets cannot be created there has been a remarkable search for market surrogates, in the form of quasi-markets with quasi-competition and quasi-customers);

2   the emergence of forms of welfare pluralism or 'mixed economies' of service provision and funding, which are not simply reducible to market-influenced approaches, but imply a complex fragmentation and the development of diverse forms of 'outsourcing' and blurred forms of 'partnership' between different parts of the reconfigured state, newly formed 'independent' agencies, commercial providers, not-for-profit agencies and the informal networks;

3   the search for more efficient and more responsive forms of service delivery, involving the organizational and spatial relocation of policy decisions away from conventional national and local government decision-making forums, which is often expressed in the language of devolution, decentralization, empowerment, enabling and the flattening of hierarchies;

4   a complex process of labour force restructuring, with the deregulation of employment relationships producing sharper and highly gendered distinctions between core, periphery and subcontracted and casual labour, and changes involving reskilling and deskilling;

5   the installation of new forms of organizational accountability, with 'the dead costs' of political and bureau-professional accountability being replaced by transparent organizational/departmental/team performance indicators and 'benchmarking' and individualized appraisal systems, renewable contracts, incentives and sanctions.

Very often these changes have been explained and understood through the prism of Thatcherism, or in terms which simply emphasize the process of recommodification – the decline of the state sector and the growth of privatization (Johnson, 1990; Marsh and Rhodes, 1992). While such forms of analysis are helpful in highlighting some aspects of the new arrangements, we believe that they tend to leave writers endlessly revisiting the 1980s, viewing the process of change as being completed, either confirming the success of the Thatcherite political project or proving its failure. We believe that such a reading fails to grasp the key processes of change which underpin the present reconfiguration of social policy in the 1990s. One of the key arguments developed throughout this book is that to produce an adequate level of understanding of the changes it is necessary to recognize, first, the degree of complexity and diversity of the *ongoing reconceptualization and restructuring of the state* itself and the relationship between the two and, second, what *links* the different innovations. As each chapter in this book indicates, change has tended to be developed through and supported by an elevated and enhanced role for new forms of public management. We are not just talking about the appointment of managers or the adoption of private sector management discourses and techniques. What is taking place, we would argue, is a deeper ideological process of managerialization which is transforming relationships of power, culture, control and accountability. In this sense managerialization is a dynamic, transformative process which cuts across the domain of social policy, 'unlocking' the old welfare settlement and making the quest for a definitive political reading of the new arrangements a problematic endeavour.

The process of managerialization

It is generally agreed that there are two important dimensions to the role that management has played within the reform of the public sector. The first concerns the 'strategic' sense of management, that is the way in which it is concerned with providing central leadership and direction for organizations. A key feature of the new managerialism (in the private as well as the public sector) is the stress that it places on the 'heroic' and 'bold' role of senior managers in inspiring and enthusing workforces with a broader understanding of and commitment to the 'missions' of the organizations for which they work. The second, equally important aspect of management is the operational emphasis on the devolution of responsibility, which implies an increased importance for local management in 'downsized' organizational settings and requires a closeness to and interaction with customers. In a sense, this openness to consumers is the other side of the 'strategic' coin, since it points to a containing process of interaction between different levels of organization so that it may, in turn, influence wider strategies. Consequently, we would argue that managerialism is the connecting thread linking markets, partnerships, an emphasis on customers and the recomposition of the labour force. In certain respects, 'management' is what the public sector learns from the business world, but it also, perhaps more significantly, increasingly links the two worlds by offering solutions to comparable problems faced.

With some important exceptions, such as Pollitt (1990), Hoggett (1991), Hood (1991) and Taylor-Gooby and Lawson (1993), within social policy this process of managerialization has generally been discussed in ways which fail to grasp its meaning and significance. Where there has been engagement with the changes taking place, supporters of the changes present and discuss them in terms which suggest they represent an alternative (usually superior) form of technical rationality to that of the welfare professions and the public administration tradition. The emphasis in these texts is prescriptive, 'teaching' public sector managers how to change their practice (see, for example, Metcalfe and Richards, 1990; Willcocks and Harrow, 1992). The main critical view of the new public management, on the other hand, has dismissed it as little more than a 'fad' or an ideological smokescreen behind which disinvestment, privatization and increased exploitation of labour are hidden (see, for example, Johnson, 1990). This leaves such critics in the uncomfortable position of having to defend the 'old' arrangements (and traditional bureau-professional control) of which, in the past, they themselves have frequently been the harshest critics. In contrast, this book is organized around the proposition that the process of managerialization is more profound than either of these versions allows. We view it as being neither merely a rational information-processing/decision-making black box nor a smokescreen which conceals more significant events. Instead, it is argued that managerialization constitutes the means through which the structure and culture of public services are being recast. In doing so it seeks to introduce new orientations, remodels existing relations of power and affects how and where social policy choices are made. This is why the new public sector management matters.

Questions of management

Each chapter in the book details a particular story of managerialization which not only utilizes specific chronologies, time frames and articulations, but also grapples with wider debates about the nature of managerial change in the public sector. Although each author has her/his own view of the significance and meaning of managerialism there is general agreement that we need to keep a series of themes in mind regarding the overall features of the process.

Which managerialism?

There are a number of different 'managerialisms' at work in the restructuring of the public sector. Like other commentators, we have found it useful to distinguish between Taylorist or neo-Taylorist approaches on the one hand and 'new wave management' (variously called post-bureaucratic management, the 'excellence' approach and the new human resource management) on the other. This distinction reflects the profoundly differing views of organizations, management roles and employee motivation that underlie the approaches. The Taylorist or neo-Taylorist approaches deriving from Frederick Taylor's efforts to establish 'scientific management' are primarily focused on the strict control, regulation and supervision of work processes by managers. They rest on an assumption that employees are fundamentally recalcitrant and productivity improvements can only be achieved by the direct and continuous exercise of management control. 'New wave management' has a more optimistic view of employee motivation and has tended to emphasize the importance of managers 'enabling' or even 'liberating' the creative and productive potential of their workforces, while developing commitment to corporate 'missions'. Despite these differences, both are united in their view of management as the fundamental coordinating force in organizations and the necessity of managers being free to manage.

Although there is some value in distinguishing different managerialisms and paying attention to their different genealogies, assumptions and practices, it is also important to remember that both of these approaches – and a variety of hybrid offshoots – are embedded in the present process of managerialization. Sometimes they simply coexist in an uncomfortable combination. At others, they may be directed at different groupings of the workforce within the same organization.

The political meaning of managerialization

It is difficult to read managerialization politically not just because it represents itself as being 'apolitical' and technical. Managerialism in the public sector has a confused and contradictory political history. It has a respectable pedigree in left approaches ranging from Fabianism through to new urban left thinking on urban governance in the early 1980s. Indeed, it could be argued that the latter pioneered many of the ideas that became more generally politically acceptable in the late 1980s and 1990s. Consequently, because of its apparent capacity to be rearticulated within various political positions, managerialization is likely to outlive neo-conservative administrations.

A new order?

Managerialization does not, in itself, constitute a new settlement. It does not conform to such static, conservative conceptualizations. By their very nature the particular clusters of managerialism presently taking hold in the public sector are dynamic and in motion. There is no crude rupture with the past, just wave after wave of managerialization. This process, by very definition, is radical, unfinished and destabilizing. There is every indication that we are witnessing a process of unravelling and fragmentation which will make a re-unification project virtually impossible. This is why it is so difficult to slow its momentum or disrupt its logics and why, we would argue, there can be no going back to the old welfare order.

A contested terrain?

Nevertheless, these defining characteristics also produce new sites of conflict and generate new contradictions. Consequently as a process and a strategy, managerialism's impact is uneven and remains open to contestation, negotiation and resistance. The public sector remains different from the private sector. Social policy decision making continues to be a deeply political process and in practice the new managerialism has made many of those decision-making processes apparent. It is this transparency, and indeed the resilience of the overall framework, that ensures complex forms of negotiation at both the organizational and political levels. Management has been centrally involved in such struggles, surrendering, in certain instances, concessions to the workforce, the public and interest groups in order to protect the new reform agenda and, in others, attempting to wrest further autonomy from the politicians and organizational opponents. The resilience of the old order also, ironically, provides the necessary justification for the introduction of new waves of managerialization.

Questions of power

The new managerialism operates to redefine power relations within social policy along two principal axes. The first of these is concerned with the redefinition of relations with 'clients', 'consumers', 'users', 'customers', 'citizens' and even 'communities'. In doing so it helps to undermine previous models of social welfare in which professionals tended to have the responsibility for identifying and representing the interests of 'client' groups, the implication being that professionals always knew better than their 'clients'. But the question which remains is the extent to which old definitional forms have simply been replaced by new ones whose impact is similar. Who now defines needs? In certain versions it looks as if the new managers take on this role, simply replacing the professionals. Put crudely, reference to 'customers' may simply allow managers the freedom to make a rhetorical claim to have their interests at heart in their conflicts with the staff whom they manage, without the actual position of the 'customers' necessarily being improved. Redefining those for whom welfare organizations are responsible as 'customers' may make it easier to manage staff from above. The result may be that the 'needs' and 'demands' of customers are essentially defined by managers.

The twin promises of 'empowerment' and 'enabling', on the other hand, suggest that those groups traditionally excluded from the policy-making process – such as those reliant on forms of welfare support, who are disproportionately women and members of minority ethnic groups – may be able to have some influence over those delivering services or allocating resources. It may even suggest that, in certain instances, non-state community and user groups will be given access to their own resources, whose use they can determine themselves. The extent to which new opportunities are opening up, or being closed down, in practice, is an issue that is debated in each of the chapters.

The second axis of change involves a redefinition of the public sector workforce, principally because of the ways in which managerialism challenges existing assumptions about professional structures. The old professions are weakened by a meta-narrative which is at the same time able to incorporate and undermine them. The new managerialism is highly critical of the ways in which human resources in organizations are wasted by the inflexible boundaries of professional practice. Challenging the old structures might be expected to encourage substantial changes by questioning the arrangements which have tended to ensure that white men reach the top in most social welfare organizations. It might be expected that new opportunities are being opened up for those who have in the past been excluded by the 'objective' rules of professionalism. It has certainly been argued forcibly that the new world opens up real possibilities for advancement within organizations on the basis of merit rather than gender or 'race'. Indeed, some have claimed that women are better suited to be managers of the new flexible, open organizations in which domineering – or 'macho' – managerial styles are said to have less of a future. On the other hand, it is within the welfare state that 'caring' professions with large numbers of women members are concentrated. Some women have been able to gain the necessary credentials which give them access to secure professional employment, which is not so easily accessible in the private sector. By undermining such professional arrangements, the new managerialism may be undermining this status too. In other words, potential gains at a senior level, themselves possibly illusory, may have as their corollary, significant losses at the other levels of the system. These important issues are explored in more detail by Janet Newman in the final part of this book.

The structure of the book

Managing Social Policy includes general chapters about the process of managerialization as well as chapters exploring the impact of managerialism in specific fields of social policy. We believe that the interaction and linkage between these two elements strengthen and reinforce the arguments which run through the book, as the points made in the general chapters are illustrated and developed in the more specifically focused ones, and the points made in the social policy oriented chapters are generalized in the others. Although we make no claims to provide an exhaustive survey of management in all fields of social policy, we believe that the changes we discuss are of general significance. The following chapter, by Janet Newman and John Clarke, sets the overall framework of the book by exploring the political, ideological and theoretical significance of the managerialization of the public sector. Its conclusions help set up the arguments of the later chapters by establishing the wider context of managerial change.

Later we return to consider some of the features of the emerging world of social policy, which are rarely explored effectively in general discussions of management, when Janet Newman (in Chapter 9) looks specifically at the gendered nature of organizational reform by evaluating women's experience of the changing nature of managerial work and the new organizational structures and cultures in which it is situated. This chapter critically considers the extent to which new opportunities for women are being created by the restructuring, pointing to the ambiguity of the process and arguing for the need for conscious political intervention if more than cosmetic change is to be achieved. The following chapter, by Norman Flynn, assesses both the various facets of the present managerial restructuring and the likely future prospects for public sector management. He sets out a series

of options which need to be considered carefully because of the ways in
which they are likely to shape our experience of the welfare state in the
future. He concludes by assessing the prospects for developing alternative
forms of public sector management which can both take account of the new
realities and enable commitment to be the basis of control and future
development of public services. In the final chapter the editors consider the
overall impact of the new managerialism on the public sector, asking
whether there has been a 'cultural revolution' and what its lasting impact is
likely to be.

The substantive chapters take on a range of social policy areas which are
somewhat more broadly conceived than conventional definitions allow. So,
for example, we have included chapters considering the broader demands of
local government for a strategic management role, and others which focus
on the restructuring of leisure services and the criminal justice system. In
part this choice reflects our desire to detail just how thorough the process of
managerialization has been, but it also reflects our view that the traditional
boundaries of 'social policy' tend to be somewhat arbitrarily defined.

As the chapter on local government by Allan Cochrane (Chapter 7)
makes clear, moving outside of the traditional social policy framework is
important because it is becoming increasingly apparent that welfare needs to
be understood as being dependent on a wider set of relationships, for
example, being explicitly linked to forms of local economic well-being and
economic regeneration. The rise of managerialism implies a move beyond
conventional models of welfare because it questions the assumptions of
welfare professionals which focus on specialist forms of service delivery, as
well as questioning traditional notions of local democratic accountability.
Instead, accountability is increasingly 'delivered' through new 'non-
political' arrangements, the monitoring of contracts, quality management
and fragmented charter-specified relationships with customers. It is in this
context of significant changes in the nature and scope of local governance
that a discussion of the new claims of strategic management competence by
local government and its attempted self-redefinition and re-legitimation as
'enabling' or community government rather than as a service delivery
system becomes important.

In the case of leisure provision, although public responsibilities and
provision extend back into the nineteenth century, and the government has
recently see fit to appoint a 'Minister of Fun', leisure has traditionally
somehow seemed to belong to a more frivolous world of voluntary and freely
chosen activity than to the serious world of welfare. Beveridge had little to
say about such activities! In the world of the 1990s, however, as Alan
Clarke's chapter (Chapter 8) confirms, looking at leisure services is much
more central to debates about social policy, both because of the early links to
market-style arrangements, but also because they relate to the broader
conceptions of welfare which are emerging. The development of international leisure (and conference) facilities has been the cornerstone of a
prestige – 'civic renaissance' – model of urban regeneration which took hold
in Britain during the 1980s and early 1990s. Post-industrial provincial cities

(Glasgow, Birmingham, Sheffield, Manchester) now vie with each other to re-present themselves as centres of European culture and compete with other global cities for the 'honour' of holding major sporting events, such as the Olympics. Success in these endeavours will, it is claimed, attract much-needed public and private infrastructural investment which will, in turn, regenerate the local economy, produce local prosperity and enhance the quality of life and individual well-being.

The circumstances of the criminal justice system are different again. For the most part, analysis of this particular part of the public sector has hovered uneasily between criminology and socio-legal studies. But given the continuing concern about inadequate community safety, debates about the causes of crime are being increasingly connected to wider social policies and effective solutions are being explicitly framed within a managerially based multi-agency framework. At first it seemed that the commitment of successive neo-conservative administrations to spending more on law and order while cutting back elsewhere seemed to guarantee the protection of the criminal justice system from the changes sweeping through other areas of the public sector. Criminal justice professionals, who were the beneficiaries of generous government patronage, viewed themselves as bystanders in the reform process. More recently, however, as Eugene McLaughlin and John Muncie argue (Chapter 6), radical changes, comparable to those executed in other parts of the public sector, have been implemented right across the system. The likely outcome of this 'silent revolution' is the shift from a relatively unmanaged and unregulated system to a much more tightly managed but essentially mixed economy of law and order than anyone could ever have imagined in 1979.

The other chapters concentrate on areas which will be more familiar to students of social policy, since they focus on the Benefits Agency (Chapter 2), the health service (Chapter 3), education (Chapter 5) and personal social services (Chapter 4). These chapters highlight the different organizational forms taken by the changes, but also point to some of the shared features across different sectors of the welfare state, particularly as reflected in the managerial discourses underlying them. As Tom Ling notes, the Benefits Agency was set up in the wake of extensive debates within the civil service as one among many 'autonomous' agencies, breaking up traditional hierarchies and forms of accountability. It appeared to offer new hope to those it was supposed to serve with promises of reduced bureaucracy and more flexible styles of management, more clearly focused on the needs of its 'customers' (that is, those in receipt of, or entitled to, benefits). However, in practice the outcomes have been much more ambivalent. This chapter also details how the new managerialism is fundamental to the social management of the long-term unemployed and the regulation of the wider labour market.

In a sense, the National Health Service was already an 'agency' with its own chief executive, long before the reforms of the 1980s. Here the emphasis was on breaking up centralized structures and introducing market reforms of resource allocation. In doing so it has been claimed that a further intention was to undermine the traditional dominance of senior medical professionals and to challenge existing internal hierarchies of power. Sylvia Walby and June Greenwell explore the consequences of the changes for those working in the health service by asking whether workers and consumers have been empowered by the managerial changes. After discussing the reasons for the bitter struggles over the various waves of reform, the chapter points to the importance of recognizing that different forms of managerialization have been used for different sections of the workforce. As a result, a series of complex and unfinished occupational re-orderings is taking place in which certain sections of the workforce have enhanced their status while others have been sidelined by the reform process.

In education the reforms have begun to break up local education authorities, while apparently strengthening the position of the Department for Education (through funding arrangements and the fostering of a national curriculum). At local level, as Ross Fergusson explains, the local management of schools and the gradual growth of grant-maintained schools has transformed the position of school governing bodies, headteachers and the management of individual schools. In this case, as in the others, management is expected to deliver higher standards as well as lower costs, but fragmentation has also required the new managers to construct their own locally based networks. Throughout this chapter, we are made aware of the unintended contradictions and outcomes produced by this particular reform agenda, and the impact that they are having not only on educational provision but the organization of the labour process within schools.

Mary Langan and John Clarke remind us that at the beginning of the 1980s it was not clear whether personal social services such as social work would survive the government's ideological attacks. What has happened instead is that the internal and external environments of social work have been reorganized and the chapter notes the extent to which the emphasis of the reforms has, from the start, been explicitly based on working through networks. The old arrangements have been effectively challenged with the 'promise' of care management through community care, linking the public, private, not-for-profit and informal sectors, and child protection through forms of joint inter-agency working and the participation of parents in child protection conferences. In this context, social work becomes the management of others and of systems through which a range of organizations have to work. The emergent local mixed economy of care involves an extensive process of inter-organizational management.

In their different ways we believe that the individual chapters reinforce and reflect and explore the dominant themes of the book. We hope that they succeed both in highlighting the impact of managerialization on quite distinct areas of the public sector and in forcing us to think about the particular ways managerialism is, itself, reshaped to fit with the demands of those different areas while still retaining its core messages. They also illustrate the ideological power of the new management across the field of social policy, as well as helping us to delineate some of its key features as they are worked out in practice.

Conclusion

We are highly conscious that this book aims to explore issues which have not traditionally been a focus of attention either in traditional social policy or for those undertaking the study and teaching of management in the public sector. The former have tended to focus on the specifics of particular policy areas, while the latter have tended to produce more or less universal templates supposedly suitable for implementation across the public sector. We are interested both in exploring change across the field of social policy and in critically examining the implications of the new managerialism. Because of this, as readers will have gathered from our previous discussion, we are clear that the book does not represent a final and definitive statement. Rather it is exploratory, attempting to make the processes of change visible, asking questions about them and beginning to assess their implications for the restructuring of social policy. We believe that it is neither enough merely to dismiss with cynicism the new arrangements, nor to welcome them uncritically as the panacea to all the problems of the welfare state. We do believe that only by attempting, in a relatively open-minded manner, to understand what is happening will it be possible to develop, where necessary, convincing alternatives and to learn from the 'new' as well as the old. At the end of the book we hope that some of the implications for the future will be clearer, that it will be easier for those working in as well as those served by the present welfare regime to make informed judgements about the nature of the changes. We hope that the arguments of this book will not only be helpful in identifying ways of surviving in the new world, but will also contribute positively to the debates about the future of welfare.

References

Hills, J. (ed.) (1990) *The State of Welfare. The Welfare State in Britain since 1974*. Oxford: Clarendon Press.
Hood, C. (1991) 'A public management for all seasons', *Public Administration*, 69: 3–19.
Hoggett, P. (1991) 'A new management in the public sector?' *Policy and Politics*, 19(4): 243–56.
Johnson, N. (1990) *Restructuring the Welfare State*. London: Harvester Wheatsheaf.
Krieger, J. (1986) *Reagan, Thatcher and the Politics of Decline*. Cambridge: Polity.
Le Grand, J. (1990) 'The state of welfare', in J. Hills (ed.), *The State of Welfare. The Welfare State in Britain since 1974*. Oxford: Clarendon Press.
Le Grand, J. and Bartlett, W. (1993) *Quasi-Markets and Social Policy*. Basingstoke: Macmillan.
Marsh, D. and Rhodes, R. (eds) (1992) *Implementing Thatcherite Policies*. Buckingham: Open University Press.
Metcalfe, L. and Richards, S. (1990) *Improving Public Management*. London: Sage (second edition).
Mishra, R. (1990) *The Welfare State in Capitalist Society*. London: Harvester Wheatsheaf.
Pierson, C. (1991) *Beyond the Welfare State*. Cambridge: Polity.
Pollitt, C. (1990) *Managerialism and the Public Services. The Anglo-American Experience*. Oxford: Blackwell.

Taylor-Gooby, P. and Lawson, R. (eds) (1993) *Markets and Managers*. Buckingham: Open University Press.

Willcocks, C. and Harrow, J. (eds) (1992) *Rediscovering Public Services Management*. London: McGraw-Hill.

1

Going about Our Business? The Managerialization of Public Services

Janet Newman and John Clarke

'A measure of the success of our first ten years is that we have restored management to its proper place in our society.'

(Kenneth Clarke, then Home Secretary, interviewed on the BBC *Today* programme, Radio 4, 12 March 1992)

It is difficult to miss the importance of management in the restructuring of the state during the 1980s and 1990s. No policy initiative has been taken without a reference to the need for a supporting infrastructure of 'good management' to achieve its objectives. No self-respecting senior figure of a public sector organization would be without a strategy, vision or mission statement. Devolved budgets, business plans and sensitivity to customers are to be found everywhere.

It is harder to identify why this particular transformation has taken place. What is it about management that has produced this sense of playing an inevitable and indispensable role in the creation of the new public services? Social policy analysts have tended to focus either on the big idea of restructuring (stressing mixed economies, welfare pluralism, quasi-markets or post-Fordism, for example) or on the detail of policy implementation and outcomes in particular policy spheres. Management features, if at all, as a peripheral element in these studies. Its presence is noted rather than analysed.

Management texts, including the growing number of books dealing with the apparently distinctive hybrid of public sector management, tend to identify the cause with policy innovation by Conservative governments since 1979 before going on to look at the issues involved in the management of public sector organizations. At this point a preoccupation with what managers do (or should do, since the line is ambiguous) tends to take over. As a result, we arrive too quickly at a view of management understood as a set of determinate skills, competences, abilities or functions.

We want to argue that the place of management in the transformation of public services needs to be seen as arising from a more complex set of relationships. First, we need to understand that management is more than a technical specification of functions or skills, it is also a social group with a particular ideology (managerialism) through which it lays claim to both social and organizational power. Secondly, this ideology is historically (and culturally) specific. Its content, as well as its claims, vary in relation to changing economic and political circumstances. Thirdly, we need to address why management was seen as an appropriate vehicle for bringing about the transformation of the public sector in Britain. Exploring this relationship between politics, policy and the process of managerialization means giving attention to the ways in which the existing organizational regimes of public services were seen as an integral part of the problem of the state. These issues organize the first five sections of this chapter which, in turn, explore the ideology of managerialism; its changing economic and political conditions; the emergence of a 'new' managerialism; and management's place in the restructuring of welfare. The final section explores some of the implications of the installation of managerial regimes in public services.

'Trust us': the ideology of managerialism

One of the few sustained analyses of managerialism as an ideology in relation to public services is provided by Pollitt (1990). His book begins with a treatment of the ideology of managerialism which we believe to be well worth repeating. He argues that, at the broadest level, there are a number of principles which underpin the prescriptions of management as a cure for economic and social ills. These centre on defining 'progress' and the central role of management in achieving it:

> The main route to social progress now lies through the achievement of continuing increases in economically defined productivity. . . . 'Management' is a separate and distinct organizational function and one that plays the crucial role in planning, implementing and measuring the necessary improvements in productivity. . . . To perform this crucial role managers must be granted reasonable 'room for manoeuvre' (i.e., the 'right to manage'). (Pollitt, 1990: 2–3)

These general principles form the 'mission statement' of managerialism: its diagnosis of social and economic conditions, its identification of the way forward, and the appointed role for its practitioners in making progress. Pollitt also emphasizes the claim to power – the 'right to manage' – which we consider in more detail later. Beneath these general principles of the ideology of management, argues Pollitt, are two other levels. One concerns the field of theories, approaches and models of management, subject to change and conflict in their proposals for how managers should manage. At this level, there have been, as we shall see, different 'managerialisms' or managerial discourses, each offering distinctive views about organizational life and the place of managers within it. Finally, there is the most detailed level of prescriptions for particular features of management practice, usually derived from the different managerialisms and transforming their 'visions' of the management role into a set of techniques and practices for managers to execute. In this chapter we shall be focusing mainly on the first two of these (the general ideology and the contemporary discourses of management) and their intersection with public service organizations in Britain.

Pollitt's study details the political recourse to 'management' as the device which would rescue and revive the public sector in Britain in the 1980s. The Conservative party in power after 1979 identified management as a necessary condition for transforming the public sector from its staid bureaucratic paternalism (the legacy of post-war social democracy) into a dynamic and effective series of organizations able to deliver 'value for money' services on a competitive basis. In an early incarnation as Secretary of State for the Environment, Michael Heseltine offered an exemplary statement of management's role in this transformation: 'Efficient management is a key to the [national] revival. . . . And the management ethos must run right through our national life – private and public companies, civil service, nationalized industries, local government, the National Health Service' (Heseltine, 1980, quoted in Pollitt, 1990: 3).

Pollitt has argued that there are at least two varieties of managerialism currently circulating which have significance for the restructuring of public services. The first, and most influential, in the 1980s is what he terms 'neo-Taylorism', exemplified in the Heseltine quotation's concern with 'efficiency'. This refers to a model of management primarily devoted to the rational analysis of organizational inputs and outputs, and committed to the creation of efficiency and increased productivity as its over-riding objectives. As such, it provided the managerial analogue for wider political concerns with the financial 'burden' of public sector spending: the drive to impose the 'three Es' (economy, efficiency and effectiveness), to create 'value for money' services, and to deliver 'more for less' by driving down the labour costs of public services. Neo-Taylorist beliefs and practices manifested themselves in all public sector organizations, framed by the prolonged 'fiscal squeeze' from central government. Put crudely, most organizations found themselves trying to deliver 'more for less', simply because they were given less and asked to do more.

Overlapping with neo-Taylorism was a rather different version of managerialism, sometimes referred to as the 'new managerialism', sometimes as the 'Excellence School' and sometimes as 'new wave management' (Wood, 1989). Where neo-Taylorism focuses on intensifying the systems of control (of resources and effort), the new managerialism offers a model of the organization which is 'people centred' and views bureaucratic control systems as unwieldy, counterproductive and repressive of the 'enterprising spirit' of all employees. Its notion of the route to competitive success is to loosen formal systems of control (within what was tellingly termed a 'loose–tight structure') and to stress instead the value of motivating people to produce 'quality' and strive for 'excellence' themselves. Managers become leaders rather than controllers, providing the visions and inspirations which generate a collective or corporate commitment to 'being the best'. This managerialism stresses quality, being close to the customer and the value of innovation.

This 'new managerialism' overlaps with neo-Taylorism both in time and in its objectives, since it too stresses getting 'more for less' and providing 'value for money'. But it differs in its view of organizations and management role within them as to how such objectives are to be achieved. Pollitt has argued that, although this new managerialism played a rhetorical part in the changes of the 1980s (with statements about quality, staff development and the like), it was neo-Taylorism which shaped most of the practice of public sector management. We would differ from this assessment in two ways. The first is that, by the end of the 1980s, the new managerialism had come to take on a greater significance in practical terms as more emphasis came to be placed on the necessity of transforming the 'culture' of public services such as the police, civil service agencies and social services, especially in the context of moves towards greater devolution and decentralization. The second is that public service organizations have been increasingly marked by the coexistence of these two models of management, rather than a succession between one and the other. Organizations have been trying simultaneously to carry out neo-Taylorist models of productivity improvement through resource and effort controls and new managerialist models of inspirational leadership, corporate culture formation and excellence/quality commitments (see the chapter by Flynn in this volume).

Such a coexistence is not a theoretical problem, although it may cause many practical ones for those involved in the processes. Ideologies are not singular, coherent or homogeneous entities – indeed they are often characterized by an ability to carry conflicting or contradictory messages. In this context, conflicts between different models of management are harmonized by their being subject to a higher level of integration. Both models of management fall within the wider ideology of managerialism – the commitment to 'management' as the solution to social and economic problems, particularly those of the public sector; the belief in management as an overarching system of authority; and the view of management as founded on an inalienable 'right to manage'.

It is precisely these characteristics of management which were deployed in the neo-conservative political project of restructuring the state. Management provided a new system of authority, a new mode of control, which could be drawn on to unlock the bastions of bureaucratic and professional power. This is not, however, a simple case of the transfer of a set of techniques and modes of authority directly from the private to the public sectors to strengthen the political project of restructuring the public sector. Our argument is that the new public sector management has been forged out of a complex articulation between changes in the realms of both politics and management. The reshaping of public policy around a new set of ideologies connected with changes which were taking place in the managerial domain in the context of economic reorganizations in the 1970s and 1980s.

Much of the work on public sector management has focused exclusively on the first of these – the political domain – and has seen change as resulting from the agency of government. This debate is well covered in the literature and we do not wish to repeat it here. However, such a focus has the result of treating management as if it were a static entity able to be lifted from one setting (the private sector) and installed in another (the public sector). In this view, the main interest focuses on issues of adaptation to the new environment – the similarities and differences at stake in public sector management. In our view, this misses important shifts in internal regimes and modes of power operating within organizations – the nature of the managerialism on offer in the private sector. We turn to this in the following section before looking at the ways in which it was transposed to the public sector.

Virility restored: rediscovering the right to manage

Economic and political changes in the 1970s and 1980s opened up the possibility of a reconstruction of power relations within industry and commerce. One central feature of this reconstruction was the demand for the restoration of the 'right to manage' on the part of managers. Although this idea of the right to manage is a generic feature of managerialism, both the content of the claim and what rights managers exercise in practice are historically variable. The extent of organizational power demanded by managers has shifted and the changing balance of economic, political and organizational power between capital and labour has resulted in different sorts of settlements about the scope of and constraints on managers' rights to manage. The 1970s and 1980s saw a concerted effort to shift the balance of power:

> Managers for twenty years have had a buffeting and beating from government and unions and we have been put in a can't win situation. We have an opportunity now that will last for two or three years. . . . Then the unions will get themselves together again; and the government, like all governments will run out of steam. So grab it now. We have had a pounding and we are all fed up with it. I think it would be fair to say that it's almost vengeance. (Collinson, *The Financial Times*, 5 Jan. 1981, quoted in MacInnes, 1987: 92)

This reassertion of the 'right to manage' needs to be understood in its historical context. In both Britain and the USA, the post-war settlements between capital and labour over the range and scope of managerial power came apart during the economic recession in Western economies from the mid-1970s.[1] These economic conditions formed the ground on which a more expansive claim to regain the 'right to manage' was asserted. They were simultaneously the conditions in which the new managerialism was developed and flourished (Clarke and Newman, 1993a).

Both appear in the context of processes of economic restructuring under way from the mid-1970s in Britain and the USA which had the effect of changing the social composition, place and shape of labour forces. To some extent, this may be about what has been called 'flexible specialisation' (Piore and Sabel, 1984), registering the impact of new technologies, new patterns of work and new systems of control. But it is also about de-unionization, the greening of labour, the feminization of labour, the casualization of labour, the reorganizing of core/peripheral labour and the mobility of the enterprise in national and international terms (see, for example, Bluestone and Harrison, 1982; Hudson, 1988; Sayer and Walker, 1992). Becoming 'lean and mean' was both an imperative of the new managerialism and an economic requirement of capital recomposition in face of declining profit-ability and increased global competition. Its dominant manifestations were the continual concern with 'overmanning' and the need to 'shake out' excess capacity and excess labour, combined with increased managerial power to bring about improved productivity.

Such economic processes also affected the relationship between capital and the state, particularly in the form of what Kim Moody (1987) has called the 'business agenda'. Moody argued that in the late 1970s and 1980s, corporate capital elaborated a set of demands about the conditions which needed to be established by both local and national states in order both to attract capital investment and to ensure the success of such investment. These demands focused on the need to 'liberate' capital from the shackles of the post-war settlements. The business agenda sought capital's release from the state in the form of over-taxation and over-regulation; from the unions in the form of restrictive practices, and from its own corporate 'deadweight'.

Both in Britain and the USA, the expanded state resulting from the post-war settlements was identified as a major inhibition to continued or renewed capital accumulation. Its actions interfered with the free market, producing distortions in labour markets and capital markets, and inhibiting the exercise of managerial discretion within the enterprise through excessive regulatory activity (see Friedman and Friedman, 1985: Chapter 6, for example). Such concerns underpinned the commitments of the transatlantic new right to 'roll back the state' in pursuit of greater freedom and led to programmes of state disestablishment in both Britain and the USA through privatization and deregulation (Swann, 1988). At the same time, the business agenda targeted the patterns of corporate and personal taxation that financed the activities of the expanded state, arguing that these had anti-enterprise effects by reducing the rewards for initiative and hard work (Adams, 1984; Cronin and Radtke, 1987).

The other feature of the post-war settlements seen as requiring treatment was the place of organized labour. Although there were significant transatlantic differences, the business agenda in both Britain and the USA identified the position of unionized labour as a major blockage to the proper workings of both the free market and effective corporate management. Organized labour prevented the efficient operation of 'free' labour markets by disrupting pricing mechanisms and blocking labour mobility (the extra-organizational dimensions of union power). Trade unions also interfered with managerial discretion within the organization, especially getting in the way of management's control of the labour process through such phenomena as demarcation agreements and shop-floor power (see, for example, MacInnes, 1987). As well as being left stranded by 'capital flight', organized labour was the subject of an elaborate battery of attacks: new ·industrial relations legislation; displacement from national 'corporatist' institutions; new single or non-union workplace deals; and the surrender or diminution of negotiating rights.

Whatever rhetorical form these demands of the business agenda took (and they variously spoke in the names of the market, the customer, the nation and the spirit of enterprise), their objective was to remove the 'shackles' from the processes of capital accumulation. In this way, they constructed a particular affinity between the 'free market' and the 'free manager' as the practical embodiment of capital within the enterprise. Consequently the central effect they sought was that of re-establishing the 'right of managers to manage', freed from unreasonable restrictions and impediments. The political conditions of the 1980s provided the opportunity for the vigorous reassertion of this right and also saw a more dynamic vision of management being developed to make use of the new right to manage.

Visions of excellence: the emergence of the new managerialism

The new managerialism, developed in the USA in this period most visibly in the work of Tom Peters (see, for example, Peters, 1989; Peters and Austin, 1985), was the beneficiary of these wider economic and political transform-ations. It promised a management equipped to take advantage of the changing internal and external environments of organizations, ready to match the pace of external change with internal dynamism. Its prescriptions for management style and strategy 'make sense' within the context of these restructurings which opened up the internal domain of the enterprise for the exercise of managerial discretion. It presented an approach to managing which offers to 'fill the gap' created by the dismantling of other forms of organizational power, especially the limitations imposed by organized labour. In place of such intra-organizational defences the new managerial-ism proffered a 'climate of trust': a corporate culture of mutual commitment to the over-riding values and mission of the organization. It promised to create a homogeneous and shared culture which binds all workers to the pursuit of corporate objectives, although extra-organizational factors like rates of national and local unemployment may also promote employee loyalty (see Morgan and Sayer, 1988).

The new managerialism is profoundly critical of traditional bureaucratic modes of managerial control which its sees as stifling individual and corporate initiative. In their place it seeks to bridge the motivation gap by vision + purpose + performance through devolved processes. It stresses reduced supervisory control to achieve enhanced integration, moving employee relationships from compliance to commitment. The objective is to work on the cultural or attitudinal dimensions of work experience to produce behavioural congruence for middle managers as well as frontline workers (see Hopfl, 1992). The aim is to create the 'transparent' organiz-ation where everyone is responsible for achieving corporate objectives and everyone is enterprising in pursuit of them: 'The new vocabulary of teamwork, quality consciousness, flexibility and quality circles thus recon-ciles the autonomous aspirations of the employee with the collective entrepreneurialism of the corporate culture' (Rose, 1989: 117). It should be noted that the practice is considerably more complex than the inspirational rhetoric of the new managerialism might suggest. The 'old' control systems do not just simply wither away. Indeed, Peters and Waterman (1982) are explicit about the difficulties which managers face in 'letting go', although they are rather more reticent about the struggles over organizational power which may make managers more reluctant to take their hands off the known systems of control. More importantly, the new managerialism is also associated with new control systems concerned with attitudinal and behavioural compliance among staff.

Nonetheless, there are problems about taking the new managerialism too seriously. It has certainly provided a legitimating discourse for a variety of organizational transformations and may indeed have been practised in some of those changes. But, despite its visibility, it is by no means the only version of managerialism. It may be practised rhetorically, even though forms of control being exercised change superficially or do not change at all. In some settings the new management may extend no further than the introduction of customer care training for front-line staff or issuing mission statements. It is more likely that many organizations are relatively untouched by the new managerialism, even though they are exercising the managers' 'right to manage' in other ways: extending controls, exercising greater power over hiring and firing, changing working conditions, creating new contractual arrangements and finding other ways of exploiting the 'flexibility' of labour. What is more significant is not what particular managements do – what style or strategy they adopt – but the more generalized conditions of the enhanced freedom in which they make choices. The stripping of defences from employees both within and outside the organization creates the possibility of the 'right to manage' and exposes employees more directly to the exercise of managerial discretion. New approaches to performance measurement, the use of 'invisible' monitoring systems (through information technology, Garson, 1989) and the use of customer surveys to discipline front-line workers (Fuller and Smith, 1991) point to a continued effort to regulate labour processes.[2]

But while we should not overestimate the impact of the new managerialism in terms of its direct effect on management practice, neither should we underestimate its significance as providing a new ideological rhetoric. This rhetoric – expressed in the discourse of values, people, empowerment, customers, quality and so on – can potentially be mobilized by different interests in the pursuit of change. The rhetoric can be greeted with cynicism and dismay, or can constitute a significant motivating force for both managers and employees. There are problems in assuming that those subjected to such a discourse take it seriously even where it has become the public language of an organization. This applies to both managers and workers. Managers now know that they should 'talk management' but may still encounter problems in maintaining their corporate commitment (see Hopfl, 1992). For workers, it may be the focus of renewed scepticism, even though their dissent may be passive rather than active: a condition enforced by factors other than their enthusiasm for the corporate vision. At the same time, aspects of this discourse offer a more dynamic and powerful alternative to the grim efficiency of neo-Taylorism. In Britain, the language of the new managerialism can be seen to provide a new sense of direction and purpose for a public sector impoverished by the constant pressure to economize and the persistent rhetoric of value for money. In such contexts, the language of quality, putting customers first and valuing front-line staff represents the possibility of reasserting a value base for public services. The language also forms an important part of the terrain of the emergent new consensus between Labour and Conservative political visions of the future of the public sector. For precisely these reasons we cannot understand the shifts within the public sector as simply the consequence of the imposition of a new managerial 'right to manage' any more than we can understand them in terms of the assertion of a new political will by government. What matters is the way in which these two domains were articulated in the programme for restructuring public services.

Doing the right thing: the politics of managerialization

The changes we have been describing were primarily developed in the context of the private sector in Britain and the USA, but they have had a significant impact on the public sector in both countries. We can identify three points of connection between these changes and the restructuring of public services in Britain. The first is that the state itself was identified as a major cause of economic decline, both through its cost and through its social effects in undermining the 'enterprise culture'. The second is that these changes gave a specific sort of inflection to government messages about how the public sector needed to learn 'good business practices': such practices carried as one of their major referents the significance of a more active and dynamic role for management. Thirdly, there is an overlap between the villains identified in the new managerialism and the objects of Conservative hostility in the public sector. This overlap occurs most clearly in their mutual antagonism towards 'bureaucracy' or ossified and undynamic organizational systems.

To develop this argument it is necessary to return to the focal concerns of the Conservative assault on the welfare state. We would suggest that there have been three central concerns visible since the mid-1970s. The first of these is directed to the economic costs of welfare as imposing an excessive burden on the 'wealth-creating' activities of individuals and enterprises. This concern has focused around public spending and public borrowing and has manifested itself in the stringent fiscal disciplines applied to all aspects of state welfare, together with the imposition of a strong ethos of 'value for money'. The second concerns the social consequences of state welfare: the demoralizing, disincentive and dependency-producing effects of state provision. This has focused on the inhibiting results which state provision has had on the freedom, autonomy and responsibility of the individual and has manifested itself both in the efforts to reduce and target benefits and in the promotion of a more diverse mixed economy of welfare intended to supplant the state's 'monopoly provider' status. The third concern has been rather different. It has focused on the state itself as the site of power and as a multiplicity of points through which political resistance or opposition might be organized. This has been the core of Conservative attacks on such diverse targets as the 'monopoly provider' role; the power of professional empires; the unresponsiveness of bureaucratic authorities and the activities of 'loony left' (and other) councils. The directions implied by these three concerns do not all point the same way. Reductions in expenditure could, in principle, have been accomplished without 'markets'. So too, more rigorous benefit systems could have been achieved without 'customers'. The economic and social objectives of the Conservative attack on welfare, however, have been structured by the political logic of dismantling the welfare state as a site of power. It is this logic which is the core of the politics of managerialization. Management represents the means by which the relations of power within the state might be unlocked and transformed.

Against this background, the restructuring process inaugurated in May 1979 was driven by a number of interlinked objectives. It sought fiscal redistribution by shifting the 'tax burden' and imposing greater financial limits and controls on welfare spending. It mirrored private sector strategies in bringing about a greater flexibility of labour by dismantling established patterns of labour relations and employment in the public sector. It aimed to change the cultures of welfare which were identified as embodying disincentives, dependency and demoralization (inhibitors to the enterprise culture). It also sought to unlock the regimes of organizational and political power which the state represented as the product of the post-war social democratic consensus (Clarke, 1991: Chapter 6; Clarke and Langan, 1993).

We need to consider the changes in the disciplines and practices of organizational co-ordination in the public sector, and shifts in the modes of power on which they are based. We have chosen the phrase 'organizational co-ordination' as the closest we can come to identifying the issues of how organizations are ordered without having recourse to more specific terms such as 'administration' or 'management', each of which carries a particular and politicized inflection. While all organizations require co-ordination, there are competing versions of how this may best be accomplished. The welfare state in Britain has developed as a combination of bureaucratic and professional forms of power. Its internal regimes of 'professional bureaucracy' or 'bureau-professionalism' are based on Fabian assumptions about the proper combination of professional expertise coupled with the regulatory principles of rational administration as the means of accomplishing social welfare. This internal regime connects the structures, cultures, relationships and processes of organizational co-ordination in a specific configuration. Both bureaucracy and professionalism involve particular modes of power. They lay claim to particular legitimations for the exercise of power (varieties of expertise and neutrality). They exercise particular ways of deploying power (controlling access to resources of establishing normative judgements). They construct relationships of power between themselves and the recipients of their services (as claimants, clients, patients and so on). They both construct and constrain the exercise of particular varieties of discretion and decision making. The welfare state has drawn together these two modes – bureaucracy and professionalism – in combinations as 'bureau-professional regimes'.[3] Such regimes involve different balances of power between the bureaucratic and professional elements in particular settings (compare medicine and social work, for example) but the concept provides a general key to the organizational architecture of the welfare state in Britain. In turn, these bureau-professional regimes were articulated, again in different settings, with organized political power – in central and local governments and in health authorities, for example. Each site also involved the construction of distinctive relationships between the internal regimes of the state, forms of political representation and 'citizens'. This combination of modes of bureaucratic, professional and political power in the regimes of the welfare state is conventionally expressed in the idea of the 'social democratic consensus' – a neutral state supplementing the workings of the market (and the hidden labour of the family) in the promotion of social welfare. Its Fabian assumptions linked the realms of policy making (politics), policy implementation (administration), welfare practice (professionalism) and the academic study of social policy.

This complex of bureaucratic, professional and political power was identified by the new right in the 1970s as a major stumbling block to a radical reconstruction of the state and its role in British society. It is this which underpins the intensity of the attacks on all three modes of power represented by the welfare state. 'Arrogant' professionals were arraigned alongside 'inflexible' bureaucrats and 'interfering' politicians as preventing efficient, effective and economic public services. Each group was seen as having a self-interested stake in the preservation and expansion of the existing regime and thus likely to block attempts at reform. But the new right also identified the welfare state as a blockage whose interlocking modes of power might be disentangled and defused by the combination of markets and management – aided by a judicious degree of fiscal strangling through the Treasury or legislative execution where needed (the metropolitan counties and the GLC).

Management has been identified as a transformational force counterposed to each of the old modes of power. By contrast with the professional, the manager is driven by the search for efficiency rather than abstract 'professional standards'. Compared to the bureaucrat, the manager is flexible and outward-looking. Unlike the politician, the manager inhabits the 'real world' of 'good business practices' not the realms of doctrinaire ideology. In each of these areas, the manager is also more 'customer centred' than concerned with the maintenance and development of organizational 'empires'.

Management, then, was the agency which inherited the task of dismantling the old regimes and providing a new regime (a new mode of power) around which organizations could be structured. The significance of management as a regime lies in the claim that managers 'do the right things': that is, they are able to make judgements, decide priorities and use resources flexibly to achieve an end result. This contrasts with the administrative concern about 'doing things right' – being able to demonstrate that the rules have been followed correctly. It is this claim which underpins management as a mode of power and is associated with the insistent demand that managers must be given the 'freedom' or the 'right to manage', and which subordinates concerns about the right way of doing things to the greater good of producing results.

Flexible friends: transforming organizational regimes

Of course, managerialization has not been the only strategy for the restructuring of the welfare state. It has been interwoven with a range of other approaches to dismantling the old regimes. Most of these are well known and have been extensively documented: for example the pressures of fiscal constraint; the exposure of organizations to competition, market testing and compulsory competitive tendering (CCT); the fragmentation of organizations into internal trading or business units, and the development of new forms of contractual relationships; the combined centralization and decentralization of power away from intermediate institutions such as local government; and the transfer of powers to non-elected bodies or 'quangos'. Each of these has, of course, included the appeal for more and better management, even though they have accentuated different versions of managerialism (see Flynn, in this volume). Less visible, and less documented, has been the recomposition of the internal regimes of organizations, and the transformation of modes of power within them. The process of managerialization has proceeded via a number of different routes.

First, there has been the expanded recruitment of managers from the private sector to public service organizations. This is visible both in the expansion of general management and in particular areas of functional expertise (finance, information technology and marketing, for example). It can also be seen in the greater use of management consultancies by public sector organizations and in the highly visible roles taken by leading business figures in government reviews of the public sector.

Secondly, it has featured in the growing representation of 'business expertise' in the management boards of public sector organizations and activities, resulting from both the perceived intrinsic desirability of 'real world' experience and from the growing salience of the idea of 'partnership' between the public and private sectors. Thirdly, the process of managerialization has been fostered by a variety of semi-public agencies either newly created (such as the Audit Commission) or reincarnated (the Local Government Training Board which became the Local Government Management Board). Alongside this has been the rapid expansion of management education and development, including the growth of public sector management programmes of varying kinds.

Finally, although perhaps less visibly, there has been a widespread transformation of bureau-professionals themselves into managers in the context of devolved or decentralized management systems. Examples range from the management of educational establishments (schools, colleges and universities) through fund-holding GP practices to most of the service delivery departments within local government (Clarke and Newman, 1993b).

At stake in these processes is the transformation of bureau-professionals into managed and managers – their subjection to the discourses of neo-Taylorism and the new managerialism. Like all discourses, these managerialisms aim to construct identities in and through relations of power and practice. In the context of the welfare state, this has involved trying to find the principles which will either subordinate bureau-professional identities to the process of being managed, most visibly in the introduction of 'general management' in the NHS, or will transform bureau-professionals into managers, in local authorities or in locally managed schools, for example (see the chapters by Walby and Greenwell, and Fergusson, in this volume).

Managers are those who 'understand' markets; who can extract the untapped potential from the 'human resources'; who are sensitized to the 'needs of the customer'; who can deliver 'results' and who can be relied on to 'do the right thing'. The unlocking of trade union organization, bureau-professionalism and local political representation requires 'management' to provide an alternative mode of power. If 'markets' and 'customers' have been the ideological cutting edge of these changes, then 'management' has been the eagerly sought principle of articulation for a new organizational regime for the welfare state. The salience of 'management' for the emergent shape of the welfare state in Britain is located in the way it links the wider context of restructuring to the specific 'problems' identified as requiring change in the organization of welfare. Management is the necessary corollary of the dismantling of the structures of bureau-professionalism.

It is this context which helps to make sense of managerialization as a process which is explicitly concerned with organizational power and as a strategy for the recomposition of previous modes of power within and around the welfare state. What is at stake is the diminution of other models of power in order to establish the conditions for managerial discretion. Nevertheless, the strategy of managerialization has not involved the simple displacement of one internal regime by another. The regime of bureau-professionalism has been established deep in the interstices of the welfare state as it has developed in Britain – in its various manifestations it had become the 'taken-for-granted' way in which public services were organized and provided. It bound together the organizational structures, cultures and routines of welfare with the occupational identities, assumptions and careers of those working within welfare in the post-war era. While the various legislative changes of the post-1979 Conservative governments have unlocked many of the structural supports of the old regime, the looked-for cultural change in identities, attitudes and practices has been (predictably) harder to accomplish. To some extent, the stubbornness of such dimensions of the old regime explain the sense of 'constant revolution' in the Conservative approach to public welfare as they search for further means of unlocking the past's persistence in the present.

The depth of resistance to change among those in bureau-professional regimes has a number of dimensions, not all of which are encompassed by Conservative explanations about their unwillingness to surrender power.[4] One is the profound suspicion about the likely fate of the ethos of 'public service' in the creation of a new mixed economy of welfare with a diminished role for the state. Another is the fear of what happens to both professional and bureaucratic 'standards' in these changes which are viewed as (however inadequately) guaranteeing certain minimum and universal norms of welfare provision. Related to this is a level of scepticism about the rhetoric of markets and management in terms of their ability to 'deliver the goods', even in the absence of fiscal restraint. Doubt is also expressed about the transferability of 'good business practice' from the private to public sectors, given the differences in conditions, processes and desired outcomes between the two sectors.

But at the same time we cannot explain the depth of the transformation which has occurred merely in terms of an imposed set of legislative and fiscal initiatives, nor in terms of an ideological trick by the Conservative governments of the 1980s. It was not only the neo-conservatives who were critical of the paternalism of state welfare, its concentration of political and professional power, its limited conceptions of the needs of service recipients, its intrusive and oppressive bureaucratic processing of people as cases. The process of unlocking these regimes can hardly be resisted in terms of nostalgia for the good old days. The old bureaucracies are having to learn to look outwards and to think about their performance in terms of the perceptions of their customers and users. Some of the intractable power bases are having to open themselves up to scrutiny, and the old exclusive clubs are having to unlock their doors to new membership. The people-centredness and the quality focus of the new management represents a welcome antidote to the economism of the '3 Es' and the impoverished style of neo-Taylorism. As we move out of the Thatcher era, we can see the emergence of a new political consensus about public service management (across all three political parties, with minor differences of style and emphasis). The new wave management of Tom Peters and others provides a value base and set of techniques which has an interesting correspondence with the customer focus and quality orientation around which this consensus is constructed. What is as yet unclear, however, is how far managerialism in the public sector can be seen, not as an imposition of a distinctive set of business-derived skills and techniques, but as a contested domain within which new practices and approaches can be forged. Indeed, some argue that we are now seeing the emergence of a 'new public management' which distances itself from the private sector, which recognizes the public sector as distinctive, and which is organized around public sector values.

Management as a contested domain

It should be clear from our approach to managerialism as an ideology and managerialization as a process that we do not view management as having a single or fixed character. As well as being championed as promoting flexibility, management itself is a flexible formation. What managers do and how they think about what they do tends to be socially and organizationally shaped by the context in which they work. This fluidity of management (what Willcocks and Harrow, 1992, call its 'contingent' nature) means that the outcomes of the managerialization of public services are difficult to predict. This imprecision relates both to the ends which managers pursue and the ways in which they pursue them.

The idealized model of management (attributed to the private sector) views management as the means of achieving the efficient pursuit of clearly defined and limited objectives – profitability or increased profitability. This is an objective established by the one significant authority in the enterprise – its owners – who devolve their authority to managers. Even if this model were true in practice, it would, as many others have argued, raise problems about the transferability of management to public sector organizations where neither the goals nor the relationships of power and authority are as clear cut.

However, studies of management in the private sector suggest that the reality is rather more complex. Organizations develop multiple goals – both formal and informal – such that managers have to negotiate their way between competing pressures and interests. Interdepartmental rivalries and competition coexist with business rivalries and external competition. Organizations are characterized by diverse power bases and networks through which power is organized and used. Managers have to deal with the demands of a range of 'stakeholders' rather than one superior authority. Organizations are complex and intractable rather than malleable or open to being shaped by the exercise of managerial will (Kanter, Stein and Jick, 1992). In such respects, the 'real world' of private sector management is both murkier and closer to some of the issues present in public service organizations than the ideal would suggest.

Transposing such issues to the public sector settings, it will be clear that, rather than resolving or transcending the dilemmas, problems and contradictions of the old regimes, the process of managerialization has the effect of changing their shape. It affects the way they are articulated: the languages in which they are represented, the places in organizations where they appear, and the principles which are applied in search of solutions. We want to end this chapter by exploring this proposition in relation to two features of the managerialization process: the regimes of organizational power and the discourse of managerialism.

The new regime of managerial power sits in the middle of a dislocated old regime with the ambition of being able to exercise the right to manage in the face of the old power bases – diminishing their influence and enhancing its own. But bureaucratic, professional and political forms of power have not been abolished and managers will confront the problem of how to exercise the right to manage in the face of continuing challenges from elsewhere. That problem manifests itself most visibly in relation to central government with its power to change the 'rules of the game' at short notice – for example, maintaining the role of Regional Health Authorities to monitor and co-ordinate the internal market to the dismay of Trust managers. But it is also present in a variety of other ways in service organizations. Professionals will seek to use specialist knowledge and skills to inflect managerial objectives and their implementation in particular directions. Political representatives will engage in conflict over who is best equipped to represent the views of 'customers'. Does a councillor's surgery give a truer view than a customer survey?

The shift to a managerial regime has also opened up wider questions about how customer power is to be exercised. The changes have emphasized the greater salience of users' views and the requirement that service organizations be responsive to them. Less has been said about the mechanisms through which individual and collective users may affect decision-making processes. But there is clear potential for users to take such promises seriously and insist on effective, rather than nominal consultation. Such issues are not just 'rearguard actions', although it is true that the old power bases have been placed on the defensive. Rather they can be viewed as struggles to determine the directions in which the newly created managerial discretion is to be exercised.

We can see this clearly if we consider the role managerialization plays in relation to the structural dilemma of matching needs and resources. The promise of managerialism is that the pursuit of organizational effectiveness will bridge this gap by the more flexible and dynamic use of existing resources (see Langan and Clarke, Chapter 4 in this volume). This will be true in certain respects, given that some of the resources have been rendered more flexible (labour in the public sector, for example). Nonetheless, there continue to be arguments about whether enhanced efficiency is the same as a more effective service. In the process, a variety of perspectives have been mobilized not against the managerial discourse, but through it, using its terms to articulate their interests. Arguments over the state of the NHS which use different empirical indicators (through-put versus health outcomes; waiting times versus degrees of urgency; local versus national priority setting; budget meeting versus need matching, for example) have their roots in competing definitions of effectiveness in addressing the gap between resources and needs (see Walby and Greenwell, Chapter 3 in this volume). Within such definitional struggles, not only are different interests being articulated, but the potential for new alliances of interests are explored and developed.

The issue of need also links to the final aspect of management as a contested domain – the discourse of managerialism. Much resistance to the process of managerialization has focused on arguments that the 'business culture' which it embodies is inappropriate to the world of public service. In particular, critics have focused on the emptiness or hollowness of its language – usually when confronted by visions, mission statements or strategic plans. This is conventionally taken as evidence of one of two things. On the one hand, it indicates that managers do not comprehend the rich complexity of how services are provided and, in particular, fail to appreciate the complex of skills, knowledges and judgements which professionals bring to bear on their work. On the other, its emptiness is seen as testimony to the fact that managerialism is just an ideological con trick or smokescreen being used to conceal 'real' changes. We prefer to think of this hollowness in a rather different way, one which recognizes that the impact of managerialization is itself a significant change to the organization of public services.

The basis of this emptiness of managerialism as a discourse is to be found in management's social location. It is derived from management's position as a recipient of devolved social and economic power – historically rooted in the separation of ownership and control in private enterprise. In that sense, management possesses no superordinate goals or values of its own. The pursuit of efficiency may be the mission statement of management – but this is efficiency in the achievement of objectives which others define (ideally, competitiveness and profitability as prescribed by the enterprise's owners). Management in the private sector has become such a 'taken-for-granted' or naturalized social phenomenon that we have come to assume that profitability or competitive success is management's own objective. It is not – it is devolved from others (the company's absentee owners). In the managerialization of the public sector, however, this absence of superordinate goals becomes more visible.

In discussions of management in public sector or not-for-profit organizations, this is conventionally discussed as a matter for managers faced with the task of balancing the competing claims and success criteria of multiple stakeholders (Kanter and Summers, 1987). Indeed, one key dimension of managerial discretion or autonomy may be the ability to represent and trade off the different interests that have a stake in the particular service. However, this also means that the 'hollow' language of managerialism is open to contestation by different interests. Statements about making services more effective or improving their quality open up spaces for different groups or alliances to give such words particular inflections (see Cochrane, Chapter 7 in this volume). Professional definitions of quality or effectiveness will rarely be the same as political ones. Neither is likely to be the same as those of service recipients (although both professionals and managers may wish to 'speak for' users). Similarly, the language of responsiveness and consultation does not contain inherent limits as to how user groups may seek to shape the nature of services, even though the intention may be limited and rhetorical. The creation of a discourse of public sector management as distinctive in texts and management development programmes represents one strand of intervention in this context. It seeks to articulate the values, culture or ethos which mark out managing in the public sector as different. In doing so, it addresses the hollowness of managerialism by trying to provide a superordinate value framework and set of orientations for what efficiency should serve in the public sector.

The very hollowness of managerial discourse constitutes it as the site of conflict between different interests. In the act of transforming old regimes of organizational co-ordination and the power bases they involved, managerialization opens up new front of contestation and struggle (see Newman,

Chapter 9 in this volume). These are, of course, not merely language games in the sense that the meanings of all words are fluid. Nor are they likely to be resolved by merely restating the importance of some values over others. In the specific political context of the restructuring of the public sector, many elements of the discourse come with meanings in which there are heavy investments (see Flynn, Chapter 10 in this volume). But the attempt to fix meaning, to give a specific stabilized inflection to the discourse, is not the same as its accomplishment. While managerialism may have been used to discount some claims to power, it has also created a field of conflict in which new routes to legitimate claims have been opened up. The process of managerialization has shifted rather than abolished the potential for attempts to articulate power and interests through meaning – ideological or cultural struggles in a new contested domain.

Notes

1. One feature of the 'special relationship' has been its impact on management education. The much sought-after learning organization has predominantly looked to learn from the USA – and the USA in the context of competitive relationship with Japan – rather than from Europe.

2. The new managerialism shares with other 'managerialisms' the promise to be the mode of management which overcomes the intractability of labour. Each identifies the non-integration of the worker as a problem, and then claims to be able to resolve it. For one striking example, see Analoui and Kakabadse (1992) whose grippingly titled *Sabotage* promises that the introduction of Total Quality Management will do away with recalcitrant or disaffected labour forces.

3. These arguments draw on a variety of approaches to the study of professionalism in routinized settings. See, for example, Mintzberg (1983) and Johnson (1972).

4. The monopolization of power by either established professions (the BMA) or other bureau-professional occupations (often lumped together as the 'polyocracy') has been a consistent thread of justification for Conservative welfare changes, especially but not exclusively in the NHS. In the US, neo-conservatives and neo-liberals have articulated this in a more extensive attack on the 'new class' composed of state professionals, drawing on critiques of state power in communist regimes. See Clarke (1991: Chapter 5) and Ehrenreich (1987).

References

Adams, J.R. (1984) *Secrets of the Tax Revolt.* Orlando, FL: Harcourt Brace Jovanovich.
Analoui, F. and Kakabadse, A. (1992) *Sabotage: How to Recognise and Manage Employee Defiance.* London: Mercury.
Bluestone, B. and Harrison, B. (1982) *The Deindustrialization of America.* New York: Basic Books.
Clarke, J. (1991) *New Times and Old Enemies: Essays on Cultural Studies and America.* London: Harper Collins.
Clarke, J. and Langan, M. (1993) 'Restructuring welfare: the British welfare regime in the 1980s', in A. Cochrane and J. Clarke (eds), *Comparing Welfare States: Britain in International Context.* London: Sage.
Clarke, J. and Newman, J. (1993a) 'The right to manage: a second managerial revolution?' *Cultural Studies,* 1(3): 427–41.
Clarke, J. and Newman, J. (1993b) 'Managing to survive; dilemmas of changing organisational forms in the public sector', in N. Deakin and R. Page (eds),*The Costs of Welfare.* Aldershot, Avebury: SPA.

Cronin, J.E. and Radtke, T.G. (1987) 'The old and new politics of taxation', in R. Miliband, L. Panitch and J. Saville (eds), *The Socialist Register 1987*. London: Merlin.

Ehrenreich, B. (1987) 'The New Right attack on social welfare', in F. Block, R. Cloward, B. Ehrenreich and F. Fox Piven, *The Mean Season: The Attack on the Welfare State*. New York: Pantheon Books.

Friedman, M. and Friedman, R. (1984) *The Tyranny of the Status Quo*. Orlando, FL: Harcourt Brace Jovanovich.

Fuller, L. and Smith, V. (1991) 'Consumers' reports: management by customers in a changing economy', *Work, Employment and Society*, 5(1): 1–16.

Garson, B. (1989) *The Electronic Sweatshop*. New York: Penguin Books.

Hall, S. (1989) *The Hard Road to Renewal*. London: Verso.

Hopfl, H. (1992) 'The making of the corporate acolyte: some thoughts on charismatic leadership and the reality of organisational commitment', *Journal of Management Studies*, 29(1): 23–34.

Hudson, R. (1988) 'Labour markets and new forms of work in "old" industrial regions', in D. Massey and J. Allen (eds), *Uneven Development: Cities and Regions in Transition*. London: Hodder & Stoughton.

Johnson, T. (1972) *Professions and Power*. London: Macmillan.

Kanter, R.M. and Summers, D. (1987) 'Doing well while doing good: dilemmas of performance measurement in nonprofit organizations and the need for a multiple-constituency approach', in W.W. Powell (ed.), *The Nonprofit Sector: A Research Handbook*. Yale, NH: Yale University Press.

Kanter, R.M., Stein, B.A. and Jick, T.D. (1992) *The Challenge of Organizational Change*. New York: Free Press.

MacInnes, J. (1987) *Thatcherism at Work: Industrial Relations and Economic Change*. Milton Keynes: Open University Press.

Mintzberg, H. (1983) *Structure in Fives: Designing Effective Organizations*. Englewood Cliffs, NJ: Prentice-Hall.

Moody, K. (1987) 'Reagan, the business agenda and the collapse of labour', in R. L. Panitch and J. Saville (eds), *The Socialist Register 1987*. London: Merlin.

Morgan, K. and Sayer, A. (1988) 'A "modern" industry in a "mature" region: the remaking of management–labour relations', in D. Massey and J. Allen (eds), *Uneven Development: Cities and Regions in Transition*. London: Hodder & Stoughton.

Peters, T. (1989) *Thriving on Chaos*. London: Pan.

Peters, T. and Austin, N. (1985) *A Passion for Excellence: The Leadership Difference*. London: Fontana.

Peters, T. and Waterman, R. (1982) *In Search of Excellence*. New York: Harper & Row.

Piore, M. J. and Sabel, C. F. (1984) *The Second Industrial Divide*. New York: Basic Books.

Pollitt, C. (1990) *Managerialism and the Public Services*. Oxford: Basil Blackwell.

Rose, N. (1989) *Governing the Soul: The Shaping of the Private Self*. London: Routledge.

Sayer, A. and Walker, D. (1992) *The New Social Economy: Reworking the Division of Labour*. Oxford: Blackwell.

Swann, D. (1988) *The Retreat of the State: Deregulation and Privatisation in the UK and the US*. New York and London: Harvester Wheatsheaf.

Willcocks, L. and Harrow, J. (eds) (1992) *Rediscovering Public Services Management*. London: McGraw-Hill.

Wood, S. (1989) 'New Wave Management?', *Work, Employment and Society*, 3(3): 379–402.

2

The New Managerialism and Social Security

Tom Ling

The way in which social security is managed matters not just because such large sums of money are involved. It also matters because it involves choices and judgements about how the public sector intertwines with old age, family life, the transition from youth to adulthood and the operation of the labour market. Whilst few would deny the importance of this, approaches to the subject usually focus on policy outcomes and ask such questions as 'How much does social security cost?', 'Has it abolished poverty?' and 'What is its relationship to economic activity more widely?' In all of this, 'management' tends to be constructed as a neutral activity.

In contrast, this chapter asserts the importance of management. In common with the rest of this book, it does so not in order to suggest the causal supremacy of managerial style over other processes, but to demonstrate how fundamental public management is to the wider political economy. Neither does it suggest that shifts in management are merely a response to, or consequence of, wider changes. Throughout this book there are examples of how the 'new managerialism' in different parts of the welfare system is associated with its own distinct processes and outcomes. In this respect social security is no exception.

In order to explore these processes and outcomes, the focus of this chapter shifts backwards and forwards from the more detailed matters of managing social security to the wider context. The chapter starts with a brief outline of the factors underlying the creation of 'Next Steps' agencies and this is followed by an even briefer outline of social security expenditure. The next section locates this expenditure within its administrative context at the Department of Social Security. The immediate managerial consequences of these changes are then assessed before focusing on the implications for social change more widely. Two aspects in particular are addressed: the management of the labour market and the long-term unemployed. In this way, it is hoped that the full significance of the changes within the Department of Social Security can be appreciated.

The background to the creation of Next Steps agencies

As noted, the 'new managerialism' has had different emphases and consequences in different parts of the welfare system. In this chapter we have the opportunity to look more closely at how it is associated with changes in a central government department. These changes have been, to some extent at least, driven by key strategists within the cabinet and senior levels of Whitehall where, from the 1960s onwards, there were growing concerns over the capacity of the centre to secure the overall financial and political direction of the state system (and especially the welfare regime). A broad sketch of the backdrop to these concerns helps to explain why the central state has taken this strategic role of management increasingly seriously since the 1970s.

The modern state is a distinct legal, financial and bureaucratic entity. Yet, because it is dependent upon non-state activities for revenue, legitimacy, military recruits and so forth, the state is locked into processes most of which it might influence but which it cannot fully control. For heuristic purposes we can talk about two different types of managerial problems. The first concerns the internal management of each agency (for example, government department or public body) to ensure that they impact upon their environment in a coherent and effective way. The second concerns the capacity of the centre to manage the overall pattern of intervention across all state agencies to secure a degree of financial control, political coherence and legality. This encourages tensions within the state system both between the non-central agencies and the central state, and amongst the different, more locally based, state agencies. Throughout this book there are examples of distinctive, overlapping and partially conflicting managerial systems. For example, the same financial controls might help to maintain the financial integrity of the state but weaken the requirements of legitimacy or reproducing the tax base. Thus, in the chapter on the mixed economy of care (Langan and Clarke, Chapter 4 in this volume) we find that the attempt to impose tight financial controls has the consequence that the successful pursuit of community care policies is undermined. Equally, what might be necessary to maintain the legality of state action may directly conflict with political objectives. Far from having any automatic 'stabilizers' which guarantee the internal coherence of the state system, therefore, we find a system which requires active management.

In the UK, as elsewhere, the fundamental periods of political upheaval and settlement have been associated with equally fundamental managerial settlements within the state. The period from the latter part of the nineteenth century to the end of the First World War saw a settlement in which the working class secured representation (or incorporation) within the state system. It coincided with the gradual implementation of the Northcote–Trevelyan proposals to create a professional, male, Oxbridge elite, recruited for life through examination (rather than patronage). This elite constructed systems of financial control and legal regulation alongside a particular conception of the public service ethos which jointly provided the basis for a depoliticized 'public administration'. Gowan (1987: 30) describes this as an expression of 'dynamic conservatism' and, in an allusion to the impending democracy, 'a safety net for the leap in the dark'.

Following the First World War, this system was more deeply entrenched with the steering role of the Treasury enhanced still further, a role which it continued to enjoy until the Second World War when it was temporarily eclipsed. In the context of the post-war settlement there was an opportunity to construct alternative core institutions within the state to match the new welfare and economic commitments which were to so absorb the non-core agencies in local government, the NHS, education and so on. Partly because the left had rarely considered what sort of state institutions were appropriate, partly because it had more pressing demands on its time, and partly because of the great skill of Treasury civil servants in regaining the centre-stage, the post-war period saw a resurrection of the pre-war civil service structures. This managerial settlement both expressed and contributed to the wider post-war settlement which was centralist, patriarchal, technocratic and paternalistic.

If the Northcote–Trevelyan system had been a safety net for British democracy it became the cage of British Labourism. There were to be a number of developments which made this cage less and less comfortable. Not only did it inhibit democratic mobilization in its own support, but also it became increasingly incapable of sustaining central managerial control over the rest of the state in general and the welfare regime in particular. Problematic trends included the growth of professionalism as a relatively independent source of power within welfare agencies; the tendency for welfare agencies to be 'colonized' by non-state interests; and the increasing complexity of interventions which called into question the clumsily centralist managerial structures of Northcote–Trevelyan. This prompted a plethora of attempts in the 1960s and 1970s to make the existing system work better – many of which were imported from North American corporate management – but no genuinely radical reappraisal of public sector structures and management. This may not be surprising since any fundamental reconsideration of the management of the state would have required a wider examination of the Keynesian welfare state as a whole, and with it the location of public sector professionals, public bureaucrats and the old Establishment in the post-war state. Critically, their support had been institutionalized in the very fabric of the state system which was at the same time breaking down.

The Conservative Party coming to office in 1979 recognized that the success or failure of its political project depended, amongst other things, upon its ability to marginalize and undermine these institutional bases of support for the Keynesian welfare state from within the state. The fundamental vehicle for this was to be (in various guises) the 'new public management'. It was in this context that an avowedly radical neo-liberal government came to approach such a restructuring in the 1980s but, before examining these reorganizations in more detail, it might be helpful briefly to outline the full cost of the social security budget.

Social security expenditure

By the beginning of the 1990s, social security expenditure accounted for 30.4 percent of all UK public expenditure (HMSO, 1992: 24). At £58.6 billion this represented 9.8 percent of GDP and was easily the largest single item of public expenditure. This massive system of transfer payments involved over 60,000 staff in delivering benefits to over 20 million people at an administrative cost of some £2 billion (see Michael Bichard's comments on this in HC, 1991, 496: 27). Just one benefit (income support) determined the living standards of one in seven people, including 17 percent of pensioners, 24 percent of disabled people and the long-term sick, 68 percent of lone parents and 77 percent of unemployed people (Bradshaw, 1991: 25). The awful reality for these, and other poor people, is graphically expressed in *Hardship Britain* (Cohen et al., 1992). But if the living standards of poor people remained miserable, the overall cost of social security was nevertheless substantial, with the money to pay for this coming from general taxation (44 percent), employers' National Insurance contributions (30 percent), employees' National Insurance contributions (24 percent) and a small sum (2 percent) from investment income from the National Insurance Fund (HMSO, 1991a: 8). These are laid out in Figure 2.1.

It is conventional to divide the different types of social security expenditure into contributory benefits (such as retirement pensions and

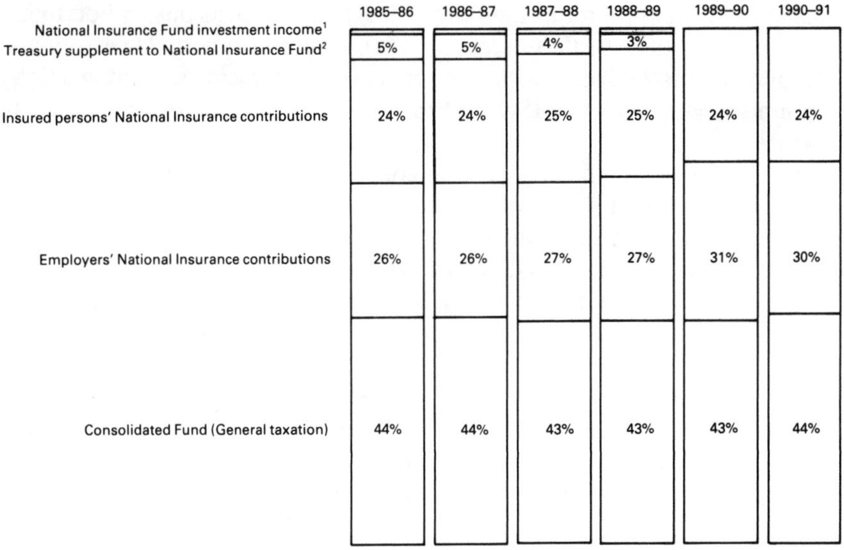

	1985–86	1986–87	1987–88	1988–89	1989–90	1990–91
National Insurance Fund investment income¹ / Treasury supplement to National Insurance Fund²	5%	5%	4%	3%		
Insured persons' National Insurance contributions	24%	24%	25%	25%	24%	24%
Employers' National Insurance contributions	26%	26%	27%	27%	31%	30%
Consolidated Fund (General taxation)	44%	44%	43%	43%	43%	44%

Figure 2.1   *Analysis of sources of National Insurance finance, 1985–86 to 1990–91 (HMSO, 1991a: 8)*

Totals may not sum due to rounding.
[1] In the years from 1985–86 to 1988–89 investment income was 1 percent; in 1989–90 it was 2 percent; in 1990–91 it is estimated to be 2 percent.
[2] The Treasury supplement to the National Insurance Fund was abolished with effect from 6 April 1989.

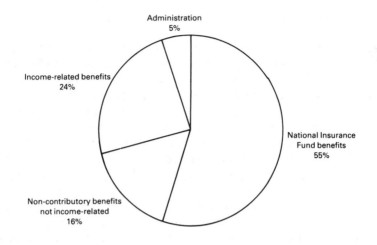

Figure 2.2   *Analysis of social security expenditure, 1990–91 (HMSO, 1991a: 8)*

unemployment benefit), non-contributory income-related benefits (such as income support, family credit and housing benefit), and non-contributory benefits which are not income-related (such as war pensions and disability pensions). In 1990–91 these accounted for some 55 percent, 24 percent and 16 percent respectively, with the remaining 5 percent accounted for by administrative costs (HMSO, 1991a: 8). These figures are presented in Figure 2.2.

In the same year, the beneficiaries could be categorized as elderly people (51 percent), long-term sick and disabled people (18 percent), families (18 percent), unemployed people (9 percent), widows and orphans (2 percent), and short-term sick and disabled people (2 percent) (see Figure 2.3).

All of the available evidence suggests that social security spending will rise throughout the 1990s with Bradshaw (1991) estimating an increase of £8.3 billion assuming no policy changes and 5 percent unemployment. This follows on from an increase in total social security spending by 44 percent in real terms between 1978/79 and 1991/92. In the short run, at least, social security expenditure is hard to control because it is demand-led with demographic changes and changes in unemployment having a substantial and direct impact. Increases in expenditure are predicted partly as a result of the ageing of the population, but also as a result of the number of children aged under 16, which fell by 6 percent during the 1980s and is now rising again. In addition, the government anticipates increased expenditure on long-term sick and disabled people and on lone parents (HMSO, 1991a). Less easy to predict are changes in unemployment and homelessness and the consequences of changes within the European Community, not least the implications of equal treatment for men and women.

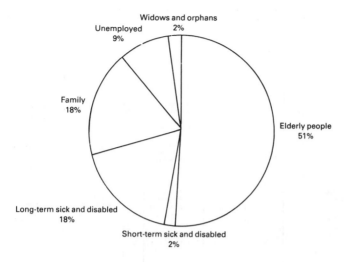

Figure 2.3   *Expenditure on benefits by broad groups of beneficiaries,
1990–91 (HMSO, 1991a: 6)*

Next Steps agencies and the Department of Social Security

Added to the wider managerial and financial pressures outlined above, more immediate circumstances gave the reforms substance and direction. These more contingent pressures included the personal distaste for senior civil servants which Mrs Thatcher did little to conceal (see Hennessy, 1989: 632–3). Ponting, himself a civil servant in the 1980s, claimed that the 'New Tory administration elected in 1979 made it clear that they appeared to despise the civil service . . .' (Ponting, 1985: 7). Many civil servants were unhappy about this (producing a form of civil service resistance by leaks) and Fry, with typical understatement, comments '[T]he career civil service having "captured", if in part by default, higher ground than constitutional theory allowed, did not seem always to be gracious about conceding to a Thatcher government . . .' (Fry, 1986: 546). Apart from the almost personal antipathies, the intellectual arguments put forward by the neo-liberal new right were openly hostile to public bureaucracy (see, for example, Niskanen, 1973; Mitchell, 1988). But, perhaps above all was the political association perceived to exist between the senior civil service and the pre-Thatcherite political consensus. For conservative historians such as Corelli Barnett, senior civil servants were amongst the 'New Jerusalemists' whose post-war attempt to construct a green and pleasant land was based on little more than a 'wish list' and who are responsible for many of the problems facing Britain at the end of the century (Barnett, 1986).

Consequently, whilst there would probably have been civil service reforms under any government in the 1980s, those which were to be implemented were less influenced by senior civil servants than would

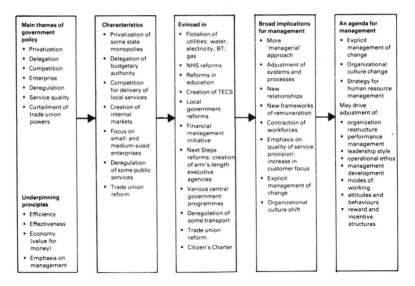

Main themes of government policy	Characteristics	Evinced in	Broad implications for management	An agenda for management
• Privatization • Delegation • Competition • Enterprise • Deregulation • Service quality • Curtailment of trade union powers **Underpinning principles** • Efficiency • Effectiveness • Economy (value for money) • Emphasis on management	• Privatization of some state monopolies • Delegation of budgetary authority • Competition for delivery of local services • Creation of internal markets • Focus on small- and medium-sized enterprises • Deregulation of some public services • Trade union reform	• Flotation of utilities: water; electricity; BT; gas • NHS reforms • Reforms in education • Creation of TECS • Local government reforms • Financial management initiative • Next Steps reforms: creation of arm's-length executive agencies • Various central government programmes • Deregulation of some transport • Trade union reform • Citizen's Charter	• More 'managerial' approach • Adjustment of systems and processes • New relationships • New frameworks of remuneration • Contraction of workforces • Emphasis on quality of service provision: increase in customer focus • Explicit management of change • Organizational culture shift	• Explicit management of change • Organizational culture change • Strategy for human resource management May drive adjustment of: • organization restructure • performance management • leadership style • operational ethos • management development • modes of working • attitudes and behaviours • reward and incentive structures

Figure 2.4   *Main themes of government policy 1979–91 and their
implications for the management of human resources in the public sector
(Thomson, 1992: 34)*

normally be the case in Britain. Cuts in civil service numbers were immediately announced, securing a 15 percent cut in its total staffing in the years 1979–85 (although the bulk of these were industrial civil servants). Civil service pay was de-linked from private sector pay, the Civil Service Department was abolished, a new Efficiency Unit was set up with Lord Rayner from Marks & Spencer at the helm, and the attempt to institutionalize cost awareness and efficiency was launched with the creation of the Financial Management Initiative (FMI). The FMI was not a complete success, at least in the minds of the authors of the so-called *Next Steps Report* (or, to give it its full title *Improving Public Management in Government: The Next Steps*, Efficiency Unit, 1988; also referred to as the Ibbs Report). The report advocated the radical breaking up of the service into separate agencies which would be responsible for carrying out quasi-contractual obligations (established in the 'Framework Agreement'). This would then leave only the 'core' of each department which would be responsible for creating and monitoring the Agreements. The implementation of many of these proposals constitutes the most radical break in the history of the civil service since the Northcote–Trevelyan report of the 1850s and it is worth noting that the report itself contains no systematic analysis of the strengths and weaknesses of either the existing system or of the proposed alternative. Alongside these initiatives, the National Audit Office and the Audit Commission were to conduct management audits which, amongst other things, were intended to root out alleged 'loony leftism', professional self-serving and bureaucratic inertia.

The overall purpose behind these reforms was to enhance the strategic control of the core over the state system by devolving non-strategic decisions

Table 2.1   *The organization of the Department of Social Security*

Department of Social Security Headquarters				
BENEFITS AGENCY Launch: April 1991	CONTRIBUTIONS AGENCY Launch: April 1991	IT SERVICES AGENCY Launch: April 1992	RESETTLEMENT AGENCY Launch: May 1989	CHILD SUPPORT AGENCY Launch: April 1993

Source: HMSO, 1991a: 35.

downwards. Thus resources and objectives would be centrally controlled whilst entrepreneurship concerning how best to achieve these targets would be encouraged. Thomson identifies seven main central government themes in support of this objective. These are: privatization; delegation; competition; enterprise; deregulation; service quality; and curtailment of union powers. She outlines the wider implications of these in Figure 2.4.

One consequence of these reforms for the Department of Social Security (DSS) was its reorganization into five agencies each with a quasi-contractual relationship with the central department (see Table 2.1).

The result of this reorganization is that 95 percent of social security staff are now employed by the agencies leaving only a core of less than 2000 staff under the Permanent Secretary at headquarters. This core has responsibility for advising ministers on policy and for drawing up strategic plans for the Department, setting targets for agencies, and monitoring their performance.

Whilst there was a general trend throughout government departments towards agencies, certain problems were especially associated with social security. A review team within the DHSS produced a report in 1988 which was highly critical of existing standards:

some offices pride themselves on virtually a same day service on supplementary benefit claims. Others take 25 working days . . .

waiting times in offices vary from 10 minutes to 90. Waits of three to four hours have been recorded. The actual interview takes, on average, only about 5 minutes . . .

accuracy in making payments is declining overall. The declared error rate ranges from the exemplary, 5%, to the awful, 40% . . .

Freefone is a super initiative which has proved a great success but some groups of customers are still largely unaware of its existence. (DHSS, 1988: 5)

The report's main conclusion was that 'the service provided to the public is too variable to be acceptable. In some places it is very good indeed. In some places it is absolutely unacceptable' (DHSS, 1988: 1).

This candid report is similar in tone to reports being produced elsewhere within the state, all of which helped to generate a sense of crisis and a conviction that change must be immediate and radical. It inhibited a careful evaluation of both existing management systems and the proposed alternatives but it also undermined effective resistance from professional groups, trade unions, pressure groups and the like. This atmosphere helped to prepare the ground for the creation of the Next Steps agencies. The one with primary responsibility in relation to social security was the Benefits Agency, which accounts for over half of the administrative costs of the DSS. Like all Next Steps agencies this operates within the quasi-contractual 'Framework Agreement' between itself and the core department (the Department of Social Security). This requires the Agency to 'promote the economic, efficient and coherent administration of social security services', to do so in a non-discriminatory manner which gives the public all the necessary information to allow claims to be made, and to contribute to departmental policy making. Indicators for performance-related payments were also established for senior management. These included certain levels of 'customer' satisfaction and the achievement of progress towards the implementation of the Operational Strategy.

The Operational Strategy involved the computerization of the administration of social security as outlined in *Social Security Operational Strategy: A Framework for the Future* (DHSS, 1982). It had three main objectives: to improve efficiency and reduce costs, to improve the quality of service to the public, and to improve the work of social security staff (p. 1). It began to be implemented in April 1988 and almost all local offices were computer-linked to the Departmental Central Index and the Income Support and Retirement Pensions Computer Systems by July 1991. Since then further work has been carried out on computerizing the Disabled Living and Working Allowances (see Adler, 1992: 4–6) although in the case of the Disabled Living Allowance the ombudsman found the DSS and the Benefits Agency guilty of maladministration in 1993 when it allowed a backlog of 250,000 claims to build up (HMSO, 1993).

There are four other agencies in the Department of Social Security. These are the Contributions Agency, with responsibility for maintaining records of individuals' contributions; the Information Technology Services Agency, responsible for all the information and communications systems in the DSS (primarily the Operational Strategy); the Resettlement Agency, responsible for providing hostels for single homeless people; and the Child Support Agency, primarily concerned with ensuring that payments for child maintenance are made by 'absent parents'. In Northern Ireland there is a separate Child Support Agency and the Social Security Agency (Northern Ireland).

Assessing the administrative changes

It is important to note that even apparently neutral things such as the computerization of the DSS need to be unpacked with some care if their value-laden contents are to be identified. The main stated objectives of the Operational Strategy have not been treated equally. 'From the start', according to Adler (1992: 4), 'the interests of the government were put first, those of the staff next and those of claimants last'. This implies not only that administrative savings were prioritized over the quality of service, but also that 'the quality of service' was given a very narrow meaning. As Adler goes on to argue, the conceptions underlying 'the quality of service' vary radically and may include a concern with bureaucratic cost-effectiveness, the professional quality of the service delivered to the client, or the legal rights and forms of redress available to the individual. To these one could add a more 'democratic' conception of quality in which individuals with shared problems and grievances are given the opportunity to organize collectively and contribute to the solution of those problems or satisfaction of grievances. Adler points out that by selecting error rates and the speed of dealing with the 'customer' as the crucial performance indicators, other dimensions have been sacrificed. User-friendly systems could have provided claimants (actual and potential) with more explicit explanations concerning their level of entitlement, more staff could have provided more home visits and more personalized access to information, and more systematic rights of collective representation could have enhanced the field of social security as an area where 'the people' (however defined) have an opportunity to democratically shape the public agencies which most directly concern them.

In this light it may be too easy to be cynical about the publication of the *Customer Charter* by the Benefits Agency in 1992. On the face of it, it was an attempt to widen the meaning of 'quality' and entrench this wider meaning in administrative practices. According to the Charter, the service provided by the Agency should be courteous, fair, confidential, private and accessible. It sets clearance time targets for income support payments at an average of four days and promises to pay 60 percent of family credit payments in thirteen days and 95 percent in thirty days. Furthermore, it promises that disabled people and people from ethnic minorities will be consulted over ways to improve the service and that it will assess and improve levels of 'customer satisfaction'. However, the charter creates no new institution which will act robustly on behalf of the claimant (such as a Benefits Ombudsman with effective powers) and the charter itself gives only limited guidance concerning how to complain other than by addressing complaints to the Customer Service Manager at the local benefits office. Furthermore (and this is anecdotal), in my local office not only were no charters on display but also staff found none in the building.

Any claims that the Benefits Agency's *Customer Charter* will lead of itself to a significant improvement in the quality of service must therefore be doubted. Individuals, lacking organizational backing, may find it difficult to bring about lasting change. In the words of Adrian Randall, 'it is difficult to imagine a serious audience for claimants' views without co-ordinated activity by existing or new organisations representing those interests' (Randall, 1992: 8). The Benefits Agency is publicly committed to consultation and organizations representing disabled people and black people do indeed have some access to the Agency, but the impact of these has been limited (if difficult to quantify).

In the absence of powerfully established individual and collective rights capable of applying pressure from without, we must look to the internal operations of the agency to find guarantees of quality of service. Here there is a tension between such objectives as saving costs and improving average response times, and other objectives such as ensuring that the most vulnerable and weakest claimants are supported and their needs met. The latter sort of objective might include targets for take-up of benefits and yet Michael Bichard, Chief Executive of the Benefits Agency, told the Treasury and Civil Service Select Committee that not only were there no such targets but neither did he know what the take-up rates were (HC, 1991: 29–30). It was, however, noted that targets for clawing back over-payment were set.

A similar tension exists in relation to the adjudication of benefits. The objective of value for money savings which the Treasury extracted as the price for funding the Operational Strategy, has tended to work against the objective of a fair and accessible system of adjudication. The *Annual Report of the Chief Adjudication Officer* (CAO) for 1991 is typical in noting only 'limited improvement in some aspects', adding that 'there remain areas of concern' (HMSO, 1991b: 5). The CAO also commented that 'the tension between good adjudication and the need to clear claims quickly is still evident' (p. 9).

Agency status was also expected to usher in a new era of transparency between the administration of social security and the central Department. The Framework Agreement, by which the Chief Executive enters into a quasi-contractual relationship with the DSS, is the key mechanism charged with securing this new degree of clarity. However, in practice, it often remains unclear where responsibility lies. Agreements are negotiated and responsibility for their content is spread. The *Treasury and Civil Service Committee Report* states that 'while Next Steps may not have changed the formal position of a Chief Executive as a civil servant who appears before a Select Committee, in practice it will have a profound effect' (HC, 1991: xxiii). Of the Chief Executive of the Benefits Agency, Kaufman (1992) writes 'Bichard keeps writing to me and I want him to stop. Whenever I have a constituency case involving a social security problem, I write about that case to the minister responsible . . .'. Kaufman complains that the minister then writes to Bichard who writes back to Kaufman saying that the case is being considered and eventually he might receive a full explanation. According to Kaufman this is part of a 'creeping abnegation of ministerial responsibility'. This concern is also expressed from the right of the political spectrum by Pliatzky who insists: 'In the absence of fresh legislation, so it seems to me, ministers cannot abrogate responsibilities placed upon them by existing legislation . . . and that is what is involved in the Next Steps agencies' (Pliatzky, 1992).

The government were presented with a choice between creating agencies which were either inside government (and hence accountable to the Secretary of State) or formally free from government. In opting for the former they chose the easy option which required neither legislation nor a change in the constitutional myth of ministerial accountability. In doing so they created a hybrid which was supposed to share the culture of the private sector within the context of a public body. Yet, as Vernon Bogdanor reminds us, '[T]he cultures of business and the civil service are more different than the government understands' (in Phillips, 1992). Worse still for the success of their reforms, in adopting this myth they avoided taking a fundamental step towards a hived-off governmental system: the reconstruction of the core department. As one analysis of the Next Steps reforms comments:

> Conspicuous by its absence is any sustained attempt to change the way that core departments do their own work. The challenge to their traditions is at least the equivalent of the challenge facing operational managers. Preparing the strategic specification of policy, and then negotiating its implementation calls for skills of a new order. No department seems to be taking a strong line on this, and the project manager's attention seems to be directed almost solely at the task of getting agencies into shape, and ticking them off on a list. (Metcalfe and Richards, 1990: 235)

In the Department of Social Security the fewer than 2000 officials left face a considerable task. The extent to which they are able to drive hard bargains over Framework Agreements and to establish effective systems of monitoring remains unclear. Indeed, the emphasis in the Framework Agreement is upon minimal interference from outside the agency and a heavy dependence upon the achievement of certain targets. As we shall see below, there are general problems with the use of quasi-contractual relationships in a policy area such as social security, but there are also specific problems relating to the actual targets set. For example, with the 85 percent satisfaction rate amongst 'customers' it will be very unclear whether 'customers' are expressing views upon the quality of the service provided by the Benefits Agency or the benefits set by the government. Furthermore, it will not include any of those who have been so badly served that they are unaware that they are entitled to make a claim. Even more problematically, the extent to which the Benefits Agency achieves its targets will fluctuate not only with factors within the control of the agency but also with (unanticipated) fluctuations in unemployment. In this atmosphere, accountability will be genuinely hard to establish and, given state secrecy, the weak powers of parliamentary scrutiny, the weakness of individual rights of redress within the law, and the weakness of institutionalized forms of representation within the social security system, it is hard to believe that this uncertainty will not be exploited to conceal failures and protect the powerful.

Thus agency status was used to justify enhanced managerial power and this in turn has been used to introduce political and ideological values in the name of technical efficiency. It has also been used to deny that these actions should be the proper object of democratic scrutiny. Yet on the grounds of managerial efficiency, individual rights and even constitutional propriety, this status is questionable. The full implications of this become clearer if we consider the importance of social security in relation to wider social change.

Restructuring social security and managing social change

In this section we explore some of the relationships between the management of the social security system and the wider changes taking place in society.

Management systems reflect the strategic response of an organization to its changing environment and these responses in turn alter than environment. For example, management systems which give considerable autonomy to professionals also shape the identity of the 'clients' and possible forms of resistance (for example, appeals to pressure groups or to professional bodies). Alternative systems which are driven by managing the response to changes in 'customer' preferences also bring with them 'customer' identities and forms of resistance (for example, appeals to the law courts). For this reason, we need to build upon some of the simpler models of the relationship between social security and wider social change in order to incorporate an appropriate sense of the significance of management. Simpler models include:

1 social security is a response to popular unrest and reflects the need to make concessions when faced with organized dissent;
2 social security is designed to secure the daily reproduction of social relationships in a society divided by gender, class, ethnic and other inequalities; it reinforces and disciplines the patriarchal family, the labour process and other forms of subordination (for example, disability);
3 social security is a part of the wider process of legitimation through which the state and the economic system are made acceptable to society as a whole;
4 social security is a result of politicians promising more in order to win elections and bureaucrats providing more in order to build up their empires;
5 far from securing the wider social order, social security actually undermines both the moral basis of capitalism (reward should be linked to effort) and the discipline of the labour market (by making the alternative to labour too attractive);
6 social security reflects the genuine desire amongst politicians, pressure groups and the public to live in a society in which certain needs are met irrespective of the ability of the needy to pay for them.

It can quickly be recognized that the first three belong to more radical critiques of patriarchal capitalism such as may be found within Marxist and feminist writings. The third is associated particularly with those approaches which stress that since the capitalist market is not based upon principles of fairness or justice it cannot automatically legitimize itself, and state-provided welfare is a necessary price to pay for the survival of capitalist democracies. The fourth and fifth interpretations relate to the politics of the new right and reflect their general hostility to both the state and attempts to modify the working of the market. The fourth argument might lead to demands to cut social security whilst the fifth might lead to demands for workfare in which those social security recipients who are able to work should do so before receiving benefit. The final and sixth model is a liberal democratic model in which the good intentions behind welfare are taken at the face value and where the main concerns would be about the impact of party politics, pressure groups and administrative systems upon the pursuit of this objective. Note also that the first three tend to see the politics of social security as an outcome of wider processes, whilst the rest see the politics of social security in a more voluntaristic sense.

Explanations which identify the causal primacy of 'external' processes have a certain force behind them. The existence of certain 'structural' factors is suggested by the tendency for Western capitalist states to become immersed in systems of income maintenance at relatively early stages of capitalist development. In each case the most potentially disruptive (usually skilled workers in relatively secure employment) and those seen to have the most legitimate needs (typically the elderly) were prioritized in a system of income maintenance which always also reflected the need to maintain discipline in the labour market. At the same time, such systems typically reflected patriarchal assumptions about the dependency of women upon a male income-earner, patronizing assumptions about disabled people and so forth. More subtle accounts can also explain different types of welfare regimes by identifying (amongst other things) different patterns of cross-class support (Esping-Andersen, 1990), by locating welfare within particular forms of patriarchy (Pascall, 1986) and by pointing to varying state capacities (Scharpf, 1991).

Scharpf's concern with the institutional fabric of the state system reminds us that the organization of the state itself has consequences for non-state identities and actions. Discourses which are institutionalized within organizations have a transformative capacity beyond the reach of discourses which are not. Therefore it would not be adequate to suggest that welfare regimes can be explained solely as a consequence of other processes (no matter how multiple and complex these are assumed to be). The challenge is to locate the welfare regime (and with it the social security system) in relation to wider social change without reducing welfare to an expression of those changes. Perhaps the most cavalier claim, and a useful starting point for our discussion, is that a shift towards post-Fordism characterizes current Western capitalist regimes. Stoker, for example, even asks if institutional change within the state should not be seen as an expression of the requirements of post-Fordism (Stoker, 1989). The use of these terms is debated but it generally indicates a shift from:

1   mass production technology applied in large workplaces;
2   mass marketing of mass-produced goods;
3   an urbanized and relatively homogeneous culture; and
4   a welfare system and/or other forms of state expenditure which sustain high levels of demand and relatively full employment,

towards circumstances in which there exists:

1   batch production using flexible technology and working practices in small units of production;
2   niche marketing of 'customized' products;

3   a fragmenting culture in which locality plays a less important role in
    shaping identity;
4   a welfare system which is concerned with flexibilizing the workforce and
    sustaining international competitiveness either through downward
    pressure on wages (as in the UK) or through training and promoting
    economic restructuring.

Jessop develops an approach to post-Fordism and, within this, puts
forward particular claims relating to the welfare regime. He argues that the
West is witnessing a general shift from the Keynesian welfare state to the
Schumpeterian workfare state (see Jessop, 1992).

This claim is worth exploring for the light it sheds on the management of
social security. The first step in the argument is to suggest four changes in the
conditions which helped to create the long period of economic and political
stability which characterized the West in the thirty years after the Second
World War. These are:

1   the rise of new technologies;
2   growing internationalization;
3   the paradigm shift from Fordism to post-Fordism;
4   the regionalization of global and national economies (Jessop,
    1992: 199).

From this we may deduce certain consequences for the British welfare
regime.

1   The perceived need to encourage the adoption of new technologies (or
    face economic defeat at the hands of the newly industrializing
    economies) has propelled choices in welfare towards policies intended
    to attract inward investment and stimulate domestic interest in applying
    new technologies. It has also encouraged the implementation of large
    information technology systems within the welfare system (often with
    less than great success). And it has encouraged the view that industries
    based upon old technologies should be allowed to decline and collapse
    (with important knock-on consequences for welfare agencies).
2   The strategic choices made in welfare policy have been strongly
    influenced by calculations concerning the best way to restore the UK's
    economic competitiveness. An amalgam of views has shaped these
    calculations including the need to encourage the poor to work for less,
    to police the unemployed with more vigour, to encourage private
    insurance rather than public benefits and the supposition that markets
    are better than bureaucracies.
3   In response to so-called post-Fordist trends in the economy, the welfare
    regime is no longer predicated upon full (male, full-time) employment
    but upon flexibilized labour markets in which part-time (often female),
    insecure and non-unionized workers would become increasingly preva-
    lent. Rising unemployment may be accepted as a 'price well worth
    paying' to induce such flexibility.
4   The regionalization of the world has meant that the welfare regime is

not simply shaped by global forces but specifically by European trends. In particular, the EC is likely to have growing influence over gender relations within social policy, employers' obligations, training policies, and restructurings following the implementation of the single market.

Taken together, Jessop (1994) describes the emergent trends as the 'Schumpeterian Workfare State'. The term 'Schumpeterian' is used to symbolize the institutionalized permanent innovation characterizing both the welfare regime and the society with which it is concerned (forthcoming), and 'workfare' to capture the sense in which the state has developed an enhanced institutional role in ensuring the availability of a flexible and disciplined workforce during times of mass unemployment.

Jessop's approach avoids many of the problems associated with attempts to use macro-theoretical accounts to explain micro-level institutional changes. There exists an emphasis upon contingency and strategic choice through which the causes and consequences of particular institutional changes can be explored. Leaving to one side wider concerns about this approach (see Ling, 1991) there are important questions to be asked concerning the extent to which the managerial changes identified earlier in this chapter are inter-related with the changes identified by Jessop. Amongst the most important changes which he identifies are the return to mass unemployment and the so-called 'flexibilizing' of the labour market.

Labour market flexibility, mass unemployment and social security

The return to mass unemployment, coupled with the British government's attempts to enhance the flexibility of the labour market as its main response to growing international competition, has had important implications for the management of social security. Social security involves particular objectives and priorities when, in times of full employment, most families most of the time receive the vast bulk of their income through the labour market. The labour market is then a site of social reproduction organized through the mechanisms of collective bargaining, managerial power and consumerism. However, as poverty in the low-wage sector, long-term unemployment, short-term contracts and part-time work all became more widespread, the labour market became a potentially disruptive force both in the economy and in society more widely. Between 1979 and 1990 some 1.3 million workers moved from full- to part-time work and now more than 40 percent of workers enjoy no redundancy pay with many more outside the National Insurance system (see Hutton, 1993). It therefore became the likely object of a series of government policies – each with implications for social security.

Immediate consequences of these policies were felt both in relation to the transition from youth to adulthood and in the 'management' of the long-term unemployed. Young people had been identified as of particular concern to the Conservative government from as early as a 'Think Tank' report of 1980 (CPRS, 1980: 7) and its 1981 report which was leaked by *Time Out* in 1983.

This concern underlay the government's change from open hostility towards the Manpower Services Commission (MSC) in 1979 to the announcement of a £1 billion one-year training scheme for all 16-year-old school leavers (see also MSC, 1981). The government accepted:

1 youth unemployment would continue to rise for the predictable future;
2 the previously dominant idea that training should be through the Industrial Training Boards (apprenticeships) was becoming redundant and, in any case, failed to reach the bottom 40 percent of the workforce;
3 the attitudes of young people needed to be changed;
4 wages needed to be brought down and the easiest place to begin this process was by altering the circumstances under which new recruits entered the workforce.

The result was the creation of the Youth Training Scheme (to replace the Youth Opportunities Programme). This included training in such 'skills' as the importance of keeping clean, understanding about loyalty to the workplace and how to use a telephone (MSC, 1984) despite the absence of evidence to suggest that the lack of such skills had contributed to the rise in youth unemployment. As the MSC put it '[T]he overall aim of the youth training scheme will be to produce a better motivated and more adaptable workforce' (MSC, 1983) and, in the chair of the MSC's words, employers 'now have the opportunity to take on young men and women, train them and let them work for you entirely at our expense, and then decide whether or not to employ them' (David Young in *The Director*, October 1982).

The success of this scheme from the government's point of view was dependent upon young people entering it. However, young people's disillusionment with the scheme was widespread and successive attempts to make it compulsory failed in the face of united employer and trade union hostility. Therefore the disciplining mechanism of social security was steadily introduced. Fundamentally, the principle of 'less eligibility' was applied (that is, that the choice of not going on a YTS scheme should be made more unpleasant than the choice to participate). YTS could only become the new 'bridge from youth to adulthood', in Dan Finn's (1987) perceptive phrase, if other bridges were knocked down.

In 1988 the Social Security Act denied 16- and 17-year-olds entitlement to income support and this was linked to the guaranteed offer of a Youth Training place (although they have some entitlement under the Act for up to sixteen weeks if they are estranged from their parents, have just left local authority care, have no living parent or guardian, could not return home because of abuse, are mentally or physically disabled, or have parents in prison or parents who are chronically sick).

In the years following the 1988 Act the Social Security Advisory Committee was continuously critical of this aspect of social security. In 1992 they wrote:

> We would strongly recommend, yet again, that the DSS reviews the procedures for young people claiming income support and makes changes that will ensure that those who are suffering hardship may claim benefit without having to deal with

complicated and, in our view, unnecessary and daunting procedures . . . (HMSO, 1992: 37)

The fact is that the provision of social security to young people was never intended to be an attractive alternative to Youth Training and the rules governing eligibility were more concerned with policing than protecting young people.

Young people over 17 but under 25 are eligible for lower age-related rates (also criticized by the Social Security Advisory Committee). One intention here is to encourage new recruits to the labour market to accept lower wages and show greater 'flexibility' in their job-hunting. It had already been recognized in the early 1980s that training would only provide part of the response to this situation. Patrick Jenkin, then the Industry Secretary, in a letter leaked by *Time Out* (27 May 1983: 5–7), accepted that long-term unemployment would continue to grow (among both the young and adults) and that the advantages of this could only be fully realized if Wages Councils (responsible for ensuring the payment of a minimum wage in certain industries) were abolished. The so-called advantages of this, however, could also only be realized if the gap between the low-wage sector and benefit payments was kept sufficiently wide. Once again, the implications for the management of social security are clear as it becomes involved in policing the bottom end of the labour market.

Governments since the 1970s have been increasingly concerned that, for the long-term unemployed in particular, just keeping a gap between social security payments and the low-wage sector may not be sufficient to maintain a ready supply of low-paid workers. A fundamental concern was that the experience of long-term unemployment may, of itself, remove the necessary will and the self-discipline to keep the unemployed genuinely 'available for work'. It is reflected in Jobclubs, Restart Courses (intended 'to bring job expectations in line with reality' according to 'Action for Jobs', Department of Employment, 1987), the New Workers Scheme (in which employers taking on young workers were paid a subsidy of £15 on condition that they pay sufficiently low wages), the Jobstart Allowance (an equivalent reward lasting for six months to the long-term unemployed if they agree to work for low wages). (For more on these see Meacher, 1989.) In its *Jobseeker's Charter*, the Department of Employment (1991) offers a package of experiences to unemployed people, including 'back to work' planning, Jobsearch seminars, Job Review workshops and Restart interviews. They are also offered the chance to participate in Jobclubs, Employment Action ('to keep your skills active'), access to employment training, a Job Interview Guarantee and a Restart Course ('to boost your confidence').

As early as the 1982 budget speech, the Chancellor announced a number of 'benefits-plus' (that is, a sum of money on top of benefits payments) community-based programmes 'intended to help the labour market work more flexibly, to help make wage levels more responsive to economic reality and so to lead to the creation of lasting jobs'. As with Youth Training, the government was forced to back-pedal in the face of considerable opposition, but when in 1993 John Major apparently supported the idea of 'workfare' (that is, no benefits without work of some sort) it should not have evoked such surprise (see *Guardian*, 5 Feb. 1993). The Employment Secretary's comment at the same time that 'it is important to keep the jobless in touch with the world of work' (*Guardian*, 5 Feb. 1993) reflects the persistence of a view held by figures within the Conservative Party throughout the period since 1979.

There are important implications in this for the management of the social security system. The Beveridge image was of a social security system catering for the tiny number of cases who fell through the full employment/ unemployment benefit net. For Beveridge, social security was never intended to be a system of mass provision, nor one massively concerned with meeting the income requirements of men and women who wanted to work but could not, or could only work for rates of pay which tied them to poverty. In the 1980s and 1990s, the social security system operates not only in the context where many of its 'customers' are expected to provide the labour market with added flexibility by being prepared to work for less money or in insecure employment or with poorer working conditions. Beveridge anticipated that those who became dependent upon National Assistance would be outside the labour market. In the Conservative policy of the 1990s the poor are regarded as a crucial part of it, providing it with the necessary flexibility to face up to foreign competition. The result is that these people cannot be managed as the marginalized and powerless recipients of welfare, dependent and rightless. The Jobclubs and Youth Training is one side of a coin and the Benefits Agency's *Customer Charter* the other. The discourse in each constitutes the poor as choice-making, independent, consumerist workers who are flexibly choosing between the wide range of options facing them. The fact that the reality facing many Benefits Agency 'customers' is not like this does not stop the discourse having real consequences.

The reality facing many claimants is, of course, that they find the benefits they receive inadequate. The first Minister for Social Security under Mrs Thatcher, Reg Prentice, should have prepared us for this when he commented in 1979 that 'If you believe economic salvation can only be achieved by rewarding success and the national income is not increasing, then you have no alternative but to make the unsuccessful poorer' (in Loney, 1987: 8). This is not only to make life on benefits 'less eligible' than life in the workplace but it is also in pursuit of another objective of government policy since 1979: the curtailment of public expenditure. As we saw at the beginning of this chapter, attempted reductions in public expenditure were largely unsuccessful but nevertheless its reduction remains central to many strategies aimed at restoring the UK's international competitiveness (because it is believed to 'crowd out' private investment, reduce incentives and to be inflationary). Furthermore, the belief that low wages and low taxation are crucial to the UK's capacity to attract inward investment is well established (if unsubstantiated). This belief lay behind the British government's suspicions of the social chapter of the Maastricht Treaty and it explains the importance of anti-fraud work within the Agency and the low priority given to take-up rates. It also lies behind the emphasis given to means-tested benefits (with the attendant administrative costs and problems). Barr and Coulter (1990) estimate a real increase in means-tested benefits of 171 percent during the 1980s compared with an increase of insurance benefits of just 17 percent during the same period (quoted in Bradshaw, 1992: 92). The overwhelming majority of registered unemployed people now receive income support rather than unemployment benefit (either because they are long-term unemployed or have not been employed for long enough to make sufficient national insurance contributions). Obviously, means-tested benefits involve more investigations and monitoring than insurance benefits and are more complex and expensive to manage.

Paradoxically, the resources available to the social security budget have been constrained partly in order to ensure that the better off receive substantially lower rates of income tax on higher incomes and gain substantially more through tax expenditures (and especially mortgage tax relief). Meanwhile those at the margins of poverty have found themselves more dependent upon benefits than would otherwise be the case because of the shift towards indirect taxes, real increases in rents, the council tax and water rates, increases in national insurance contributions and tax thresholds, rising only in line with prices (and not average earnings). Taking this into account, the genuine achievements in improving the administration of local offices may be cold comfort to the poor. Political choice has led to a managerial system of delivering benefits more heavily dependent upon top-down targets than upon home visits and a personalized service. It has also led to a treatment of the poor which is amongst the worst in Western Europe.

Thus the managerial systems currently applied within the DSS agencies are neither accidental nor arbitrary, but they are not simply the product of a narrow set of causes (whether these be seen as government indifference, the transition to post-Fordism or whatever). Jessop's notion of the Schumpeterian workfare state provides a valuable way into exploring these causes but it cannot carry the whole explanation. It is also worth emphasizing that far from only being an outcome of processes generated elsewhere, the new management of income maintenance has social effects of its own. It further individualizes the experience of dependency both by the manner through which payment is made available and through the limited nature of collective participation in the provision of the service. In addition, it gives this individualizing a particular content through its focus on 'customers', 'charters' and the like. This (combined with other policies) is an attempt to shape the identity of the poor and includes the repeated insistence that poverty no longer exists. Developments within the labour market and in the organization of production make it inevitable that income maintenance systems in all developed capitalist societies will be under pressure to change, but the particular direction and content of this change in the UK are also bound up with deeply rooted conservative assumptions about the patriarchal family and the poor as well as neo-liberal assumptions concerning the nature of poverty (perhaps expressed particularly clearly in the creation of the Child Support Agency to ensure that 'absent parents' – usually fathers – at least make a financial contribution to the upbringing of their children). As the right-wing Peregrine Worsthorne observed, 'Thatcherites think of poverty as a disease: largely self-induced' (Worsthorne, 1987: 38).

Conclusions

Comparing this chapter with others in this book, it is clear that the 'new managerialism' has had distinctive consequences for social security. There are no powerful professional groups which had to be overcome or won over. The clients of the department are also politically weak and whilst they may enjoy public sympathy they lack powerful political backing. This has produced a style of management similar to that presented as typical by Kelly (1991) in Table 2.2.

Partly because of the emphasis given to innovation within the new managerialism, partly because social security is by its nature responsive to changes in demography and the labour market, and above all because social security is locked into other policies concerned with managing the poor and policing the labour market, we have not arrived at a stable managerial settlement within the Department of Social Security. The notion of institutionalized permanent innovation describes this sense of flux well.

However, the recognition that the new public management has no stable basis in social security should not lead to the conclusion that the managerial changes are therefore trivial. They have had, and continue to have, real effects because they institutionalize and give organizational content to a new set of power relationships. The politics of the post-war boom were inclusive, a paternalistic one-nation politics in which everyone's basic needs should be met by a caring Establishment. The appropriate managerial style was a centralized, permanent bureaucracy which delivered the services deemed appropriate by a social or professional elite. Since the 1970s the divisive and two-nations effects of policies and structural changes has led to the need to manage the agencies most concerned with those excluded in new ways. It was never a likely political outcome that these people could simply be ignored by the state, but neither was it likely that professionals and paternalistic bureaucrats would be given a free hand. The result has been a halting and incomplete project to create a system of management which enhances the ability of the new political leadership at the centre to control the financial and political activities of the state system, and which attempts to encourage a particular set of identities within the excluded nation. Thus new forms of managing the state have become implicated in a complex set of processes through which public problems are experienced as personal grief and individual entrepreneurial choice is seen as the solution to social dislocations.

This suggests the real significance of the development of citizens' charters, for example. There can be no doubt that citizens' charters are genuinely

Table 2.2   *Changing management styles in the public sector*

	Administrative management	The 'new' managerialism
Management goals	system maintenance and stability	system performance and change
Resource strategy	reliance on state resources	proactive search for non-state resources
Resource allocation	by rules of eligibility and professional needs judgements	by target 'norms' and charges
Financial management objectives	to ensure probity	to inform management decision making
Cost reduction pressures	internal search for cost efficiency	external search for 'opportunities'
Incentives	rewards for conformity	rewards for innovation
Supervision style	rule/procedure based	review-based achievement
Employment relationship	long career hierarchy	short-term contracts
Orientation to consumers	defensive, paternalistic	receptive, responsive

Source: Kelly, 1991: 182.

intended to improve the quality of services and that they are taken seriously by public agencies. Equally, it is important to people claiming benefit that their claims should be quickly dealt with and that they should be treated in a courteous and professional manner. However, it does not help all of those who are unaware that they are entitled to benefit, those who are unaware of the existence of the charter, those who do not understand it, and those who are reluctant to complain to the same office which handles their claims. Arguably, these are the very people who need help most. Yet, should they fail to use it they have no-one to blame but themselves. Furthermore (and perhaps more importantly) for those who take advantage of the charter, it gives them a very institutionally limited option to influence the public agencies which most affect them.

Citizens' charters pose a fundamental question which concerns the nature of the relationship between the government and the citizen. With the new managerialism, government bodies would be managed like private organizations and citizens would have the opportunity to register complaints in the same way that they may wish to complain to (or even sue) their local supermarket. In this model the proper concern of government (that is, of democracy) is restricted to setting targets. Concern with how agencies are run is ruled off-limits for democracy. It is important to question the justification for such a decisive shift when, as we have seen, it is not possible to detach questions of management from questions of values and political choice.

The Benefits Agency is one institution amongst many Next Step bodies intended to secure this shift. These institutions have been created with limited political debate despite their constitutional significance. They mark the end of a unitary civil service but, it should be noted, they do not signify the radical dissolution of the unitary nature of the state. Rather, they are an attempt to regain financial and political coherence with a different strategic orientation through new institutional means. The Framework Agreement allows for this but does not guarantee it. There are two major drawbacks, from any government's point of view, of using contracts in this way. First, there are always interstices between the clauses in the contracts. In other words, it is not possible to design a contract which rules out the possibility of perverse incentives or ensures that 'grey areas' will not be exploited against the public interest. Indeed, discretion and judgement are usually necessary features of the work of many agencies. Secondly, there are many agencies whose work directly impinges upon other public bodies. In order to meet its targets, it is tempting for one agency to 'externalize' its costs by saving itself money in such a way that it compels other public bodies to spend more.

However, as has been argued throughout this chapter, it is important not to view the new management of social security as simply an exercise in technical efficiency. Wider processes of change are taking place and the new managerialism is part of these. It is 'part of' them in the sense that it is both shaped by them and gives them a particular institutional form and direction. In a sense, the search for a new managerial settlement within the state drove much of the politics of the 1980s and this has left a legacy of managerial flux and instability in the 1990s. The new public management was, in this sense, a vehicle for rearticulating the relationship between the state and civil society whilst simultaneously marginalizing hostile interests within the state.

The relative absence of political and academic debate around these questions is alarming. This is not only because it allows fundamental political choices to go uncontested (never a good thing in a democracy) but also because it has stunted the debate about alternative systems of management. Can agencies be run in different ways with different political values? Can some values simply not be incorporated into Framework Agreements? Could citizens' charters be so constructed that they would genuinely empower weaker members of society as well as improving the quality of service? These important political questions are also suitable areas for academic enquiry requiring further theoretical and empirical investigation. This would require subjecting 'Next Steps' and the new managerialism to more serious investigation than has usually been the case.

Note

A number of people have directly commented on this chapter and I would like to thank them all. In particular, the editors of this volume, Bob Jessop, Kevin Bonnett and Bryan Wendon have all helped in different ways. It is an unfortunate but necessary convention that they can share any credit whilst any errors must be mine.

References

Adler, M. (1992) 'Realising the potential of the operational strategy', *Benefits*, 4 (April/ May): 4–6.

Barnett, C. (1986) *The Audit of War: The Illusions and Reality of Britain as a Great Nation*. London: Macmillan.

Barr, N. and Coulter, F. (1990) 'Social security: solutions or problems?', in J. Hills (ed.), *The State of Welfare. The Welfare State in Britain since 1974*. Oxford: Clarendon Press.

Benefits Agency (1992) *Customer Charter*. London: Benefits Agency.

Bradshaw, J. (1991) 'Social security expenditure in the 1990s', *Public Money and Management*, 11(4): 25–30.

Bradshaw, J. (1992) 'Social security' in D. Marsh and R. Rhodes (eds), *Implementing Thatcherite Policies, Audit of an Era*. Buckingham: Open University Press.

Cohen, R., Coxall, J., Craig, G. and Sadiq-Sanster, A. (1992) *Hardship Britain: Being Poor in the 1990s*. London: CPAG (Child Poverty Action Group).

CPRS (Central Policy Review Staff) (1980) *Education, Training and Industrial Performance*. London: HMSO.

Department of Employment (1987) *Action for Jobs*. London: HMSO.

Department of Employment (1991) *Jobseeker's Charter*. London: Department of Employment.

DHSS (1982) *Social Security Operational Strategy: A Framework for the Future*. London: HMSO.

DHSS (1988) *The Business of Service: The Report of the Regional Organisation Scrutiny*, May. London: HMSO.

Efficiency Unit (1988) *Improving Management in Government: The Next Steps*. London: HMSO.

Esping-Andersen, G. (1990) *The Three Worlds of Welfare Capitalism*. Cambridge: Polity Press.

Finn, D. (1987) *Training Without Jobs. New Deals and Broken Promises*. London: Macmillan.

Fry, G.K. (1986) 'The British career civil service under challenge', *Political Studies*, 34(4): 533–53.

Gowan, P. (1987) 'The origins of the administrative elite', *New Left Review*, 162 (March/April): 4–34.

HC (1991) *Treasury and Civil Service Committee 7th Report 'The Next Steps Initiative'*. House of Commons, Session 1990–91 496.

Hennessy, P. (1989) *Whitehall*. London: Secker & Warburg.

HMSO (1991a) *The Government's Expenditure Plans 1991–1992 to 1993–1994, Social Security*, Cmnd. 1514. London: HMSO.

HMSO (1991b) *Annual Report of the CAO for 1990–91 on Adjudication Standards*. London: HMSO.

HMSO (1992) *Social Security Advisory Committee 8th Report*. London: HMSO.

HMSO (1993) *Sixth Report of the Parliamentary Commissioner for Administration*. London: HMSO.

Hutton, W. (1993) 'A country of casuals', *Guardian*, 30 March.

Jessop, B. (1992) 'Changing forms and functions of the state in an era of globalization and regionalization', paper presented at EAPE Conference, Paris.

Jessop, B. (1994) 'The transition to post-Fordism and the Schumpeterian workfare state', in R. Burrows and B. Loader (eds), *Towards a Post-Fordist Welfare State*. London: Routledge.

Kaufman, G. (1992) 'Privatising the ministers', *Guardian*, 7 December.

Kelly, A. (1991) 'The "new" managerialism in the social services', in P. Carter, T. Jeffs and M.K. Smith (eds), *Social Work and Social Welfare Yearbook 3*. Milton Keynes: Open University Press.

Ling, T. (1991) Review of *State Theory: Putting Capitalist States in their Place* by Bob Jessop, *Capital and Class*, 44 (Spring): 129–35.

Loney, M. (1987) 'A war on poverty or on the poor?' in A. Walker and C. Walker (eds), *The Growing Divide. A Social Audit 1979–1987*. London: CPAG.

Meacher, M. (1989) 'Employment', in M. McCarthy (ed.), *The New Politics of Welfare*. Oxford: Macmillan.

Metcalfe, L. and Richards, S. (1990) *Improving Public Management*, 2nd edn. London: Sage.

Mitchell, W.C. (1988) *Government As It Is*. London: Institute of Economic Affairs.

MSC (Manpower Services Commission) (1981) *A New Training Initiative, A Consultative Document*. London: MSC.

MSC (Manpower Services Commission) (1983) *Scheme Design and Content, Youth Training Scheme YTS B1*. London: MSC.

MSC (Manpower Services Commission) (1984) *Notes of Guidance, Occupational Training Families*. London: MSC.

Niskanen, W. (1973) *Bureaucracy: Servant or Master?* London: Institute of Economic Affairs.

Pascall, G. (1986) *Social Policy: A Feminist Analysis*. London: Tavistock.

Phillips, M. (1992) 'The tender trap of the civil service plc', *Guardian*, 21 July.

Pliatzky, L. (1992) 'Quangos and agencies', *Public Administration*, 70(4) (Winter): 555–64.

Ponting, C. (1985) *The Right to Know. The Inside Story of the Belgrano Affair*. London: Sphere Books.

Randall, A. (1992) 'Service planning – an agenda for the Benefits Agency', *Benefits*, 4 (April/May): 7–9.

Scharpf, F.W. (1991) *Crisis and Choice in European Social Democracy*. New York: Cornell University Press.

Stoker, G. (1989) 'Creating a local government for a post-Fordist society: the Thatcherite project?' in J. Stewart and G. Stoker (eds), *The Future of Local Government*. London: Macmillan.

Thomson, P. (1992) 'Public sector management in a period of radical change: 1979–1992', *Public Money and Management*, 32(3) (July–September): 33–42.

Worsthorne, P. (1987) *By the Right*. London and Dublin: Brophy Books.

3

Managing the National Health Service

Sylvia Walby and June Greenwell

Introduction

The managerialization of the NHS has been a bitterly contested process over the last decade. It has been a complex change, partly because there have been a series of quite different attempts at managerialization, and partly because of the diversity of the workforce in the NHS. The reconstruction of the agenda over which struggles take place has been fast and fluid, with 'the best interests of the patient' acting as the contested high ground.

The quantity of complexities in the reshaping of health work may initially appear to be specific to the NHS, but they actually share many features with those in the rest of the public services, albeit with different labels.

Diversity of managerialisms

There is more than one way of doing management. Although the Taylorist type of managerialism is sometimes treated as if it were the only form (for example Braverman, 1974), this assumption needs to be rejected (see Elger, 1979; Wood, 1989). Indeed the changes in the NHS can only be understood in the context of the partial development of 'new wave management'. The tensions between these two main types of management theory and practice underlie the complexity of the managerialization of the NHS. They are espoused by different groups, and have varying impact in different areas, and at different levels of rhetoric and practice.

The distinction between management styles, described in more detail in Chapter 10 (by Norman Flynn), is essentially between two ostensibly opposed forms of control over the worker and the production process. Taylorism (referred to by Flynn as 'scientific management') has at its core control through detailed supervision, and efficiency improvements created by breaking complex tasks down into simpler ones which can be performed by less skilled and cheaper workers. New wave management (sometimes called 'new human resource management') is different in attempting to utilize a worker's human capacity to treat work as a creative arena. It works by trying to create positive worker commitment which leads to harder and more creative and engaged work. Taylorist management presumes a model of social relations and human nature in which workers will only work if pushed by wage incentives and surveillance. New wave management presumes a model of society in which workers will work if their commitment can be engaged by treating them as creative sensitive human beings. The perspectives also differ on the wider context of financial constraint, the former seeking to centralize in order to control; the latter seeking to decentralize in order to engage front-line workers' expertise and self-discipline. Taylorism controls through standardization, centralization and bureaucratization, while new wave management seeks to increase productivity through flexibility and decentralization (Peters and Waterman, 1982; Peters, 1987; Wood, 1989).

These perspectives underlie the series of attempts to managerialize the NHS over the last decade. They have been drawn on to different extents in the different waves of reorganization, and for different groups of workers, as will be explored below. While they may appear diametrically opposed alternatives, they also coexist, producing a dissonance that encourages scepticism rather than enthusiastic commitment.

'Managers' and 'managerialism'

The distinction between introducing 'managers' and 'managerialism' is important for understanding the NHS. Conventionally management has been thought of as being performed by people who have 'manager' in their job title. The division between management and worker has often been presumed to be that between two different groups of people: 'managers' and 'workers'. However, this is inappropriate in the analysis of management in the NHS for three reasons. First, this has never been really appropriate for professional workers, who have often performed management functions (nor for other workers with such responsibilities). Senior professional workers, such as medical consultants, GPs and ward sisters, have usually organized and regulated the work of junior members of their professions. Secondly, the most recent changes have attempted to enhance the management role of doctors, especially consultants and GPs, implicating them more deeply in budget and other management decisions. Thirdly, management is best conceptualized as a function or set of tasks which are performed by various people to various extents, rather than as a single distinct set of people. Indeed, it may be thought of as involving a discourse which permeates conduct and involves actors, rather than being an identifiable set of actors. Contestations over meaning by actors with different power resources are important. Indeed, there is an argument for using a term different from management, with its heavy ideological baggage, referring perhaps instead to organizational co-ordination, as Clarke and Newman suggest in Chapter 1.

The importance of the distinction between 'managers' and 'managerialism' can be seen in the shift within the managerializing strategy between the mid-1980s and the early 1990s. It is shown up most sharply in the relationship of doctors to management.

The influence of Taylorist management in the NHS was massively strengthened with the introduction of general managers into the NHS in the mid-1980s following the Griffiths report in 1983 (DHSS, 1983). Managerial initiatives had been implemented in the NHS prior to Griffiths, with the introduction of planning systems in 1974 (DHSS, 1972) and increasing use in the NHS of the monitoring mechanisms instituted in Whitehall by Rayner in the early 1980s (Hennessy, 1989; Harrison, Hunter and Pollitt, 1990). Cox suggests that the industrial disputes of the late 1970s were a significant factor in transforming administrators into managers well ahead of Griffiths (Cox, 1991), and the introduction of competitive tendering for hospital ancillary services was another indicator of a stronger managerial ethos preceding the introduction of general management (Cousins, 1988). The significance of Griffiths was that this was a very overt attempt to introduce managerialism by bringing in traditional-style managers. Griffiths, whose experience was based in the retail grocer, Sainsbury's, explicitly sought to introduce conventional private sector forms of management into the NHS. General managers were expected to subordinate the health professions, especially medicine, to a single chain of command. It was supposed to overcome the syndicalist structure which had developed in the post-war period in which each profession was effectively self-governing (DHSS, 1983; Owens and Glennerster, 1990; Strong and Robinson, 1990).

These changes were bitterly fought by health service workers, in particular by the medical and nursing professions. They were regarded as an attack on their professionalism. Nurses derided the general managers in a poster campaign as being unable to distinguish between different parts of the anatomy. The debate was between a defence of professional expertise as essential to the taking of decisions in the NHS, against the general managers' claim to be able to improve efficiency (Strong and Robinson, 1990; Butler, 1992).

The campaigns by the health professions failed to prevent the imposition of the new general managers. However, at a local level the power of the general managers to enforce change was significantly circumscribed by their dependence upon the professions to carry out the work and the professionals' possession of the effective knowledge.

The debate over the causes of the troubles of the NHS in the late-1980s was primarily between those who attributed these to lack of funding, and those who blamed the professions and the lack of a directive management structure. Political arguments over the funding of the NHS were the precursor of the major round of changes introduced by the White Paper *Working for Patients* (Department of Health, 1989a). In the winter of 1987–8 there was a growing political storm over what was described in the press as the underfunding of the NHS. Indeed, in 1986 the House of Commons Social Services Committee, which had a Conservative majority, reported that between 1980–1 and 1986–7 underfunding of NHS hospitals and community health services in England ran to £1.325 billion (Butler, 1992: 3). The financial squeeze had been operated through a number of mechanisms, including demands for regular 'efficiency savings', that is, funding was reduced on the presumption that efficiency had been improved as demanded as well as unrealistic assumptions about wage and price inflation. Further, there was a geographical dimension in that Resource Allocation Working Party (RAWP) formula was redistributing resources towards the previously underfunded Midlands and North away from the South-East, increasing the resource reduction in the area closest to national media and politicians. The media reported many stories, particularly ones about ward and bed closures and sick babies. The underfunding of the NHS became an issue in the 1987 general election. In the first six months of the 1987–8 Parliamentary session the House of Commons held nine debates on NHS cuts (Butler, 1992: 3). Popular opinion wanted more spending on the NHS, as suggested by an opinion poll in May 1988 where only 3 percent thought enough was being spent and 49 percent thought extra money should come from general taxation (Butler, 1992: 5). Such a policy of spending more money on state services was inconsistent with Thatcherism. By January 1988 Thatcher announced that an internal government review was under way.

Doctors into managers via finance

The next wave of managerialization took place on the basis of the 1989 White Paper *Working for Patients* (Department of Health, 1989a) which introduced markets into the NHS. Among its changes it sought to turn doctors into managers rather than setting managers to control doctors. Rather than professionals being set against managers, as in the changes of the mid-1980s, the senior medical professionals of today are being encouraged to become more managerial. The development of managerialism within existing professions, rather than in opposition to them, is a more subtle and possibly more effective strategy for the introduction of managerialism than that of introducing outside managers. While resistance to general managers was overt and forceful, that to managerialism within professions is much less strong. Resistance to the changes invoked by *Working for Patients* (Department of Health 1989a) was located at a different level, in particular resistance to the development of hospitals into Trusts and GPS into fund-holders. Why should doctors resist taking on the role of controller of a budget, which can appear to enhance their decision-making role? The priorities and discourses of new wave management can be seen here with their emphasis on pushing decision making down to the front-line worker, here the doctor, who is conceived to be closer to the needs and wishes of the customer. Increased overt involvement in financial allocation is a key feature in the new management of medical care by doctors. The post-1989 changes in management form introduced more overt discussion of finance and the ostensible devolution of financial decisions downwards. Doctors have become more involved in financial decisions as part of their managerialization. This can be represented as part of the decentralizing thrust of new wave management.

However, while the form of the development of the role of the doctor as controller of budgets is new, doctor control over resources is not. Doctors have always regulated access to medical care. They have always taken decisions as to whether patients should be treated and with what level of intervention. This has been understood within a discourse of clinical freedom, in which the doctor makes the decision 'in the best interests of the patient'. The sub-clause of 'in the context of the available resources' has always been present, but less frequently spelt out in public debate than is now the case. Doctors have always decided among themselves the priorities of resource allocation – should there be a new dialysis machine in the renal unit, or another baby incubator? However, these decisions have previously been articulated in a medical terminology focused around need. The change has been the introduction of finance at a lower level of decision making and a more overt recognition of the salience of financial matters in the setting of priorities.

The increasing managerialization of medicine can be understood in some ways as one inspired by new wave management theory. This is the case in the ostensible increase in the financial decision making of doctors. However, there are simultaneous changes which have more similarity with Taylorism, especially in the greater control over the consultants' contracts and work timetable and the greater surveillance over their practice. A third element of surveillance over the work of health professionals is the process of evaluating the outcomes of treatment. This appears to fit as easily into a service ethos as it does to a management process, and the fact that it has been so slow in establishing itself as part of the UK health service may be a comment on the strength of paternalistic and corporate traditions in both UK health managers and professionals rather than a conflict between them.

Donabedian has described three different aspects of health service provision amenable to evaluation, and therefore surveillance: the structure, processes and outcomes of health care (quoted in Coulter, 1991). Evaluation mechanisms for all three have been developing over the last three decades. The significance of the changes in the last decade is not that they have sprung into life within a service that previously had no management function, but that management has been given a central role within the NHS. Both the Griffiths changes, and the NHS reforms required managers to manage professionals, in contrast to an administrative cadre that had previously existed to support professional services. These are inherently different functions, but since the outcome of service provision is determined by professionals, the intention to manage professionals is likely to have variable results.

Involving doctors in management has been developing since the first 'Cogwheel' report in 1967. Resource management has its origins in clinical budgeting systems that allowed clinicians to have an understanding of the cost implications of the decisions that they made. Since the selection of particular waiting-list patients for treatment rather than others can determine whether a health authority or hospital achieves a balanced budget for the year, reviews of case mix are an element of clinical budgeting. A recent initiative, encouraged by *Working for Patients* (Department of Health,

1989a) and designed to involve professional staff more closely in budgetary management is the establishment of clinical directorates.

Medical audit was initiated in the UK by doctors, with the survey of peri-operative mortality as a prominent early example, but was rapidly developed following the publication of *Working for Patients* (Department of Health, 1989a) when it became obligatory practice. Medical unease has centred on the possibility that medical audit may be used by general managers to serve non-medical agendas, not on the process of medical audit itself. The stance taken by government in establishing medical audit, that 'the quality of medical work can only be reviewed by a doctor's peers' (NHSME, 1989), may have been less of a firm policy than a placatory and transient message to encourage doctors to put aside their misgivings about government's intentions. Managerial control of the clinical agenda is more likely to be expressed through clinical budgeting and the management of case mix rather than through medical audit. Nevertheless, contested control of audit information is an indicator of the determination of medicine to absorb and retain managerialism within the profession, rather than maintain opposition to managerial initiatives.

Consultants have traditionally had very considerable autonomy in organizing their own work. The 1989 changes included the specification of a timetable as part of annually renewed contracts (Department of Health, 1989b). This level of surveillance in a documented form was previously unheard of for consultants who, in practice, were accountable to no one, except in most exceptional cases of abuse or error for which they could be sanctioned by the General Medical Council. This new surveillance of doctors, especially consultants, thus introduces a Taylorist type of control at the same time as the other types of new wave management.

Nurses

So far the discussion of management in the NHS has followed the two groups traditionally examined in this regard – doctors and managers. However, this conventional approach has a serious problem in its neglect of the management of other groups of workers, in particular, nurses and ancillary workers. The NHS is a large diverse employer and to a considerable extent utilizes different forms of management for different types of workers, despite, to some extent, a common identity and goal.

Nurses have long been subject to more conventionally Taylorist forms of management than doctors. The organization of nursing involves a more bureaucratic form of governance, closer supervision, greater accountability for mistakes and a clearer hierarchy of command than medicine. This occurs despite the sometimes isolated working conditions of some nurses, especially at night. Nurses have a management hierarchy within the profession with job titles which reflect this – Charge Nurse, Nurse Manager, District Nursing Officer. Thus it would be incorrect to say that the NHS does not have a strong Taylorist element in its management system. Yet, too often, accounts of the management of the NHS appear to suggest that the only relevant category of workers is that of doctors.

Nurses have in recent years made strong efforts to reorganize in a manner which is similar to the more traditional professions. This has involved some elements which are the same as those in new wave management. This is clearest in the development of the 'New Nursing'. This is a new form of nursing philosophy and practice which emphasizes the holistic treatment of the patient, rather than its fragmentation into a number of specialist functions carried out by many different people. It finds expression in the practice of primary nursing where each patient has a primary nurse who organizes their care. This is in contrast to nurses performing the same task across the whole ward. It is a practice which attempts to be patient (or consumer) oriented. It is a good example of functional flexibility (Atkinson, 1986; Walby, 1989). It is associated with the drive to improve the levels of training and breadth of education of nurses, as represented in *Project 2000* (UKCC, 1986) which takes nurse training into general higher education rather than units attached to hospitals and tries to raise the standard. A recent change in the *Code of Practice* for nurses by their national body, the UKCC, states that there is to be a move away from minute certification for detailed skills, the 'extended role', and towards a general professional training and judgement (UKCC, 1992).

The assessment of the effectiveness of these changes for patients, which is the yardstick accepted by nurses as well as managers, is complex. The study by Carr-Hill et al. (1992) assessed the benefit to patient care of nurses being more highly trained. The response to this was an unequivocal affirmative, but the complexities of the analysis, and the importance the authors attach to the organization of nursing care and the provision of post-qualification training belie the author's claim that the overall conclusion is simple.

At the same time as this increase in the level of training of new nurses there has been the introduction of a new grade of health care assistants, who have only six months' training, instead of the Registered Nurse's three years. While nursing leaders are seeking to upgrade the whole profession, some fear that the outcome will be a polarization between the more highly trained, fully qualified *Project 2000* nurse and an increasingly numerous layer of semi-skilled nursing assistants. These workers, the new health care assistants, will not have the same pay and conditions as fully trained nurses.

Some fully trained nurses do not work on permanent contracts, but rather are employed on a short temporary basis, as bank or agency nurses. Such temporary nurses are unlikely to develop the ongoing knowledge of the ward and patients of permanent staff, and hence detract from the New Nursing project. There is a question as to how much this practice will grow; indeed, some commentators fear that it might lead to a collapse in the conventional nursing career (Davies, 1990). The growth of part-time working has also occurred in nursing, as elsewhere among women workers.

These developments potentially undermine the development of a skilled more professionalized nursing occupation. We see, therefore, the ongoing tension between different logics of management: on the one hand the fully committed permanent highly trained worker; on the other the temporary and less skilled workers who are unlikely to be part of the same culture of commitment.

In the wider structure of the hospital nurses have a historically varying place on governing bodies. The heyday for nursing may be thought to be the 1970s when the two major health professions were regarded as complementary and when consensus management was the order of the day. The Griffiths changes of the mid-1980s removed nurses' automatic right of representation on health authority management teams, a move which was bitterly contested. In the new regime most arrangements are discretionary and some nurses have come back into senior management with job descriptions relating to quality assurance. Robinson (1992) is very critical of the lack of consideration of nursing and the nursing viewpoint in high-level health decisions, referring to it as the 'black hole of nursing'.

The direction of change in nursing is thus away from Taylorism towards new wave management, insofar as the highly trained nurse remains the typical nurse. This significantly overlaps with the notion of developing professionalism. Perhaps more than any other group of health workers, nurses have managed to go with the 'new times', merging the discourse of new wave management concern for the customer and individually tailored products with their own project of upgrading the training and autonomy of their profession. This, if it is actually achieved, might be an instance of the golden scenario of new wave management. However, the wider context of pressures on the nursing budget means that this is by no means an inevitable outcome. The alternative scenario is that managers will introduce more of the less trained, cheaper, health care assistants in more conventional Taylorist style.

Ancillary workers

Ancillary workers are essential to the working of the NHS, even though they are the least frequently discussed group of health workers. It was ancillary workers who were the first to experience the attempts by the Thatcher government to introduce its ideas on management and cost cutting on the NHS. The management restructuring here takes a quite different form again. The workers here include many hygiene workers, such a laundry workers, pest control and ward cleaners, as well as cooks, and many others (Cousins, 1988).

There was an attempt to separate each group of these workers from the conditions and solidarity of other hospital workers. The work became subject to compulsory competitive tendering (CCT). In the early 1980s one of the first attempts to cut costs and control workers in the NHS (and in local authorities) was government insistence that certain forms of work must go out to tender rather than be automatically performed in-house. This had a diverse outcome since hospitals were allowed to tender alongside outsiders and some bids were won in-house. The overall impact was to drive down wage levels and conditions of service, such as job security, whether the contract was won in-house or not. It was a practice which was strongly resisted by the relatively well unionized workers, but without much success. These workers were then subjected to conventional and severe forms of management. CCT has been the subject of litigation at a European level and there is currently some uncertainty as to the legality of replacing one set of workers with another with worse conditions of service in such a deliberate way.

The management of doctors, nurses and ancillary workers is quite different and the tendency to consider that the treatment of the doctors is the same as the treatment of the NHS is a mistake.

Marketization

The structural changes which generated the managerialization of doctors via finance were deliberate. The 1989 White Paper *Working for Patients* (Department of Health, 1989a) explicitly introduced markets into the NHS for the first time (with the exception of ancillary functions). This was part of the Conservatives' belief that markets would produce more efficiency than state-run services. Buyers and sellers were created by separating purchasers from providers. Purchasers were of two sorts: all the District Health Authorities and those GPs who successfully asked to become fund-holders. Providers were hospitals and other health organizations, such as ambulance services.

The original White Paper concept of a competitive internal market was rapidly scaled down. In the first year of the new system purchasers were required to place their contracts with their traditional suppliers. The Secretary of State moved rapidly to issue 'guidance' on the way hospital consultants should relate to GP fund-holders (NHSME, 1991). Applications from London hospitals to become NHS trusts were deferred to allow the Tomlinson Commission time to pronounce on the future pattern of health provision in London. Nevertheless, even a scaled-down and managed market represented a massive change in NHS organization.

Purchasers were presumed to choose providers on grounds of both cost and quality and to change their providers as necessary to achieve greater efficiency (after the first year). The choice of two types of purchasers appears to have been both an experiment and a compromise. The District Health Authorities are large bodies which had previously run the provider units, such as hospitals. Recently they have been encouraged to group together to form even larger purchasing consortia. The GP fund-holders, by contrast, are much smaller units, albeit that the smallest practices were not allowed to apply for this status.

Provider units were invited to apply for trust status which gave them considerable autonomy from the Health Authority in their internal organiz-ation. There have been annual rounds of applications for trust status and now the majority of hospitals, or hospital groups, are trusts. Trusts have had the freedom to vary the conditions of employment of staff, although they were strongly discouraged from utilizing this in the early years of the new system.

The relationship between purchasers and providers is mediated by a market and by contracts. The purchasers place contracts with provider units for a number of units of service, with a small amount of funds set aside for extra-contractual referrals. Three kinds of contracts exist: block contracts, cost and volume contracts, and cost-per-case contracts. The last of these is the form of contract that fits most closely to a market model, while block contracts resemble a more bureaucratic arrangement. Emergency services, and many medical services, are frequently paid for through a block contract, while waiting-list surgery utilizes either cost and volume, or a cost-per-case contract. These distinctions reflect the fact that emergency medical services do not fit as easily into a market structure as waiting-list surgery. Hence the budgets held by GPs are for payment for waiting-list surgery only, while emergency admissions are covered by the block contracts issued by health authorities. At the same time, the financial viability of accident and emergency units relate critically to retention of waiting-list orthopaedic contracts, which are precisely the kind of contract most vigorously competed for by the private sector.

The changing pattern of utilization of hospitals following the development of the market is an expected feature of the new system. Provider units, such as hospitals, are expected to respond to threatened loss of contracts by cutting costs and improving efficiency. The provider units which are most expensive, for whatever reason, face a shrinking future. If this were a real market then the bankruptcy of some provider units would, on occasion, be a feature of the system. The threatened financial disaster facing London's many expensive, old, specialist hospitals in areas of declining population made the government draw back from the full workings of the market. A special commission, the Tomlinson Commission, was set up to plan the orderly closure of selected London hospitals. This led to a series of campaigns run through the media to save particular hospitals. For a while it seemed that paternalistic rationalization had replaced the use of a market mechanism, but by the autumn of 1993 the internal market was threatening the financial viability of the hospitals that Tomlinson had retained. Planning and politics, or, perhaps, trial by the media, appear to be important continuing elements of the system.

There is a more general question as to the limits of the possible marketization of the NHS. Markets require large amounts of accurate information to function efficiently. For instance, both purchasers and providers need information on the pricing of the services for sale, the provider needs to know accurately the costs of production, and the purchaser needs to be able to compare prices with those offered elsewhere. Further, they each need to have good information on quality standards, since price is not the only consideration (presumably). Yet the NHS has not historically needed this information and is only now establishing the mechanisms which, it is hoped, will generate the information. The costs of this information system are significant. One of the reasons for the low administrative cost of the previous NHS compared to insurance-based health care systems was that it did not need to collect such information. The nature of the work in health is such that this information is necessarily hard to collect and that the costs of trying to do so are high. Bourne and Ezzamel (1986) argue that different types of management have developed in response to the differential ability to measure costs and quality of work, and that to ignore such differences is a mistake. They argue that Griffiths was wrong to suggest that the NHS can be placed closer to the market in the same way as is possible in the management of retail grocery. The variety of forms of marketization of public health services, and the construction of different groups between which market relations are appropriate, which has occurred in different countries, is instructive (Saltman and Von Otter, 1992).

The essential data to adjudicate the claims of the medical profession and the government is to be able to compare outcomes. Have more patients been successfully treated for less money and is the health of the nation improved? How is successful treatment measured? Unfortunately, if not unexpectedly, the data on this is highly contentious and contradictory. It would appear both that more patients have been treated and that the waiting lists are longer. This may be connected with far greater care being taken in collecting information on numbers treated when there is a direct financial value in showing an increase. The impossibility of measuring the quality of care should engender caution. The principal of *reductio ad absurdum* illuminates the issue; if all patients were discharged from hospital too early, so that all had to be readmitted, the hospital service would be statistically twice as 'efficient'.

Perhaps the greatest absurdity is that waiting lists and waiting times measure the time after the consultant has seen a patient in the clinic, whereas the total wait is from the time the GP requests that the consultant should see a patient. In effect there are two waits, but improvements in the highly publicized waiting list statistics refer only to the time between clinic consultation and admission.

A disturbing aspect of concentrating on waiting-list statistics is that reductions in the numbers waiting, or in the time spent waiting, may only be achievable by processes that reduce the quality of care that can be given to emergency admissions. The absence of statistical indicators to compare, say, the time between a GP request for an emergency admission to the admission of a patient to a ward is a measure of the potential there is for some service improvements to mask other service failings. The only objective, rational, response to the question of whether changes in the NHS have improved the efficiency of the service is an open acknowledgement that no information exists to answer the question.

Consumers

The traditional interpretation of these changes from the left has typically been to argue that they are simply part of an attempt to drive down the wages and conditions of service of workers, and to control the NHS, in order to contain health expenditure more easily. This represents the scenario as one with two sides, represented by two groups of people, workers on the one side, managers and government on the other.

However, the new feature of the debate is that of the place of the consumer or patient. It is this which makes the above account too simple. All sides claim that they are working in the best interests of the patient, but the way that this has been articulated has been changing.

Everyone in the NHS has always claimed that patients come first, as in the Hippocratic Oath of the medical profession, from the caring nurse, to the government in their White Paper of this title. New wave management has stressed the significance of the consumer and the new public battle over who cares for patients most effectively is carried out in the new discourse, rather than the old. But it means different things to different groups. The health professionals have a long history of successful claims to working for patients. They have long attempted to construct the government as the problem for the NHS on the grounds that the service is under-resourced. The doctor versus the bureaucrat became the doctor versus the manager and the state in the late 1980s.

A new consumer movement in the wider society has had a strong resonance in health (Williamson, 1992). Two successful examples of this have been that for birthing women to have more control over how they are treated on maternity wards, and that to allow parents of sick children access to their children in hospital at most times. There is, in fact, a long history of medical sociologists criticizing doctors for their insensitivity to patients' felt needs (Stacey, 1988).

There is competition for the status of the best representative of the user of health services. It is often claimed that the patient has insufficient knowledge to be able to make the choices typical consumers would have so that there are various mechanisms and persons who attempt to fill the gap. Traditionally this role has been successfully claimed by the doctor, either as general practitioner, or the hospital consultant to whom the patient is referred. Nurses are increasingly seeking a portion of this role, especially those influenced by the new nursing philosophy and by the increasing weight such nursing projects place on the care of the whole person. Community Health Councils have existed in the NHS since 1974 to represent the views of the users and potential users of health services on a local basis, but have had little statutory power, minimal budgets and a labyrinthine system of appointing members. Some have succeeded in gaining local influence in health care provision in spite of these features. After the 1991 changes following *Working for Patients* (Department of Health, 1989a), they have lost some of their statutory powers, though they have been given more symbolic status. Pressure groups have developed since the 1960s taking up special needs and cases, such as those of women giving birth, the parents of hospitalized children, MENCAP for the care of the developmentally disabled, Age Concern for the elderly.

The recent shift in political and managerial discourse has given increased importance to the interests of the consumer. New wave management seeks to make workers more sensitive to the needs of the consumer, by advocating the movement of decision making closer to the consumer. John Major's political initiatives have emphasized the consumer rather than the producer, who was perceived to have neglected the needs of the consumer. Major attempted to link the consumer with the citizen with his range of citizen's charters, including a specific one for health.

The Conservatives launched a challenge to the view that the interests of the patient were best looked after by the health professions. Welfare state professionals have been characterized as self-serving, organizing the welfare state to suit themselves rather than their customers. Popular consumerism and criticism of state bureaucrats has been called upon as the basis of a project of reducing the power of welfare professionals.

Consumers may be represented by such official democratic bodies as Community Health Councils (CHCs), or pressure groups such as MENCAP, which operate at a political and policy level. However, the Conservatives believed that the market was a better mechanism to represent the consumer than political and democratic processes. For the government, the consumer was best represented when a purchaser. Rather than create the patient as the consumer, they gave this status to the District Health Authorities and GP fund-holders. These were to purchase services on behalf of the public and patients.

Popular consumerism has been re-expressed by the government in its citizens' charters, and its policy of backing consumers against producers. There has been a popular criticism of the way that state bureaucracies treat individuals, especially when they are clients.

The left has been divided in its response to this, some ignoring the criticism of the state welfare institutions which the Labour movement had fought so hard to establish, others, especially those influenced by feminism, already moving to policies of decentralization and localism (Wainwright, 1987). On the right, the articulation of these complaints about unfeeling, self-regarding bureaucrats found a relatively clear expression in a discourse of individualism. The right was able to articulate these concerns in terms of the needs of individuals against collective state agencies, of the effectiveness of the market to treat people as individuals. There has been an attempt to equate marketization with individualization and democratization, which has been remarkably, though certainly not consistently, successful.

The success of Major's political project of creating a new hegemony around the consumer against the producer should not be exaggerated. While the government has control of sufficient levers of power to establish certain changes of organizational structure, this is not the same as winning popular consent. Indeed, popular opinion has consistently supported increased funding for the NHS throughout the 1980s and 1990s, as shown in regular opinion polls (Butler, 1992). This is not to argue that the changes are reversible, but rather that public perception has consistently and strongly adhered to the belief that the NHS is under-funded, despite the best efforts of the government to attribute the cause of shortages in services to the health workers.

The changing form of management of the NHS cannot be understood outside of the wider political context and the dominance of government and its levers of power by the Conservatives since 1979. The health workers have not lost the popular arguments, insofar as public support for increased funding is concerned, despite the weaknesses in their position. But they are subject to a determined political attempt to reshape the employment relations within the NHS, the better to control costs and the shape of the health service.

Empowerment

Are workers and users empowered by those of the changes which are consistent with new wave management? New wave management has the potential to empower both producers and consumers. The question is that of the end to which this version of managerialism is put. Quality indicators, outcome targets, performance review, peer review and so on could be used to improve the service to patients, but in the context of fierce 'cost containment' they are as likely to be used to squeeze workers. Underlying new wave management theory is a conception of human nature which is optimistic, one in which people will be productive if they are treated well and will use autonomy creatively for customers; but this rhetoric is assimilable to Taylorist techniques, with its agenda of tight control over a set of workers who are deemed untrustworthy. The final question is thus a political one, of the government's agenda for health.

Managerialization in the NHS has affected different groups of workers in different ways. Ancillary workers have been subject to peripheralization as their jobs have been put out to tender and their conditions of service and wages reduced. Nurses are divided, with some gaining autonomy and training as part of a long-run professionalization strategy, while the new grade of health care assistant is subject to a different regime. Doctors have been subject to both an attempt at Taylorism under Griffiths, and new wave management with the development of Clinical Directorates.

Managerialism in the NHS has been introduced within a discourse of putting consumers before producers. However, the context of fierce cost constraints has reduced its potential to actually improve services for patients. The NHS is still one of the cheapest health care systems among Western industrialized countries.

The market has been an important part of the recent wave of managerialization, yet the introduction of markets into the NHS has been slow and partial. The construction of a market is necessary to the Conservatives' conception of the consumer. Yet it has not been the patient, but the District Health Authorities and GP fund-holders who have been constructed as the purchasers. The outcome of market pressures, however, has not been unmitigated. The selection of London hospitals for closure has not been left to the market and bankruptcy, but to politics and planning. Instances of the market producing adverse outcomes for individuals have been subject to intense critical scrutiny in the press. The marketization of the health service must be regarded as still contested and partial, rather than complete, despite the central place of the market in Conservative management discourse.

Insofar as new wave management has been introduced, there is some empowerment of consumers and of workers, but in many instances the managerialization introduced has involved a Taylorist as well as a new wave strand. Thus senior doctors are not averse to controlling the budget for their specialty, but resent the control of general managers over the size of the budget and the increased surveillance over their practice. Those nurses who are able to participate in the upskilling of their profession and the increased autonomy of primary nursing may be enthusiastic about the changes, but those at the sharp end of budgetary restrictions and increased workloads are subject to greater restrictions. Insofar as patients receive holistic nursing care and the special attention given to the patients of GP fund-holders then they may welcome the changes, but those on the growing waiting lists, or with ailments which are considered of low priority, are disempowered. Both medicine and nursing have consistently and strongly opposed managerialization, which they see as undercutting their special commitment and ability to carry out their jobs looking after patients, but have been less resistant to the increase in the managerial components of their own jobs. The government aim of containing the costs of the NHS is still a pipe dream, in the context of an ageing population and advances in medical technology, but professional power has been directed towards cost containment by the invigorated mix of Taylorist and new wave management.

References

Atkinson, J. (1986) *Changing Work Patterns: How Companies Achieve Flexibility to Meet New Needs*. London: National Economic Development Office.

Bourne, Michael and Ezzamel, Mahmoud (1986) 'Organizational culture in hospitals in the National Health Service', *Financial Accountability and Management*, 3(1): 29–45.

Braverman, Harry (1974) *Labor and Monopoly Capital*. New York: Monthly Review Press.

Butler, John (1992) *Patients, Policies and Politics: Before and After 'Working for Patients'*. Buckingham: Open University Press.

Carr-Hill, Roy, Dixon, Paul, Gibbs, Ian, Griffiths, Mary, Higgins, Moira, McCaughan, Dorothy and Wright, Ken (1992) *Skill Mix and the Effectiveness of Nursing Care*. York: Centre for Health Economics, University of York.

Coulter, Angela (1991) 'Evaluating the outcomes of health care', in Jonathan Gabe, Michael Calnan and Michael Bury (eds), *The Sociology of the Health Service*. London: Routledge.

Cousins, Christine (1988) 'The restructuring of welfare work: the introduction of general management and the contracting out of ancillary services in the NHS', *Work Employment and Society*, 2 (June): 210–28.

Cox, David (1991) 'Health service management', in Jonathan Gabe, Michael Calnan and Michael Bury (eds), *The Sociology of the Health Service*. London: Routledge.

Davies, Celia (1990) *The Collapse of the Conventional Career*, English Nursing Board (ENB) Project Paper 3. London: ENB.

Department of Health (1989a) *Working for Patients*, White Paper Cm 555. London: HMSO.

Department of Health (1989b) *NHS Consultants: Appointments, Contracts and Distinction Awards*, NHS Review Working Paper no. 7. London: HMSO.

Department of Health and Social Security (1972) *Management Arrangements for the Re-organised National Health Service*. London: HMSO.

Department of Health and Social Security (1983) *The NHS Management Inquiry* (The Griffiths Report). London: HMSO.

Elger, Anthony (1979) 'Valorisation and deskilling – a critique of Braverman', *Capital and Class*, 7 (Spring): 58–99.

Harrison, Stephen, Hunter, David and Pollitt, Christopher (1990) *The Dynamics of British Health Policy*. London: Unwin Hyman.

Hennessy, Peter (1989) *Whitehall*. London: Secker & Warburg.

NHS Management Executive (1989) *Working Paper on Medical Audit*. London: HMSO.

NHS Management Executive (1991) *Joint Guidance to Hospital Consultants on GP Fundholding*. London: Department of Health.

Owens, Patricia and Glennerster, Howard (1990) *Nursing in Conflict*. London: Macmillan.

Peters, Tom (1987) *Thriving on Chaos: Handbook for a Management Revolution*. London: Pan Books.

Peters, Thomas and Waterman, Robert (1982) *In Search of Excellence: Lessons from America's Best Run Companies*. New York: Harper Collins.

Robinson, Jane (1992) 'Introduction: beginning the study of nursing policy', in Jane Robinson, Alastair Gray and Ruth Elkan (eds), *Policy Issues in Nursing*. Buckingham: Open University Press.

Saltman, Richard B. and Von Otter, Casten (1992) *Planned Markets and Public Competition: Strategic Reform in Northern European Health Systems*. Buckingham: Open University Press.

Stacey, Margaret (1988) *The Sociology of Health and Healing*. London: Unwin Hyman.

Strong, Philip and Robinson, Jane (1990) *The NHS – Under New Management*. Milton Keynes: Open University Press.

UKCC (United Kingdom Central Council for Nursing, Midwifery and Health Visiting) (1986) *Project 2000: A New Preparation for Practice*. London: UKCC.

UKCC (United Kingdom Central Council for Nursing, Midwifery and Health Visiting) (1992) *Code of Practice*, 3rd edn. London: UKCC.

Wainwright, Hilary (1987) *Labour: A Tale of Two Parties*. London: Hogarth Press.

Walby, Sylvia (1989) 'Flexibility and the sexual division of labour', in Stephen Wood (ed.), *The Transformation of Work?* London: Unwin Hyman.

Williamson, Charlotte (1992) *Whose Standards? Consumer and Professional Standards in Health Care*. Buckingham: Open University Press.

Wood, Stephen (1989) 'New wave management?' *Work, Employment and Society* 3(3): 379–402.

4

Managing in the Mixed Economy of Care

Mary Langan and John Clarke

'I've been interfaced, empowered, quality assured and PSId [Performance Standard Indicator] up to here.'

(Mary Black, 'Leader of the pack', *Guardian*, 30 December 1992)

Given that social work has been a continuing focus of controversy throughout the last twenty years, it is somewhat surprising that major structural changes in the organization of personal social services have only taken place in the early 1990s. The restructuring of social work – around the familiar themes of partnership, markets and management – was primarily driven by the Children Act of 1989 and the NHS and Community Care Act of 1990. The prolonged survival of personal social services as an unreconstructed 'monopoly provider' despite the public vilification heaped upon social workers during the 1980s is testimony to the complexities of legal, organizational and professional structures associated with service delivery. Nevertheless, the two Acts signalled the break-up of the last of the local state's 'bureau-professional' welfare empires and threatened the fragile professional base of social work itself. The effects of the Acts were to fragment the service, subject it (albeit unevenly) to the disciplines of the mixed economy of welfare and require that services be reconceived in terms of multiple and multi-faceted varieties of 'partnership'. The objective was not merely to change the role of the local authority social services department from that of provider of services to that of 'enabler', 'commissioner' or 'purchaser' of services from a mix of public, voluntary and private sources. There was also a broader concern to transform the character of social services from a welfare agency run by professionals, allegedly too much in their own interests, to a customer-centred network of facilities and services run by managers.

In the process, it is possible to see the characteristic juxtapositions between the alleged failings of the old regime and the transformative promise of the new. The old structure was widely condemned as centralized, bureaucratic and hierarchical in its organization, as monopolistic, inefficient, even incompetent in its mode of operation and as aloof, insensitive and inflexible in its dealings with clients and carers. The new system promises to be more decentralized and informal, more economical and more efficient, and at the same time also to offer greater choice and higher-quality services.

The case for change

The personal social services have been the target of fierce public criticism, most conspicuously in the sphere of child protection, but also in their provision for disabled people, people with mental illness and older people. There is a general perception that social services departments had failed to meet the aspirations either of those who launched 'the fifth social service' in a wave of optimism in the late 1960s and early 1970s or of the wider public and those in need of social support. These criticisms of social work have come from a variety of perspectives, from the left, feminists and anti-racists; from the disabled people's movements and other user groups; and from the anti-welfarist right (Clarke, 1993). Government arguments for the need to reshape social work linked a complex array of themes: the inefficiency and cost of personal social services; the vested interests of professional empires; the failure to provide user choice in services; and the failure of local authorities to manage personal social services effectively.

First, local authority social services were condemned for failing to use resources economically. In a period of increasing constraints on public expenditure, local authority social services were widely judged to be expensive and, according to the Audit Commission, in some areas wasteful (Audit Commission, 1986: 2). Much social services provision was tied up in institutional care, such as old people's homes, children's homes, day centres, etc. Such resources are therefore not readily available for deployment in the community, for services designed to support older people, those with learning difficulties and disabled people and their carers in their own homes. As well as being expensive, institution-bound services tend to be centralized, standardized and inflexible. As a consequence, people who seek help tend to be assessed in terms of their suitability for existing services. The result is service-led rather than needs-led assessment – the interests of the institutions and those who work in them tend to displace the needs of the individual applicant. Although it is a strong element in the Conservative case for reform, this stress on de-institutionalization and the promotion of users' needs to centre-stage carries support from much wider social work and social policy constituencies.

However, the government-encouraged shift away from local authority institutions towards private residential care for the elderly over the past decade created its own difficulties. As a result of changes to social security regulations introduced in the 1980s to encourage private provision of nursing and retirement homes, the number of such residential places expanded from 37,000 in 1979 to 98,000 in 1990, an increase of 165 percent. The cost rose from £10 million to £1.2 billion (Oldman, 1991: 4–5). This vast subsidy to the private residential sector allowed many councils to close their own homes, but simply transferred (and sometimes compounded) the defects of institutional care elsewhere. At a time when the general drift of policy was towards care in the community, the residential care allowance created what the Griffiths report called a 'perverse incentive' towards institutional care (Griffiths, 1988). The rapid expansion of the costs of the private care sector in the 1980s greatly alarmed the government. Indeed, few would now dispute Oldman's judgement that 'a major driving force behind the recent community care legislation is the desire to reduce public expenditure on residential care' (Oldman, 1991: 4).

The second major criticism of the social services departments was that they were widely judged to be inefficient in terms of providing an optimal level of services for a given input of resources. One indication of this problem was the wide variations in the provision of services and in levels of social services expenditure among local authorities. For example, the number of people receiving home help per thousand people over the age of 75 varies from 90 (Surrey) to 399 (Derbyshire) (Harding, 1992a: 26). A survey of recent studies in the child care field revealed 'huge differences in the quantity, quality and style of the services provided, in spite of a shared legal framework and broadly similar aims and policies' (Department of Health, 1991: 59–60).

There were also substantial variations in provision to different areas and different communities within local authorities, underlining the fact that the social services operate in ways that are inequitable as well as inefficient (Harding, 1992a: 27–9). People in rural areas and minority ethnic communities particularly lost out. Although the reasons for the relatively restricted access to social services for black and minority ethnic groups have been well documented – discriminatory assumptions by service providers, lack of accessible information and lack of culturally appropriate services – these differentials persisted. Again, such arguments tap much wider reservoirs of support, drawing on criticisms made by user groups and minority communities as well as from within social work itself.

For the government, however, the clearest indication of inefficiency was the way in which resources were allocated to social services departments each year, not according to assessed need, but by simply adding an inflationary increment to the previous year's budget. Social services departments lacked the kind of rigorous data on local need that was necessary to deploy resources efficiently. In the absence of specific, targeted plans or proper assessments of local needs and priorities, the past crudely dictated the future. But when users were seen to be increasingly demanding individualized home-based support, service-led, institutionally based assessments were seen as likely to lead to wasteful spending on services which people no longer wanted.

Such inefficiency was seen to be compounded by the slowness of social services managers in identifying performance indicators at every level of their departments. In 1984 the Audit Commission had noted the traditional reluctance of social services staff to accept hierarchy and formal managerial styles, with the result that performance-related pay remained 'conspicuous by its absence' for social services managers long after it had become commonplace in the private sector (Kelly, 1991: 181). For the Commission, the underlying weakness of social services departments was to be found in the 'low level of strategic rationality' in their management (Kelly, 1991: 180). This led to a reluctance to advance clear and specific policies that instead allowed 'happenstance' to dictate the persistence of anachronistic patterns of service provision and staff allocation. The lack of adequate management information systems made it impossible to make plans, set targets or decide priorities – or to monitor the impact of policy changes. Social services critics blamed the ascendancy of professional values over managerial principles for many of the failures of the past decade. They saw this leading to a preoccupation with blaming all problems on government cuts, instead of accepting expenditure restraint and working out how to deploy scarce resources more effectively. Furthermore, a rigid administrative structure, which had often promoted highly experienced and capable social workers into managerial roles for which they had little training and sometimes no great aptitude, was better suited to conserving the old order than leading a revolution against it.

In this sense, social work exemplified the case against welfare 'bureau-professionalism' (Chapter 1 in this volume). Social services departments had failed to find effective ways of managing the professionals, while their antiquated administrative hierarchies compounded the problems of in-efficiency. The combination produced services which managed to be costly, ineffective and left the 'customer' powerless. As a case of change, this argument both articulated essential Conservative themes about state welfare and linked them to wider sets of arguments about the failings of social work. These linkages provided the basis for both the major pieces of reforming legislation being relatively free of conflict in terms of their general direction and principles.

A sense of crisis?

The two major pieces of legislation – the 1989 Children Act and the 1991 NHS and Community Care Act – provided the framework and authority for the dramatic changes taking place in social services. After some controversy in the 1980s about the future of social services departments and the social work profession in general, both new acts assumed their continuation, but in a different form and context. Indeed, the Children Act made the departments key agencies in child protection within a tighter legal framework, and the Community Care Act transferred functions (and funds) from the spheres of social security and the health service to local authority social services. In this respect, the legislation pointed to an enhanced rather than reduced role for social service departments in relation to both services for children and community care. However, such an optimistic reading misses the way in which both Acts restructured not just the internal world of social work but also its relationships with other agents and agencies. The Children Act subjected social work to greater judicial scrutiny and insisted on the delivery of services through both a mixed economy of care provision and a variety of 'partnerships', ranging from those with parents to those with the private and voluntary sectors of service provision. In community care, although local authority departments were allocated the role of 'lead agency', their involvement in direct service provision was intended to decline in the context of a more 'mixed' economy of care. Most significantly, the core 'purchaser' role for care services has deliberately not been identified as a 'social work task'. The change of title to 'care managers' was more than cosmetic, marking out the distance between social work (viewed as the professional combination of assessment and provision) and the management of care services (understood as assessment and contracting for services from others who may include social workers).

Government policy and the financial levers of policy implementation were directed to pushing councils towards a mixed economy with a lower level of direct public sector provision. Management as both a transformative force and an ideal for the organization of public sector services has been the focus of recommendations from quasi-autonomous agencies such as the Audit Commission and the Social Services Inspectorate. The Audit Commission, established in 1983 under the 1982 Local Government Finance Act, has preached the gospel of economy, efficiency and effectiveness in a series of investigations into local councils documenting managerial weaknesses. It has pursued a deliberate policy of using publicity to 'intensity the belief of awareness of crisis' in social services and thereby to encourage the emergence of a stronger 'management culture' (Kelly, 1991: 180–1). Offering detailed advice on how to improve management policy, the Audit Commission has been characterized as 'a policeman constantly tempted to turn consultant' (Day and Klein, 1990: 13). The Social Services Inspectorate, which started out in the 1970s as a professional consultancy 'social work service', assumed its present title in 1985 and took on the role of 'ensur[ing] the implementation of national policies' (Day and Klein, 1990: 27). Day and Klein characterize the SSI as 'a hybrid moving fast on the spectrum which runs from the professional-consultancy model towards the inspectorial model' (1990: 25).

At the same time, there have been attempts to create stronger public voices from within social work itself. Most notable was the emergence in 1992 of the Social Services Policy Forum, bringing together the Association of Directors of Social Services, the British Association of Social Workers, the National Council of Voluntary Organizations, the National Institute for Social Work and the Social Care Association. This prestigious forum convened its first seminar in February, with 'financial and logistical support' from Price Waterhouse. Papers presented at this seminar were subsequently published in *Great Expectations . . . and Spending on Social Services* (Harding, 1992a). A second policy forum pamphlet, *Who Owns Welfare: Questions on the Social Services Agenda*, was published in November 1992 (Harding, 1992c).

Tessa Harding of the National Institute for Social Work (NISW) articulated the sense of a professional crisis, arguing that 'the certainties of a professionally-driven, local authority-controlled service system no longer exist, and few people have a clear vision or experience of the potential alternatives' (1992a: 3). What Harding described as the 'destabilization of an entire service system' had resulted in widespread uncertainty, generating both 'energy and excitement' and 'high anxiety and stress' (1992a: 3). In relation to community care, in particular, NISW chair Sir William Utting repudiated the 'myth' that there is general agreement about how to proceed with the proposed changes: 'there is no consensus, rather a gladiatorial combat of competing perspectives' (in Harding, 1992c).

Nevertheless, this 'gladiatorial combat' primarily took place between professionals and politicians. The public debate has mainly focused on the arguments about whether the reforms are being adequately funded. For some academic critics of government social policy, the introduction of community care – and the associated changes in social services departments – was nothing more than a device for reducing public spending, 'another step in dismantling the welfare state' and pushing 'all responsibility back to the family' (*Guardian*, 4 January 1993). But while many questioned whether the changes have been adequately funded, there was general public approval of their principles. Most commentators regarded the wider operation of market forces and a more vigorous management approach as badly needed solutions to widely acknowledged problems. Feedback from Department of Health workshops on community care noted 'a pretty general acceptance of the case for change' (Department of Health, 1992). More importantly, perhaps, the core principles for community care – the move away from institutions and the focus on a more individually sensitive view of needs – were central themes in the development of social work itself.

In such a context, a sense of professional and organizational confusion comes as no surprise – the 'old ways' were clearly doomed and the 'new ways' laid claim to principles which are widely held within social work. What characterizes the sense of confusion is an overwhelmingly defensive set of concerns about how to hold on to cherished 'professional values', identities and practices in the emergent new regime. These concerns have been concentrated in two main axes of opposition to the reforms. The first has involved accepting the changes, at least nominally, while questioning whether the level of resourcing will be adequate to support the new system. The second has focused on the intrusion of an alien ethos – the 'business culture' – into the world of care. The financial, commercial and managerial logics associated with this business culture are seen as antithetical to the professional, political and public service cultures in which care services have been developed (Wistow et al., 1992). At the same time, it is clear that the agencies of reconstruction had little time for such professional nostalgia.

The community revolution

If the new mixed economy of care was advanced as the solution to the failings of local authority social services departments, the new managerialism was the decisive force in effecting the transition and implementing the new arrangements. Indeed, to pursue the metaphor self-consciously adopted by the Audit Commission, managers are the Bolsheviks of the community revolution. The commission recommended that councils appoint a full-time officer to provide 'strong, committed leadership' to the revolutionary process, while newly designated cadres of 'care managers' should act as the 'catalyst for change' (Audit Commission, 1992: 22).

The main aim of shifting the balance of welfare provision from the state to voluntary, private and informal agencies (in parallel with similar measures in education, housing, health and social security) is to establish market forces within the sphere of welfare (see Flynn, 1992). Competition among independent agencies is expected to expose (and reduce) the costs of services and offer wider choice to users. The market should thus encourage a shift from service/supply-led provision to needs/demand-led provision. In practice this means that instead of directly providing services, care managers should use their devolved budgets to commission or purchase services from a variety of sources, including private and voluntary organizations as well as council facilities. It is worth looking in more detail at the conceptions of management which are embodied in the roles of both senior or strategic managers and care managers.

The 'leadership' role in community care involves formulating clear values and goals in a 'mission statement' that should establish aims and priorities (Audit Commission, 1992: 23). In keeping with the 'new managerialism', the Commission recognized that such statements are a necessary but not sufficient condition of cultural change. It argued that 'winning the hearts and minds of social services members and staff to a different role for social services is the key to the success of community care' (Audit Commission, 1992: 22). This, it recognized dryly, is 'a task of some magnitude', given that commitments, identities and loyalties are heavily bound up with the old organizational systems and structures. Such a transformation would require staff consultation and involvement, education and training at all levels. The Local Government Training Board and Nalgo Education established a joint initiative for community care to help with this process, while a variety of other agencies from university departments through to voluntary bodies offered a range of seminars, training and advice on organizational and cultural transformation.

At the level of council members, senior management should be responsible for securing commitment to specific policies that put people's needs before the demands of existing services and their staffs. 'Members must decide on competing priorities between dependency levels and user groups, setting criteria for different levels of assessment, care management and services' (Audit Commission, 1992: 26). They should also consider the spending consequences of such decisions and make appropriate budgetary allocations. More significantly, management must take the lead in 'challenging power structures and vested interests' (Audit Commission, 1992: 27). Such challenges cut across the whole organization since members, officers and front-line workers were all seen to have established 'stakes' in the old regime which they will seek to defend. Organizationally, the 'community revolution' required the replacement of the existing bureaucratic hierarchy with one dedicated to 'process'. Instead of being a comfortable reward for past efforts, management posts and their occupants should be continuously reassessed in terms of fulfilment of targets and achievement of strategic objectives. According to Michael O'Higgins, 'social services client partner' of Price Waterhouse, the aim should be to squeeze out middle management, removing intermediaries between those responsible for strategy and planning and those responsible for providing service (O'Higgins, 1992: 48). For the Audit Commission, challenging vested interests also meant the introduction of performance-related pay, cost centres and short-term employment contracts: 'Personnel departments and trade unions must agree to flexible working conditions and recruitment procedures, operated locally' (Audit Commission, 1992: 27–8). Social services departments should accommodate themselves to the contemporary 'ideal' organizational model – fitter and flatter (or leaner and meaner), stressing flexibility and adaptiveness to its business environment. This 'isomorphism' (the modelling of ideal organizational shape) is currently being promoted through the range of advisers, educators and consultants.

Senior – or strategic – management must take the lead in establishing strategy, planning change, taking stock of resources, defining and measuring local needs and establishing priorities and targets. O'Higgins emphasized the key role of information technology in facilitating 'effective management' and de-bureaucratizing the organization of services. The Department of Health produced a 'key indicators package' to assist social services departments in accurately assessing local relative dependency levels and in defining and measuring need. The publications of the CIPFA/ADSS Financial Management Partnership aimed to assist social services managers with computer systems. For O'Higgins the new information culture was necessary, not only for targeting resources appropriately, but also for allowing the development of flexible forms of service provision without necessarily incurring higher costs (O'Higgins, 1992: 50–1). Equally, such systems were seen as integral to the establishment of a widespread 'budget consciousness' in which different layers of management would come to 'own' budgets and the responsibilities which accompany them. This also required change in the 'budgetary culture' of local authorities, shifting control of resources away from the traditional combination of chief officers and finance departments. Such a change posed problems both in terms of the adequacy of financial systems and the degree of 'trust' necessary to create effectively devolved resources. One objective, then, is to create a tier of senior management with a strategic role, able to survey the environment, make informed choices and deploy more 'flexible' organizational resources in pursuit of value-for-money services.

By themselves, however, such senior managers would not constitute a 'cultural revolution'. Only if responsibility is devolved and taken up by lower tiers of management – the team leaders and care managers – will the revolution be achieved. Care managers have a distinct managerial role within the new structure, engaged with the tasks of assessing the needs of particular individuals and devising appropriate packages of care services. If 'flexibility' is to be achieved, the devolution of resources and responsibility to such levels is essential: resources must flow to the point in the organization where user needs are assessed. The role of care manager is not a simple relabelling of the social work job title. The Audit Commission was explicit about the need to see the care manager post as a way of unlocking the hold of professional 'vested interests':

> Social work professionals also have vested interests and some regard the concept of the care manager as commissioner and not provider with grave misgivings. There may be an assumption that 'care manager' equals 'social workers' and as social workers they wish both to run with the hare and ride with the hounds. . . . Other professionals such as occupational therapists, nurses as well as home care organisers should also be well placed to take on the role of care manager. . . . Social work however is a provision in its own right to be commissioned by the care manager, although the role of care manager may well encompass a degree of counselling and support. (Audit Commission, 1992: 27)

The Audit Commission favoured decentralized management and devolved budgets, considering that the task of needs assessment would be best carried out by specialized care managers who can then assemble and resource individualized care programmes. Such a combination of needs-led assessment and targeted resources is claimed to offer greater scope for flexible and innovative domiciliary services. It is also supposed to put new power in the hands of the user of social services – now less of a troublesome client and more of a valued customer. In practice, the customers' new-found power is of a second-hand variety, exercised through the proxy of the care manager who purchases care on their behalf. This change rests on the assumption that such managerial assessments would produce more 'transparent' representations of the user's needs than the much criticized forms of professional assessment.

The precise terms of the purchaser/provider split and the associated arrangements for assessment and care management have been worked out in a variety of ways in different authorities (Wistow et al., 1992). In 1991 Price Waterhouse put forward three alternative models: purchasing by contract, purchasing controlled by professional assessment and devolved financial management (Price Waterhouse, 1991). Speakers at an ADSS/PSI seminar in July 1991 discussed plans and experiences in different authorities (Allen, 1992). For example, Anne Parker, director of Berkshire social services, spoke in favour of the second model (Parker, 1992). She emphasized the importance of retaining the professional standards and values of social workers, occupational therapists and home care workers in the assessment process. However, responsibility for budgets rested with the team leader, rather than with the care manager.

Speaking at the same seminar, David Browning, associate director for health and social services at the Audit Commission, emphasized the key reversal in the relationship between elected councillors and social services staff (Browning, 1992). In the past, council members made decisions about services and in practice left the business of rationing resources to workers in the field. Now councillors are expected to make explicit political choices about which services may be purchased and for whom, by establishing clear eligibility criteria. Meanwhile care managers carry out individual assess-ments and organize individualized care packages. Such as system rests on the supposedly greater transparency of decisions in the shift from strategic choices to individualized implementation. However, it is less clear about where 'hard choices' will be made which emerge at the intersection of need and resource. Will these be strategic choices made by establishing narrow eligibility criteria (for example, by retreating to a minimalist or statutory definition of responsibility) and thereby de-legitimating a range of needs? Will they take place in the sphere of managerial 'discretion' as senior management translate the criteria into organizational plans? Or will they be left to care managers to juggle within the 'flexibility' of their budgets and care packages?

Problems of transition: managing in the mixed economy

The restructuring of welfare has been framed by a set of overarching conditions: the fiscal pressures on public spending; the growing dislocation between welfare demand and the resources made available to meet it; the tension between user and provider control of welfare decisions. It is possible to see these tensions being played out both in the general restructuring of the British welfare state and within more specific service settings. Restructuring has been dominated by the commitment to the mixed economy and the managerial transformation of state agencies as the means to resolve or reconcile the contradictions of public welfare provision. It is anticipated that, through the mixed economy, competition should both drive down costs and enhance customer choice in service provision. A managerialized service should reduce provider power, reduce costs and be more customer oriented. As a managerial vision, this sounds like an ideal resolution of the contradictions of welfare. However, we think it may be more productive to look at how the changes have the effect, not of resolving the contradictions, but changing the places where they appear and the forms in which they are represented and handled.

The over-riding problem confronting the project of transforming the world of personal social services is the wider conflict between growing demands and shrinking resources. It is the particular misfortune of the community care initiative that it is being implemented in the midst of the third, and the deepest, recession in twenty years. The resulting increases in unemployment, homelessness, poverty and distress inevitably impose greater demands on social services. At the same time, public expenditure on social services is being curtailed. The capacity of local authorities to protect social services by overspending on their budgets as many did in the 1980s has been curbed by government charge-capping. In her survey for the Public Policy forum, Tessa Harding noted that in 1990–91 thirty-two councils reduced their social services budgets, others experienced standstill or reduced growth. In 1991–92 half of all councils announced reduced or standstill budgets (Harding, 1992a: iii). A survey of local authority spending plans for 1993 conducted by the Association of Directors of Social Services revealed that 87 percent planned cuts in personal social services budgets (*Guardian*, 11 January 1993). Harding's stark conclusion was that 'government policies to improve services and government policies to control local authority spending are in direct conflict' (Harding, 1992a: iii).

Two further factors make the demand/resources conflict even more acute than these figures suggest. The first is what Melanie Henwood calls 'the community care crunch' (Henwood, 1992: 23). This is the mismatch between the rising numbers of elderly and disabled people wanting to live at home and the declining availability of carers resulting from demographic (a long-term fall in the birth rate reducing the numbers of young adults), economic (persistently high levels of women's participation in the labour market) and social changes (greater family diversity). The second is the raised public expectations resulting from the long-running debate about community care. People who never previously considered that they might be eligible for support in the community may be encouraged to apply for services publicized through the media. Thus Oldman argued that 'resources are grossly inadequate at a time when local authorities face new responsibilities' (Oldman, 1991: 5).

The revenue allocations made to cover the transfer of responsibility for residential and nursing care for older people from the Department of Social Security to the local authorities in April 1993 provided a specific illustration of the problem of under-funding of community care. In October 1992 Health Minister Virginia Bottomley announced a total of £539 million – including £399 million for existing residents and an additional sum of £140 million to cover the estimated cost of 110,000 new entrants over the coming year (*Guardian*, 3 October 1992). Although Bottomley proclaimed this an 'excellent settlement', Toby Young of the Association of Metropolitan Authorities estimated that there would be another 12,000 people coming into institutional care at an extra cost of £200 million. Such arguments about the levels of public spending created widespread concern about 'a care gap' between levels of need and available services even before the community care legislation came into effect. The managerialization of welfare promises to resolve this contradiction between needs and resources through 'flexibility'. While recognizing that resources are finite, managerialism carries the message that resources can be unlocked from unnecessary rigidities and vested interests. When 'liberated', the finite resources have the capacity to deliver the desired goal of getting 'more from less'.

Framed by such competing claims, the issue of matching resources and need increasingly resembles a game of 'pass the parcel'. The first player (central government) proclaims that it has done its sums and that it is up to local authorities to use resources more effectively and efficiently. Local government, while bemoaning the level of resourcing, nevertheless conducts its allocation of budgets, establishes its priority and access criteria, and hands the shrinking parcel on to social services managers. Strategic managers, though no doubt feeling hard done by in the budgetary allocation process, devolve the budget to care managers urging them to use it wisely –

and flexibly. Care managers, while berating the perfidy of all those above them, make choices about what needs to meet and how to meet them. At each stage, the managerial ethos requires us to believe that (a) each level makes wise decisions and (b) each subordinate layer has sufficient autonomy and flexibility to bridge the resource/demand gap. Front-line staff in social services have always had to perform 'emotional labour' to cope with the gaps between needs and resources. Devolution not only pushes decisions further towards the front line, it also devolves added stress in the responsibility for managing to bridge this gap.

The uncertainty about resources and needs is compounded by the attempt to introduce market relations into a sphere in which they have never previously played much of a role. The shift towards a new mixed economy of welfare raises many questions. Will the market really open up choice in welfare? Will the customer be able to choose her care manager? Will there be enough providers of reasonable quality to offer a real choice?

The first major study of contractual relationships between local or health authority purchasers and non-statutory providers found that 'in all but two cases, our respondents said that the existence of a contract did nothing to increase user choice of service' (Common and Flynn, 1992: 35). This was largely because the service provided through the contract became the only one meeting a particular need for a particular client group in a particular area. In addition they noted that, as there was little spare capacity in the system, in practice the effective choice amounted to 'take it or leave it'.

As Le Grand has argued more generally about privatizing trends in welfare, 'quasi-markets' is a more accurate description of the mixed economy being constructed than 'markets' (Le Grand, 1990). He has suggested that what are being constructed are patterns of relationship which attempt to 'mimic' markets, through enforced splits between purchasing and providing functions. On the supply side, there may be a tendency towards the emergence of highly fragmented private providers competing for the purchases of one social services department. In such circumstances, worries about cash flow and profits may well dictate greater concern with contract specifications than with standards of care. The outcome may well also be a tendency to negotiate long-term block contracts to minimize risks and uncertainties (Flynn, 1992: 45). One major community care simulation found that both purchasers and providers tended to look towards 'cartelization' to maximize their market power and reduce risk (South West Thames RHA and Office for Public Management, 1991: 21). Such arrangements put risk aversion over innovation, conserving the very ascendancy of service-led over needs-led services that the market was supposed to erode. Studies of 'real' markets might suggest that these are not deviations from the ideal, but are, in fact, well-established strategies for minimizing risk and maximizing market power or advantage.

Although most attention has been focused on the installation of managerial roles in the purchaser organizations, the changes are equally significant in their implications for provider agencies. There is pressure on those agencies, most particularly those in the voluntary or 'not-for-profit' sector, to develop managerial systems to enable them to be 'business-like' in their approaches to tendering and service delivery. Such demands have implications for their organizational systems, relationships and cultures, which may well have been developed with very different objectives in mind. Indeed, their ability to pursue other objectives, such as advocacy work or lobbying, may be undermined by an increasing dependence on service provision contracts. This may be intensified as relationships between voluntary organizations and local authorities shift their footing from grant aid to specified service contracts. There are similar pressures on 'in-house' service providers which become more or less autonomous 'profit centres', although their formal status may range from remaining integral parts of the social services departments to being floated off or divested as trusts or independent 'for profit' agencies.

Secondly, it is in the provider side that the main benefits of 'flexibility' are anticipated, particularly those relating to the flexibility of labour and its impact on the cost of services. Given the labour-intensive nature of care services, much managerial effort is likely to be devoted to the labour cost–productivity equation as a core component of becoming competitive. This most obviously bears on those employed in provider organizations, but the provision of care has hitherto developed around a more complex network of paid and unpaid work. There is a spectrum of 'care work' which runs from full-time employment, through part-time paid work to paid and unpaid volunteering, to the unpaid 'labour of love' of informal or primary carers (Ungerson, 1992). In a context where both volunteers and informal carers are being considered as eligible for payments, training and accreditation there will be the potential for managers to consider their labour worthy of closer attention as part of care packages and thus requiring greater direction, monitoring and supervision. Indeed, it may be reasonable to think of volunteers and informal carers as representing the most developed version of the 'flexible' labour force, given the potency of their personal motivations and the fluidity of their working conditions. Given the predominance of voluntary and informal care labour in the provision of domiciliary care, the current concern with standards and monitoring the quality of service suggests that managerial discipline cannot be limited to only those in direct employee relationships.

Quasi-markets and quasi-customers

The quasi-markets of the mixed economy of care present a number of problems for those who attempt to manage within them. On the purchaser side, the care manager allocates the budget on behalf of the customer. But although the manager controls the budget, she now has no direct control over the services themselves, depending on contract specification and monitoring to guarantee the quality of service. Indeed, in many instances it is likely that she will be 'purchasing' only nominally, within the framework of block contracts already negotiated. Block contracting serves to minimize risk and uncertainty for purchasers as well as contractors, particularly for 'first-time buyers' who have no experience of this market and little information on which to engage in bargaining. The same conditions are likely to promote contracting relationships with known and known-to-be-reliable providers, rather than producing efforts at 'market stimulation' (Wistow et al., 1992). At the same time, the customer may receive the services she is assessed as needing, but has no direct control over the assessment or the allocation of resources. The position of users is that of a quasi-customer, exercising consumer sovereignty at second hand through the care manager. Like other 'customer-centred' changes in welfare such as GP fund-holding, the changes in community care stop short of transferring power and decisions to the customer in person, assuming instead that their purchasing proxies will 'transparently' represent their needs. In this role, we can see the potential for replaying some of the contradictions of the old social work role but in a new way. Historically, social workers have occupied an ambiguous position as both a gatekeeper to resources and as an advocate or 'champion' on behalf of clients. The devolution of resources compounds this ambiguity by requiring the care manager both to 'represent' the user's needs and to ration resources directly (South West Thames RHA and Office for Public Management, 1991: 20).

Within community care there is a potential conflict between the customer asserting her entitlement, by right as a citizen, to a particular service, and the care manager acting as the custodian of scarce public resources. Local authorities are given the power and the duty to provide certain services, but this rarely gives individuals enforceable rights to such services. Although disability activists have had some successes in the courts in forcing councils to provide particular services, the extent of such entitlements remains unclear. Care managers, on the other hand, emphasize needs rather than rights, and have a wider responsibility to stay within a budget while ensuring the efficient delivery of services. Such an approach may prove particularly insensitive to the demands of disabled people and minority ethnic groups. Despite the 'user-led' language which has accompanied the introduction of community care, the pre-eminent tests of managerial efficiency are likely to remain resource centred and there is a clear danger that user pressure towards diversity of needs will not fit easily with cost-effective managerial concerns. These issues expose the ambiguities of the 'user-led/customer-oriented' discourse of community care. Although such conceptions have been deliberately directed at undermining bureau-professional paternalism in the name of empowering the customer, it is difficult to identify exactly what power has been transferred. Little attention has been given to the involvement of users in service planning or service review, as opposed to the more generalized and ambiguous commitment to consultation. Equally, it is hard to tell what effective power the individual user can exercise in relation to a personalized care package – other than 'expressing preferences'. This is a rather attentuated version of consumer sovereignty and rests on the (charitable) assumption that managerial discretion is intrinsically more user friendly than professional discretion.

For Michael Oliver the very language of community care 'serves to deny disabled people the right to be treated as fully competent, autonomous individuals, as active citizens' (Oliver, 1992: 31). He argued for a 'rights-based welfare' which would emphasize entitlement, independent living, social support, personal assistance, activity, organization and empowerment. From a black perspective, Adele Jones rejected needs-based assessments as promoting 'pathology, inadequacy and inability as the basis of who has what services' (1992: 38). For her, the focus on '"needs" rather than "human rights" is in direct conflict with the concept of "empowerment"' (1992: 38).

Some of the fears of user groups and social workers were confirmed by a confidential document circulated to local authorities by Herbert Laming, chief inspector of the Social Services Inspectorate and subsequently leaked to the press. This exposed the contradiction between needs and resources at the heart of the community care programme (*Guardian*, 30 December 1992). Laming warned councils not to tell older and disabled people of their rights under the new system unless the money was available to deliver the relevant services. He advised them that once a need for a statutory service had been identified it would 'not be possible for an authority to use budgeting difficulties as a basis for refusing to provide the service'. Where an individual's preferences could not be met he advised that it would be best to log such information 'in aggregate' rather than on the individual's file, where it might be seen. He cautioned that 'practitioners will have to be sensitive to the need not to raise unrealistic expectations on the part of users and carers'. Although the advice was subsequently withdrawn, it exposed the problems of the position of the 'customer' within the new arrangements.

Seamless care? Partnership problems

Yet another set of problems arises at the interface between social services and other welfare agencies, notably health, housing and social security. The rhetoric of community care speaks of 'seamless services' offering a warm blanket to those in need. Again those in the field remain sceptical: Tessa Harding has described a situation of uncertainty compounded by the confusion of responsibility, the moving of goalposts and shifting of costs between central and local government departments. The seamless blanket begins to resemble a net full of holes: 'As each area of public service narrows its focus, the gaps between them become larger' (Harding, 1992b: 7). The problem for social services is that people who have fallen through other nets tend to end up on their doorstep. Thus responsibility for people who are discharged early from hospitals and for those discharged permanently from closing mental hospitals tends to shift from the health authorities to the social services. The contraction of public housing and the limited availability of low-cost private housing create further difficulties for social services.

Finding suitable places in the community for young people leaving council care, for people with mental illness or those with learning difficulties is a major problem.

Nor is the pattern of relationships which is supposed to provide the 'seamless web' very clear. 'Care management' is driven by two competing injunctions. One is to use the competition inherent in the mixed economy of welfare to obtain 'value for money' services. This places a premium on contracting, looking for market advantages and exercising purchasing power. The second is concerned with the 'enabling' and 'partnership' visions of service delivery. These stress the role of the local authority in fostering alternative service providers, building up good relations, developing multi-agency working and joint initiatives. It is not clear that these two versions of the local authority role sit comfortably together. It may be that they become distributed to different levels of the partner organizations, such that competition and contracting become 'strategic' issues while lower levels of management busy themselves with building partnership bridges – or vice versa, depending on which version is given strategic priority. There is further potential for uncomfortable relationships when one considers that partner organizations may have differing strategic priorities which are likely to render partnerships highly unstable (Kanter, 1990).

More generally, the language of partnership tends to underestimate differences between the partners, attaching little significance to differences of organizational goals, structures, cultures and power which bear on the relationship. Existing examples of multi-agency or multi-disciplinary working should give cause for thought about the difficulties of constructing effective relationships, revealing the tensions engendered by different priorities, professional cultures and power. In the new situation, there is even greater potential for tensions around joint working because of issues of resource control (Family Health Service Authorities and GP fund-holders are purchasers alongside local authorities), different professional definitions of care and different management systems and cultures. In one modelling exercise of community care implementation, all of these tensions were revealed. One particularly striking feature was Health Service complaints about the slowness of local authority decision making and impatience with the need to 'consult politicians'. Managerial cultures, introduced to enhance autonomous decision making and organizational flexibility, seem to have little time for the complexities of democratic representation and accountability (South West Thames RHA and Office for Public Management, 1991: 17).

Alvin Schorr, formerly an adviser to the 1968 Seebohm Report (Seebohm, 1968) which launched the social services departments, has argued in a recent survey of social services departments that 'too much has been laid on the personal social services; and they were already overburdened' (Schorr, 1992: 3). He noted the outcome of a review of progress in implementing the recommendations for reform put forward to Brent social services in the 1985 report into the death of Jasmine Beckford, a child under the care of the council. Twelve months later it became clear that the department was so disorganized and demoralized, and resources were so short that the recommendations could not be implemented. For this local authority social services department, the lessons of one of the most highly publicized child protection scandals of the 1980s were simply 'unlearnable' (Schorr, 1992: 46). He and many others have commented on the climate of insecurity among social services staff, the siege mentality, the low morale, the high levels of staff vacancies and turnover. Tessa Jowell concluded that '[o]ur professional world is spinning so fast it is hard to maintain one's bearings and the uncertainties, real or speculative, are in danger of sabotaging competence, creativity and confidence' (Jowell, 1991).

What such comments underestimate, however, is the way in which such 'professional worlds' have been defined as part of the problem to be overcome in welfare reform. One of the objectives of the changes has been to accomplish precisely that sense of destabilization of the professional world. Only by unlocking its hold on the organization, discourse and practice of service delivery could a new regime be established.

Conclusion: the magic of management?

What are the prospects for the managerial revolution in social services? There are optimistic and pessimistic prognostications. Government ministers and sympathetic commentators have continually insisted on the generous funding arrangements that have been made for community care and on the way new legislation is encouraging diverse sources of initiative in welfare provision (see Department of Health, 1990). Dismissing the protests of local authority representatives, professional groups and social policy experts as self-interested or ideologically outdated, they confidently anticipate the emergence of seamless, user-friendly services offering wider choice and higher quality.

Optimism about the future of social services is not exclusively confined to government circles. Many workers in the welfare field and many service users have become so disillusioned by the performance of local authority social services departments that they hold out some hopes for the new order. Malcolm Dean reflected the aspirations of many social workers in his statement that they might benefit from the emergence of 'a multitude of private and voluntary agencies bidding to provide services. Once freed from their predominant town hall ties, they could emerge as a much more independent profession as they fan out' (Dean, 1992: 26). At the same time, community care promises innovatory forms of service across different sectors and agencies. Such innovations may bring services 'closer to the customer' and her needs. In such terms, the promise of community care carries considerable weight for different sorts of interests. For senior managers, it offers the prospect of transcending narrow departmental and professional interests and becoming empowered to act as 'real managers'. For lower-level managers and front-line staff, devolution promises to get the 'bureaucrats off our backs' and empower those in closest contact with users.

For users, the new system promises to take their individual needs seriously and create more responsive services.

There are, of course, less optimistic versions, such as Alvin Schorr's gloomy prognosis. Given the influence of US welfare models on recent social policy trends in Britain, he offered as 'a cautionary tale' the degeneration of American child welfare agencies over the past thirty years, which he depicts as the 'systematic destruction of a functioning organisation' (Schorr, 1992: 42). Drawing from the US experience and from his survey of current developments in Britain, Schorr made three telling points.

First he emphasized that it is 'only a theory' that a mixed economy of welfare provides greater choice. For him, 'true choice depends on whether the care that is preferred will be paid for' (Schorr, 1992: 22). In his view, government assurances that it will provide adequate resources for community care 'appear to bear no relation to reality' (Schorr, 1992: 23). Secondly, he argued that the US experience shows that community care is neither cheaper than existing provisions, nor can it be self-financing (Schorr, 1992: 35–7). Whereas keeping old people at home may be cheaper than residential care, moving disabled people, the mentally ill and those with learning difficulties out of institutions into appropriate community facilities is very expensive. Even informal care, which appears highly cost effective, requires back up services.

Finally, Schorr rejected the notion that 'care management' – a concept derived directly from 'case management' in the USA – can be a panacea for personal social services in Britain. Citing an American survey which 'fails to support most of the claims for its effectiveness', he pointed out that it demands high levels of training and expertise in budget management and contract negotiation, which are unlikely to be rapidly acquired by over-stretched 'care managers' in Britain (Schorr, 1992: 38). He acknowledges that, given adequate resources and well-organized services, care management could play a role. But it cannot itself overcome or compensate for the absence of these conditions: '[a]t the heart of the problem of care management is that it cannot, like reconstituted DNA, be inserted into a chaotic structure and organise it' (Schorr, 1992: 40).

Nevertheless, management – in both its strategic and devolved forms – has been given precisely this transformational role to play in the reconstruction of community care. It is the alchemist's stone which will transform a leaden and costly bureau-professional organization into a flexible and efficient one. For those inside the mixed economy of care, the debate about optimistic or pessimistic prognostications over whether this magic will work is somehow beside the point. They now inhabit a world whose basic elements have been transformed – the structures, cultures, languages and practices are different and the old elements cannot be recovered. The ground has changed under them and the issue is how to manage to survive in the new world. This 'cultural revolution' of community care captures precisely the magic of management: the ability to recast old assumptions and patterns into a new configuration which promises happy endings.

The real outcomes are likely to depend on what relationships between power and resources finally emerge in these transformations. At a time when community care seems to promise the 'empowerment' of everybody, it is difficult to trace the real movements of power around this system. This dispersal of power is particularly significant, given that different versions of the managed mixed economy of care will take shape in different localities. At present, it is easier to see where different sorts of 'responsibility' have been allocated, but whether these involve effective forms of power is another matter. It may be that the political test of this alchemic transformation is not whether it works in the sense of providing better services. It is whether the organizations themselves have been transformed into managerialized enterprises. Once that is accomplished, success or failure becomes a managerial rather than a political responsibility. The logic of the discourse of managerial flexibility in community care demands that once they have been 'set free' (however reluctantly) it is managers who are responsible. The buck, as well as the budget, is now well and truly devolved.

References

Allen, I. (ed.) (1992) *Drawing the Line: Purchasing and Providing Social Services in the 1990s*. London: Policy Studies Institute.
Audit Commission (1986) *Making a Reality of Community Care*. London: HMSO.
Audit Commission (1992) *The Community Revolution: The Personal Social Services and Community Care*. London: HMSO.
Browning, D. (1992) 'Purchaser/provider split: passing fashion or permanent fixture?' in I. Allen (ed.), *Drawing the Line: Purchasing and Providing Social Services in the 1990s*. London: Policy Studies Institute.
Clarke, J. (ed.) (1993) *A Crisis in Care?* London: Sage.
Common, R. and Flynn, N. (1992) *Contracting for Care*. York: Joseph Rowntree Foundation.
Day, P. and Klein, N. (1990) *Inspecting the Inspectorates*. Bath: Centre for Analysis of Social Policy.
Dean, M. (1992) 'Breakdown services', *Search*, 14 December.
Department of Health (1990) *The Government's Plans for the Future of Community Care*. London: HMSO.
Department of Health (1991) *Patterns and Outcomes in Child Placement*. London: HMSO.
Department of Health (1992) *Implementing Community Care: Feedback on the Purchase of Services and the Purchaser–Provider Workshop*. London: HMSO.
Flynn, N. (1992) 'Managing in the market for welfare' in T. Harding (ed.), *Who Owns Welfare: Questions on the Social Services Agenda*, Social Services Forum Policy Paper No. 2. London: NISW.
Griffiths, R. (1988) *Community Care: Agenda for Action. A Report to the Secretary of State for Social Services*. London: HMSO.
Harding, T. (1992a) *Great Expectations . . . and Spending on Community Care*, Social Services Policy Forum Paper No. 1. London: NISW.
Harding, T. (1992b) 'Questions on the social services agenda' in T. Harding (ed.), *Who Owns Welfare: Questions on the Social Services Agenda*, Social Services Policy Forum Paper No. 2. London: NISW.
Harding, T. (ed.) (1992c) *Who Owns Welfare: Questions on the Social Services Agenda*, Social Services Policy Forum Paper No. 2. London: NISW.
Henwood, M. (1992) 'Demographic and family change', in T. Harding (ed.), *Who Owns Welfare: Questions on the Social Services Agenda*, Social Services Policy Forum Paper No. 2. London: NISW.

Jones, A. (1992) 'Civil rights, citizenship and the welfare agenda for the 1990s', in T. Harding (ed.), *Who Owns Welfare: Questions on the Social Services Agenda*, Social Services Policy Forum Paper No. 2. London: NISW.

Jowell, T. (1991) 'Challenges and opportunities', Conference speeches delivered by Virginia Bottomley and Tessa Jowell, distributed with *Caring for People*, 4.

Kanter, R.M. (1990) *When Giants Learn to Dance*. London: Unwin Hyman.

Kelly, A. (1991) 'The new managerialism in the social services', in T. Carter, P. Jeffs and M. Smith (eds), *Social Work and Social Welfare Yearbook 3*. Milton Keynes: Open University Press.

Le Grand, J. (1990) *Quasi-markets and Social Policy: Studies in Decentralisation and Quasi-markets 1*. Bristol: SAUS, University of Bristol.

O'Higgins, M. (1992) 'Effective management: the challenges', in T. Harding (ed.), *Who Owns Welfare: Questions on the Social Services Agenda*, Social Services Policy Forum Paper No. 2. London: NISW.

Oldman, C. (1991) *Paying for Care: Personal Sources of Funding Care*. York: Joseph Rowntree Foundation.

Oliver, M. (1992) 'A case of disabling welfare', in T. Harding (ed.), *Who Owns Welfare: Questions on the Social Services Agenda*, Social Services Policy Forum Paper No. 2. London: NISW.

Parker, A. (1992) 'Purchasing and providing: what kind of progress?' in I. Allen (ed.), *Drawing the Line: Purchasing and Providing Social Services in the 1990s*. London: Policy Studies Institute.

Price Waterhouse (1991) *Implementing Community Care – Purchaser/Commissioner and Provider Roles*. London: HMSO.

Schorr, A. (1992) *The Personal Social Services: An Outside View*. York: Joseph Rowntree Foundation.

Seebohm, F. (1968) *Report of the Committee on Local Authority and Allied Personal Social Services*. Cmnd. 3703. London: HMSO.

South West Thames Regional Health Authority and Office for Public Management (1991) *Care Kaleidoscope: Futures for Community Care*. London: South West Thames RHA and Office for Public Management.

Ungerson, C. (1992) 'Payment for caring', Paper presented to Social Policy Association Conference, July, Nottingham.

Wistow, G., Knapp, M., Hardy, B. and Allen, C. (1992) 'From providing to enabling: local authorities and the mixed economy of care', *Public Administration*, 70 (Spring): 25–45.

5

Managerialism in Education

Ross Fergusson

Introduction

The provision of a publicly funded education system has long been a cornerstone of state welfare and public and social policy in Britain. Its history is inextricably bound up with them (Banting, 1985; Lawson and Silver, 1985, among many illustrate this point). Education has special significance in the politics of the New Public Management in that it is by far the largest budget of local authorities, comprising about a third of expenditure, and is the second largest item of central government expenditure, jointly with health, exceeded only by social security (Central Statistical Office, 1993). In this sense, the battles of the last fourteen years between local and central government have been, more than anything else, struggles over the control of education and education spending. Against this background, a strong and persuasive case can be argued that the reform of education is central to the public policy reform project (see for example Keohane, 1991, on the ill effects of the marginalization of education in the Beveridge Report), and that it has led the way in some areas of contemporary reform. Indeed, in some interpretations the very creation of state systems of education is axial to the development of the modern state itself (Green, 1990). Education does not deserve its role as the Cinderella of public policy studies, and its inclusion here is a reflection of its importance in any comprehensive overview of managerialism, and of its significance in state restructuring.

Ideologically, no transformation of the public sector in Britain would have been complete without transforming the education system. Education had come to epitomize much that was seen to be wrong with burgeoning state power. It was construed as expensive, not self-evidently adequately productive, insufficiently accountable, monopolistic, producer-dominated, a bastion of an entrenched professional elite, resistant to consumer demand and, at worst, self-generating and self-serving. It was at the forefront of reforms, particularly through the 1988 Education Reform Act. The focus of this essay is not on the reforms themselves as part of the restructuring of welfare provision and the new public management of which they are a part, but on the potentially more deep-rooted and enduring development of managerialism. The creation of a managerialist education system in a managerialist public sector may well emerge as the least ephemeral aspect of these reforms. Nevertheless, the reforms, and the centrality of education reforms to the overall project are the main backdrop to what follows.

Constraints of space have meant that this chapter is confined to an exploration of managerialism in the school sector. Many of the trends which will be identified find parallels in further and higher education, though their manifestations there are quite distinctive. In HE for example, many more academic autonomies are retained compared with the centralist thrust which will be identified in respect of schools; but the use of powers of central funding to promote a competitive and expansionist market (the implications of which have radically altered the culture of management in many institutions) has exceeded that which has occurred in the schools sector. Further analysis of post-compulsory education would serve to demonstrate the diversity, specificity and hence the ubiquitous penetration of managerialism.

Many of the key features of managerialism in schools cluster around the headteacher, whose changing role is one of its most evident manifestations. The extent and rate of changes in the head's role provide a convenient barometer of the advance of managerialism. This is not to imply that managerialism is only or even mainly about what managers do, as though their powers and actions can be viewed in isolation. Indeed, it is significant in itself that the massive accumulation of a literature around school management and the reforms is either oblivious to managerialism or unconsciously or covertly encouraging it (see Ozga, 1992, for example). But the narrative of heads' changing role provides a good basis for studying key elements. The proposition which will be developed here is that the managerial function of being a headteacher in a school is undergoing radical alteration, both in terms of the role itself, and the ways in which it stands in relation to the hierarchies and constellations of power and influence which exist both above and below it. As for other public policy sites described in this volume, the changes are uneven, faltering, contested, sometimes ambiguous, iterative and far from complete. But the long-term trend and its consonance with similar shifts in other public policy fields is clear.

In essence, the headteacher is ceasing to be a senior peer embedded within a professional group who has taken on additional responsibilities including a significant administrative function, and is becoming a distinctive and key actor in an essentially managerialist system, in which the pursuit of objectives and methods which are increasingly centrally determined is the responsibility of managers who must account for their achievement and ensure the compliance of teaching staff. This is a crude caricature both of the status quo ante, and of the incoming regime. It nevertheless captures some of the key distinctions and the significance of the shifts which will be explored in more detail. A great deal more work, analytical, theoretical and empirical is needed to test this proposition to any convincing conclusion. The purpose of this essay is to set out the prima-facie case, explore the advances, identify the contradictions and ambiguities, and show what further work is needed to do so.

A number of features of managerialism already identified (see especially Chapters 1 and 2) are relevant to the education reforms:

1   the reconstruction and partial circumvention of a number of democratic processes in the control of education;
2   centralization of key aspects of policy determination, coupled with devolution (or perhaps more accurately distribution) of more marginal decision making;
3   concomitant substantial reductions in the powers of managers in some spheres and increases in others;
4   a dismantling of the power bases held in the name of professionalism, or specialist or elite knowledge;
5   subordination of the exercise of professional judgement to judgements made by reference to predetermined and/or publicly available criteria;
6   managers assume a pivotal role in the determination as well as implementation of those aspects of policy which are dealt with at local level;
7   substantial changes in the social relations between managers and those whose work they manage; and between managers and service users.

The central argument of the essay is that the introduction of the education reforms of the last few years has come to rely heavily on managerialist structures to ensure implementation and the compliance of a frequently resistant profession; that the reforms have deliberately introduced such structures; that they may emerge as the most long-lasting feature of the reforms; and that the reforms themselves and the processes of managerialism have not been fully secured and may recede if the two cannot advance in tandem. Developing this argument will also develop the claim that managerialism is, as the opening chapter argued, a connecting thread which links together the major reform thrusts in the public sector, and that it is through the actions of reconstructed public sector managers that the multi-faceted new forms of service provision are expected to jell into a coherent and durable market-driven programme.

Throughout the development of this argument it is important to realize that the reforms themselves, and managerialism as an emerging new feature of public service provision, stand in a complex and mutually interdependent relationship to one another. On the one hand, managerialism may reasonably be conceived of as the means to a larger reform end within the broad political project of restructuring public service and welfare provision. Its essential promise is to achieve on the ground in every service outlet the objectives of a reformed system in a manner which would be beyond the reach and the means of the most detailed of legislation and the most diligent forms of policing of its implementation. Managers, reconstructed as key actors to function as agents of reform, can bring about a more thorough-going and far-reaching overhaul of the methods and purposes of service delivery than an army of policy-makers and inspectors, or than a panoply of committees and bureaucrats. They are in this sense a *sine qua non* of systemic reform (for an elaboration of this theme, see Inglis, 1985, especially

Chapter 6). Without them, reforms reliant on centralist determinations of policy and populist support on the ground (rather than devolved powers and local democracy) would inevitably be diluted in transmission or amended by statutory local powers.

On the other hand, the structures for the effective delivery of reforms so significantly shape the precise form in which the reforms are realized as to have a life of their own, partially independent of and beyond the control of the substantive objects of reform, and potentially larger and more durable. These structures may also establish a more responsive environment – in their purest form a conduit – for subsequent reforms not presently envisaged. In this sense, the creation of a managerialist system becomes an end in itself for a political project committed simultaneously to reasserting the right to govern and the power of government, and to rolling back the state. Insofar as managers in a managerialist system can be re-created as nodes receptive to direct central determinations, and can obviate the activities of the residua of a local democratic or state machinery, their re-creation becomes as essential as substantive reform itself.

The objectives of educational reform are in essence the same as those of the other major public policy reforms of the Conservative administrations since 1979: the creation of competitive markets in service provision, the establishment of the power and rights of consumers, the subordination and curtailment of producer power and producer interests, the pursuit of efficiency and cost cutting in the quest for reduced public expenditure, the promotion of excellence over equity, the encouragement of diversity in the interests of widening consumer choice, all driven by the neo-liberal belief in the wider social value of the enlightened pursuit of self-interest as *the* means of raising standards.

At the heart of the reforms of education these objectives have been manifested as the pursuit of choice for parents in the schooling their children receive. The reforms envisage parents who choose from a variety of schools, unimpeded by restrictions on admission, and informed by extensive information about both the approach and performance of the school. They also envisage a funding regime in which diversity is encouraged, and popular schools are rewarded and unpopular schools penalized, to ensure that schools become increasingly responsive to consumer demands and preferences. At the same time, clear parameters for the activities of schools are established through a National Curriculum and a national system of testing intended to guarantee minimum standards, consistency and a measure of comparability. Parents are enabled to exercise their powers as consumers not only by which institutions they use, but also through a direct voice on governing bodies, on which local employers and business interests, also consumers of the output of a public education service, are represented.

The other major arm of reform concerns the redirection of producer activity to bring about this rise of effective consumer power at minimum public cost. This has a number of complex and inter-related facets. They can be summarized as the erosion of professional autonomy, increased public accountability, increased centralized control over the content of teaching, and major challenges to claims to monopolies of competence over a number of aspects of teaching and of education more generally. In particular, the exclusive claims of teachers and other education professionals to determine the content of the curriculum and assess the attainments of pupils have been challenged through the imposition of the National Curriculum and testing. The relatively weak management lines between heads and classroom teachers, premised on rights of professional autonomy, have been strengthened by the introduction of systems of appraisal and performance-related pay. Changed procedures of promotion and reward for good performance through an incentive allowance scheme have taken exclusive control away from professionals by vesting responsibility for promotion with governors. The superior powers of Her Majesty's Inspectors (HMI) to endorse and sanction practices (from the highest levels of curricular policy making to the inspection of the work of individual teachers) have been severely curtailed with the introduction of a dramatically contracted core Office for Standards in Education (OFSTED) and an extensive and flexible periphery of contract staff. The role of academics in higher education in determining the content and nature of teacher education, both initial and in-service, has been radically circumscribed, as has their role in deciding what kinds of undergraduate study make a suitable preparation for a career in teaching. In all, producer power is very markedly reduced.

Managerialism is essential to the realization of both these aspects of reform. For the first, it became essential that each school have a head who could not merely manage the implementation of reforms according to statute, but who could take on the full spirit of reform and envisage her school as a distinctive and separate institution striving for excellence and ready to grow on the basis of popular support – if necessary in competition with and at the expense of neighbouring schools. This required a degree of autonomy to fashion the school in response to parents' preferences, which would in turn need powers to shape events way beyond the power of management and the right to manage which is a defining characteristic of managerialism.

The containment of producer power too is heavily dependent on a form of administration and control which gives managers sharper, more extensive and clearly defined powers, but within the legislative parameters of the National Curriculum, testing, Local Management of Schools, and the various forms of public accountability associated with them. Heads have acquired both power and responsibility to oversee the content of teachers' work, to scrutinize its outcomes as measured by tests, truancy rates and leavers' destinations, to appraise performance, and to account for all these to governors, as well as exerting a powerful influence over promotion (and, prospectively, over performance-related pay), over the professional formation of future generations of teachers and over who inspects their schools.

In both cases (empowering the consumer, controlling the producer) managerialism appears initially to be the means to the achievement of the reform end, so fundamental are the cultural changes required to achieve an effective transformation. But in both cases managerialism begins to acquire the status of an end in itself. The powers become potentially so extensive as to give them a life of their own, independent of the reforms which gave rise to them. Like many quasi-autocratic powers in senior management, this one breeds a need for its own continuous expansion to ensure effective pursuit of the centrally prescribed mission.

The next section is concerned with detailing the fine grain of how the reforms and managerialism are intertwined and the positions of heads and teachers are then considered in turn. The final section considers how this works in practice.

The interdependence of reform and managerialism

The education reforms of the 1988, 1992, 1993 and 1994 Education Acts, plus a mass of non-statutory directives, orders, circulars, etc. over the same period, have been so extensive, so all-embracing, so interlocking and, for the most part, so radical as to warrant being conceived of as a model. They have touched almost every aspect of the content, organization and control of educational provision. They have done so in such a way as to make all the parts capable of harmonizing with the whole. In the perfect model form, each element of reform appears on the surface to mesh with several others for which it has implications. Every element of reform can be explained more or less directly by reference to the core objectives listed above, beginning with competitive marketization. Conceiving of the collection of reforms as a model is not, of course, to deny that there are internal contradictions and inconsistencies. Indeed, much of what follows will be devoted to identifying manifestations of these in the implementation of the reforms. Many of the contradictions and inconsistencies are concealed; many are common to the wider reform project, not particular to this sphere.

In essence, the 1988 Education Reform Act sought to establish the conditions for a competitive market in publicly funded school provision and to enable parents to exercise choice in a free market. It removed many of the restrictions on admissions to schools which prevented parents opting to send their children to the school they preferred. It gave schools substantially increased control over how they used their budgets, to allow them to develop in the way they preferred. It sought to influence these directions of development through the powers of the market, by allocating funding according to numbers on roll, which were themselves intended to be the result of the appeal of the school to selective parents. The relative attractions of schools were to be judged by a number of instruments, principally the publication of results of pupil performance within each school on tests at ages 7, 11, 14, 16, plus details of truancy rates and the destinations of leavers. In addition, schools were to be required to publish an information booklet for intending parents, and an annual report on the school, to be presented to parents at a public meeting open to all parents. Under the 1986 Education (No. 2) Act, parents had already acquired a major role as members of school governing bodies, alongside a large number of other lay members, and together they outnumbered teacher members by up to five to one. Now their powers were very considerably extended to encompass many aspects of school life which had previously been under the control of the LEA, particularly regarding finance, staffing and the curriculum. Employers and local business interests were to share this control on governing bodies as prospective consumers of education. Schools were to be increasingly free to spend their funds in a competitive market place, rather than obliged to use the services provided by LEAs. A majority of parents could vote to take schools out of LEA control altogether, to be directly funded by central government as Grant Maintained (GM) schools. Many of these rights for parents are enshrined in a *Parents' Charter* (GB, DES, 1991).

Alongside these came a crucial cluster of reforms which considerably increased central control over the content of schooling. The National Curriculum imposed three core subjects and six or seven foundation subjects which were to be taught to all children from the age of 5 to 16, following programmes of study determined by the Secretary of State and using detailed attainment targets which would provide the framework for extensive testing, results of which were to be published.

The 1988 Act provided the bedrock of reform. Three subsequent Acts have essentially been concerned to tighten the legislation and consolidate the thrust of reform. There have, for example, been considerable adjustments to the procedures concerning schools moving towards GM status. Also a centralized Funding Agency for opted-out schools has been established. These moves, and the historical evidence that there are considerable financial incentives to opt out are indicative of the strongly centralist strand in the reforms. Ministers have not disguised their eagerness that as many schools as possible should leave LEA control, nor their readiness to use ministerial authority to make critical determinations about the nature of those schools, even to the extent of approving proposals for selective entry which would previously have required legislation and which were inimical to local preferences (covert selection in GM schools has been reported for some time, see Dean, 1992; Ward, 1993, but a GM Penrith comprehensive became the first school in twenty years to be granted grammar status, in the face of protest and unsuccessful High Court action). The centralism of the National Curriculum and testing has been deepened by the closure of separate *councils* responsible for each area and the establishment of a single *authority*. New arrangements for inspection of schools and for an Education Association charged with taking over schools which are performing badly are also profoundly centralist (Simon and Chitty, 1993). Plans to strengthen the regional representation of government departments which have a significant interface with local government are likely to enhance the centralist tendencies in education as in other spheres.

As regards reforms directly affecting the producer interest, the main elements are that teachers' hours of work were specified for the first time, and schemes for teacher appraisal were to be required. Performance-related pay is also envisaged. Considerable controls over the purposes of expenditure on staff development for serving teachers were imposed, and the forms and means of initial teacher training were repeatedly revised by directives.

The entire framework for the inspection of schools was also radically overhauled, to recast inspection as a service to be purchased by quasi-autonomous schools, and to render the results of inspection as a further piece of objective information to inform parents' choice of schools and governors' deliberations.

Other alternatives to locally funded and controlled provision of public schooling were also sought, primarily through state funding of places in private schools for those whose parents could not afford them, through the Assisted Places Scheme; and the introduction of City Technology Colleges intended as centres of excellence with specialist curricula, whose setting-up costs were to be funded in part by local businesses. Both these typify the kinds of mixed economies of service provision which have been characteristic of the wider public sector reforms.

The reconstitution of school governing bodies is a crucial element of the reform process, in giving form to the rhetoric not only of a voice, but of a measure of control for the consumer. The predominance of elected parent and co-opted local community governors over professional and political representatives is one dimension of this. The extension of their powers to cover recruitment, staffing, curricula and the allocation of budgets is the other. The relevance of this to managerialism is that, like all key figures in essentially managerialist regimes, headteachers must fuse consumer will and ministerial diktat into living policies for their schools, in a form which will be acceptable to staff whose own professional roles and standings are being reconstructed in a number of ways. Governors in a centralist system would not be possible without managerialist controls, just as a centralist system would not be tolerable in the prevailing balance of political forces without the intervention of the consumer interest.

The changing position of headteachers

It is almost self-evident even from this sketch of the reforms that they have conferred upon the managers of schools powers greatly in excess of some previously held, while eroding others. Headteachers have substantially increased powers and responsibility in conjunction with governors in the financial and other administration of schools. They also have substantial powers as a result of the introduction of the National Curriculum and assessment, but have lost other significant powers as a result of them.

It is important to note at this point that a number of changes, particularly in respect of pay and conditions, have served to separate heads from classroom teachers. At around £50,000 the salaries of heads of the largest schools are commensurate with those of managers of some commercial institutions of comparable size, and are sharply differentiated from those of their workforce, which average around £18,000. Given the strong under-representation of women in these echelons, it is also notable that managerialism has a powerful and significant gender dimension (Statham et al., 1991). This is doubly significant when seen in the broader context of gender inequalities in the labour market, in that teaching has traditionally been the profession through which women have best been able to establish their own autonomy, with the impact of a male-dominated hierarchy limited by professional codes curtailing the activities of managers (see the wider discussion of these issues by Janet Newman in Chapter 9). The gross under-representation of black teachers in the workforce, especially in management, gives managerialism an even stronger race dimension.

The main plank of empowering managers has been the introduction of a very high degree of devolved financial control to all but the smallest primary schools. Each school is allocated a budget according to a formula which leaves little discretion to the LEA making the allocation.

LEAs are now obliged to allocate at least 85 percent of their budgets in this way. Though the responsibility for the internal allocation of these budgets lies formally with governors, the effect has been markedly to increase the managerial powers of headteachers. They have a previously unimagined degree of control over staffing in particular, but also other key areas of expenditure, including books and equipment, staff development and bursary items. It is a commonplace that managers generally exploit their special accountability for budgetary matters to justify sometimes autocratic actions on grounds of being solely in possession of knowledge about financial circumstances. The basic information is often kept secret on the grounds that it cannot be properly interpreted by others who do not have full knowledge of the context. By these means managers often by-pass or truncate normal processes of consultation, or take executive action against advice or without resolving conflicting views, or allowing financial considerations to prevail over educational (Ball and Bowe, 1990, quoted in Halpin and Whitty, 1992). The Audit Commission (1993b) provides detailed evidence of important budgetary information being withheld from governors, and independent financial decisions of heads which seriously lack probity. While Located Management of Schools (LMS) does not of itself confer autocratic powers, it does so to the extent that heads become drawn into these habits. Furthermore, powers of apportioning resources as between the various budget heads are in effect powers of significantly determining the directions and priorities of an institution. The significance for managerialism of these developments is not only that they confer more power upon managers. The exercise of even the most unassailable autocratic powers of management resulting from extensive control of finances is not in itself managerialist. What makes it so here is that financial control provides not only a means of disposal of policies determined elsewhere, it partly provides the means of determining the policies themselves. To the extent that democratic controls over schools are vested in governors rather than local politicians, and governors are dependent on heads' advice, the heads' powers to create policies *post hoc* through the exercise of financial control is greater. In GM schools the power of heads in the absence of LEA checks or public financial accountability is greater still: audits are produced privately and not published (Audit Commission, 1993a).

As schools become detached from LEAs, then, a major determinant of the extent of heads' administrative powers is the nature of their relationship with governors. On the face of it governors retain extensive powers over deployment of resources, staffing, curricula, etc. What is far more difficult to tease out is the extent to which devolved powers have accrued in practice to the head and to the governors respectively. Simply reading the lines of statutory responsibility does not provide an adequate guide. The head is normally a governor. He is one of the few governors who works full time in education, and certainly knows the school best of any of the governors. Parent governors are part time and normally lay. Under the pre-1988 arrangements lay governors were of low status and ineffective compared to the politicians and full-time educationalists who were also governors, partly because of lack of time as well as of expertise (see Deem, 1990). Some research findings to date suggest that this has not changed under the new regime (Diamond, 1993; Deem and Brehoney, 1994) but its significance will have changed considerably. In reducing the number of political representatives and teachers on governing bodies in favour of parents, the 1988 Act has arguably substantially diluted effective opposition to the head. To the extent that parent and other lay governors are dependent on professional sources of factual information, advice and interpretation, they are necessarily prone to accept the views of the head. This is particularly true if they are inexperienced in operating in formal settings and public meetings. The head is also likely to be the only governor who is a member of every one of the sub-committees which most governing bodies have found it necessary to create to cope with the weight of business. Such multiple membership confers special powers, both ingenuous and disingenuous, in the name of co-ordination. Persuasive argument, appeal to popularly recognized discourses, agenda fixing, cultivation of sympathetic parents, are the familiar weaponry of those with leadership responsibilities operating in ostensibly democratic settings. Their use by heads becomes part of the potentially populist strategy of managerialism: the construction, manipulation and selective amplification of lay opinion; or, as Inglis (1989) puts it, 'to be managed is to be persuaded of something against your better judgement'. In most schools, the balance of power between heads and governors does not reside exclusively with one party. Each will be more effective on some issues than others. However, the present balance has not merely the potential to drift towards a managerialist utilization of orchestrated popular opinion, but a strong tendency to do so, for it is a key means by which heads can weld consumer will and statutory requirements into coherent school policies acceptable to and deliverable by the teaching staff.

There are other forces, too, driving heads towards this managerialist manipulation of popular power, financial responsibility and statutory obligation. First, the introduction of the National Curriculum has at a stroke redefined the role of the head as a 'director of studies'. In essence he is now the curator of his school's curriculum, not its senior architect. In curtailing the head's role as a professional academic, this serves in itself to recast him primarily as a professional administrator with academic acumen, capable of making academic judgements, rather than as a professional academic with administrative responsibilities. His investment in the effective exercise of his non-academic managerial role is considerably greater. If that is squeezed on the other jaw of the vice as the academic role has been squeezed on the first, the head faces an intolerable role as mere functionary largely deprived of autonomy and the exercise of professional judgement. Governor power has therefore to be kept in check.

Secondly, partnership with the LEA was far more acceptable to some heads than partnership with governors. LEA staff, whether inspectors or officers, were generally appointed from among the ranks of teachers, often because of their competence in staff development or as educational administrators. They were in this sense part of the exclusive expert cadre, not outsiders ignorant of its special knowledge, codes and values. Similarly, the remote if extensive powers of local councillors were to some heads preferable to the contiguous and specific powers of governors.

Thirdly, the downward pressure on managers from an increasingly centralist system makes the managerialist exercise of executive powers a pragmatic response to being required to implement changes determined elsewhere and to being judged – by exam results, inspections, enrolments and in the end by the market – on their implementation. The job-for-life head not ephemeral political or consumer masters is the person whose future is on the line.

Taken separately, each of these reasons for the drift towards managerialism will have a limited and partial influence on any head in any school. Some will be inoperative in some contexts. But taken together in their many permutations, they represent a strong tide.

The obligation on the head to ensure the translation, development and implementation of the statutory National Curriculum and assessment requirements epitomizes much of managerialism. He must comply with central requirements irrespective of his own views. The rationale for the National Curriculum is not open to debate (see Inglis, 1985, for an elaboration of this theme in the period prior to the National Curriculum). The head must oversee his staff's implementation of the requirements, and account for it to governors. On the one hand he is isolated from the decisions about what is specified; on the other he is heavily monitored in this task of ensuring implementation, both by governors directly and through inspection and assessment procedures and publication of results. Like all managers in managerialist systems the head takes orders from above (quite literally, in the shape of the so-called National Curriculum Orders issued by the Secretary of State) and applies them below. Some early studies of LMS have already noted a shift from collegial to hierarchical styles of management (Halsey, 1993). But whereas in a classic Fordist commercial business hierarchy the scope for interpretation and latitude is typically limited at lower levels of management, the devolutionary aspects of the education reforms and the truncation of intervening managerial tiers (especially in the LEA) give considerable scope to the head to occupy an expanding and expandable middle ground between staff and governors sufficient to afford him unprecedented *managerial* power. Only the head can make the link between the activities of the whole teaching staff and the governors in accounting for the school's adherence to Orders.

The National Curriculum may have produced relatively few changes both in the practices of some teachers, and in the levels of intervention by heads in the work of individual teachers and of governors in the work of heads (though there will also be many exceptions to this). Rather, the principal managerial power conferred by the National Curriculum is likely to be in the subtle yet enormously significant changes in the social relations between head and teacher, and heads and governors. For heads and teachers, their respective roles in meeting National Curriculum requirements are transformed from being those of professionals, more bound by their common professional membership than divided by their rank, to those of manager and managed, more divided by their responsibilities and objects of allegiance than united in a commitment to meet educational needs according to a shared set of perceptions and expectations. The head/manager must look to those who monitor the legislation's implementation, the managed teacher to his own understandings of pupils' needs, subject and pedagogy. However rarely these objects of allegiance clash, the possibility that they can do so without recourse to professional debate and reference to shared understandings unclouded by extraneous considerations alters at a stroke the social relations of every school (see Lawn, 1988, for a development of notions of the reconstruction of professionalism and increasing managerialism). Equally, the social relations of heads and governors more closely resemble those of the managing director and the board. However little the board's powers are exercised, the knowledge of their possible exercise alters social relations, not just between head and governor, but between head and teacher.

Finally, in the model form, a system of teacher appraisal formalizes and organizes the powers of management to ascertain and discuss the extent to which individuals are contributing to the school's pursuit of its mission, and fulfilling their statutory responsibilities. Again, while it may in practice be a rarity for matters as basic as adherence to the programmes of study and pursuit of the attainment targets to be the subject of review of a teacher's performance during appraisal, the possibility (and in extreme cases the necessity) of doing so reshapes the social and power relations of teacher and head.

To summarize, then, governors are nominally empowered as the voice of the consumer interest exercising direct control over many aspects of school life, but within the parameters of a centrally determined curriculum and testing; heads are nominally controlled by and accountable to governors, but in practice have both the motivation and the means to influence, dominate or even manipulate popular opinion as expressed by the governors, both to retain their own powers as senior officers, and to retain and enhance clear lines of managerial control over staff. Both these provide a check against the risk of governor power making a major switch from populist power to the more collectivist democratic mode which it had been designed to supersede by supplanting some powers of LEAs.

For most schools the combination of LMS, open enrolment and the

National Curriculum has hugely reduced the powers of intervention of LEA staff. To the extent that this staff was at least accountable to and at most controlled by elected members of the LEA Education Committee, managers and governors have been granted one of the most crucial requirements of any managerial system: that it be free of properly constituted democratic controls. However much the reality of most authorities was that officers and professionals, not elected members held power, the principle of democratic control was enshrined, and a deterrent to the potentially managerialist interventions of officers preoccupied with techno-rational ends (the latter are well defined in relation to schools by Inglis, 1989; see also Allan Cochrane's arguments in Chapter 7). The simultaneous diminution of that deterrent effect (as much a consequence of an atomized distribution of powers as of LMS, National Curriculum, etc.), and the by-passing of LEA central staff under LMS, have bestowed upon those heads capable of containing and fashioning the activities of their governors just the managerialist powers which their old LEA superiors could use only with subterfuge. A report by the Audit Commission (1993b) highlighting the potential for unaccountable abuses in the financial management of GM schools may be a harbinger of the kinds of losses of democratic control which may become endemic throughout the system.

The perceived power bloc of what ministers came to refer to disparagingly as 'the educational establishment' also stood in the way of managerialism. Educationalists, particularly the inspectorate and academic staff in colleges and departments of education, were identified as potential impediments to reform. They could block some changes through their statutory powers, and others by their power to question the populist underpinnings of reform, the lay wisdom of governor control and the drift towards managerialism itself. What was singular about the threat they posed was their special autonomy. The inspectorate was chartered not by the civil service and the then Department of Education and Science, but by the Crown. Similarly, academic teacher trainers, particularly those in the old universities, were protected by their academic charters. The monopolies of inspectors were broken by the decimation of HMI into OFSTED, and the introduction of competitive tendering from any body whose inspection plans could achieve OFSTED approval. By these means it was intended that the deliberations of inspectors should be more responsive to the concerns of governors, as well as more accessible to them. As regards academics, some of their fate had already been sealed by a series of non-legislative directives which had exerted unprecedentedly powerful controls over the curricula of teacher training, both initial and in-service. This was achieved by the increasingly prescriptive specification of the content – and to some extent the method – of courses which the then Department of Education and Science would fund.

Challenging the teaching profession

Other obstacles, too, had to be smoothed away under the new managerial regime. For classroom teachers, accepting a national curriculum and its associated tests, which prescribed extensive aspects of their activity and occupied the very large proportion of the school timetable, entailed some adjustment of self-concept. Similarly, accepting the subtle but unmistakable shift in the role of the head from senior colleague to institutional manager meant some reconceptualization of the teacher's role as well. A further adjustment would be required for classroom teachers to accept work which was more technicized, more routinized, more bureaucratized, more pre-scribed or more dependent on the judgements of others. There has been extensive debate as to how far teachers are becoming deskilled by curricular and other changes (see for example Buswell, 1988; Lawn and Ozga, 1981; Inglis, 1985; Mac An Ghaill, 1992) but the inception of the National Curriculum, testing and the advance in the managerial role of the head strengthen the arguments of those who make the case. In particular, the shift away from conception on the grander scales of curriculum design and teacher assessment of pupil performance, in favour of the skilled executions of programmes and activities at least partially conceived elsewhere, makes clear that the values, ethos and collective self-concept of the occupational group are being required to alter significantly.

In view of this, the reform movement and the drive towards managerial-ism prudently took the initial professional formation of teachers within its ambit. Together they have led to careful scrutiny of the sources of notions of professionalism and collective self-concept, and the values, assumptions and expectations that are associated with them: the entire gamut of the processes of group socialization, combined with the development of professional identity and allegiance to academic community.

Until very recently, the professional formation of teachers has been the exclusive preserve of academics, who trained and held the dominant influence in licensing teachers. Over the last ten years there has been a steady, progressive erosion of this position, moving from interventions in the curricula of initial teacher training described above, to the complete removal of training from HE under pilot plans set out in 1993. In this progression there have been many stages and hybrids, with a number of variants of schemes (licensed teachers, articled teachers, internship, school-based courses) experimenting with weakening the links with HE. These were followed by changes in regulations, requiring two-thirds of the time of trainee teachers to be spent in schools, then by a further experiment which handed to schools complete responsibility for training.

A scenario in which the licensing and induction of teachers is entirely located within schools and entirely the domain of heads and governors is imminent. Many elements of it are already in place. The 1994 Education Bill proposes to entirely transfer funding from HE to schools and to leave schools the option of contracting HE to contribute to initial and in-service training. The potential impact on the constitution, standing, identity, autonomy and authority of the profession is enormous. The socialization of intending teachers into the mores, values and understandings of what it means to be a teacher will switch from being developed in a collective setting of debate informed by theory, research and evidence, to one in which socialization is entirely dependent on two or three teachers. New teachers' capacities to act autonomously, work independently and, most of all, to mount well-grounded challenges to managerial diktat are likely to diminish, and their sense of membership of and solidarity with a larger body to be diluted.

Similar effects can be achieved through casualization of the labour force. Supply teachers have always provided a substantial section of the workforce. The proportion of part-time, short-contract posts, mainly occupied by women, has increased with LMS. The use of low-qualified teaching assistants is a temptation to governors eking out tight budgets and eyeing the potential of salary savings to technicize, routinize and mechanize teaching processes (especially in subjects in which qualified staff are scarce and expensive, and teaching has to be entrusted to teachers of other subjects). The Audit Commission (1993b) found that both the employment of teaching assistants and pupil–teacher ratios had risen since the introduction of LMS; and that staff leaving were being replaced by less experienced, less costly teachers. New forms of low-qualified direct entry make for potentially more transient careers, with lower 'front-end' investment by both parties. From the reluctantly abandonded 'mums' army' to licensed teachers, the idea of a short teaching career during particular stages of people's lives (first job, last job) may gain hold. In all, the pursuit of flexibility and the contractual requirement for flexible specialization which have characterized restructured labour markets and workplaces begin to find emergent parallels in schools.

If new modes of professional formation are to form classroom teachers to the precise mould of the particular workplace, trainability and flexibility are more critical qualities of managers. Their deconstruction as senior academic colleagues with an administrative function, and reconstruction as managers with primary administrative responsibilities and residual academic functions, is arguably the greater transformation. Since heads, so far at least, are always promoted experienced teachers, they cannot by definition be formed *ab initio* in their new managerialist role in the same way as a new generation of teachers. It is only relatively recently that any form of management training has come by custom and practice to be considered essential for a new head; those who were in post before reform may still remain untouched by any formative training except of the most instrumental kind. For the head in a managerialist system partly designed to bear the constant refinement and attenuation of the reform process, flexibility and flexible specialization are indispensable attributes. Management training designed to provide these has burgeoned in a variety of forms, from the instrumental to the still remarkably academic and reflective. There are clear signs that the tide is running strongly from the latter to the former. The most pronounced evidence of this is the growth of interest in MBAs specifically designed for teachers. Broadly, these tend to be focused more on the means than the ends of management (see Price, 1993), and are as such more evidently compatible with a managerialist approach.

The reforms in practice: advances and resistances

The discussion so far has concentrated on the reforms as a model. The focus
has been on the ideal form, on the potential of the reforms radically to alter
provision and the nature of education as a public service. In this sense we
have been concerned with intent rather than effect. Of course, the
implementation of the reforms in schools and LEAs has by no means neatly
and mechanically followed the model, or brought into being the ideal type.
Most of the basic technical and legal conditions for doing so have now been
or will soon be satisfied, but the arrival of a competitive market in publicly
funded education is still some considerable distance away.

Prominent among those aspects of the reforms in which the conditions for
change are satisfied is the introduction of an essentially managerialist
system. Some of the desired outcomes are already being achieved, along the
lines described. The idea of some form of managerialist approach to running
a school seems firmly implanted in many, perhaps a majority of schools.
What is far less certain is how far it has advanced, how deep is its grasp and
how far it has become out of step with the substantive reforms with which it is
so mutually interdependent. This section is concerned to explore these
uncertainties. It does so by examining the extent to which flaws inherent in
the reform model intervene; and by examining the contra-indications and
forms of resistance which have become evident to date.

One of the most fundamental criticisms of the public sector reforms has
been that they are premised on the transferability of values, methods and
approaches from systems of production based on extrinsic motivations and
rewards to systems based on intrinsic motivations and rewards. John Clarke
and Janet Newman point out in Chapter 1 that one of the disjunctures in
attempts to transfer the practices, ethos and conceptions of managers in the
private sector to those in the public is that public sector managers have no
developed value system which equates to their counterparts' use of profit
and profitability to steer a clear conception of efficiency and effectiveness,
and in the end to measure success. In other words, the private, profit-
seeking sector is essentially concerned with the extrinsic value of its
products: that is, with the value others attach to them and therefore the price
they are prepared to pay for them. Their intrinsic worth is of no material
concern to either producer or manager. Neither views the value of her work
as revolving round her own understanding of the worth of what she
produces. It is not necessary for the labour force to have a view of the
intrinsic value of the product to continue to produce it effectively.

In contrast, it is the essential absence of extrinsic measures of value which
characterizes much of the work undertaken by licensed professionals in the
public sector. Not only have there been very limited measures of extrinsic
value until recently, but self-assessment by reference to intrinsic values by
professionals in public sector service roles provides an important feedback
loop in their own self-monitoring of performance. In the case of teachers this
typically takes the form of continuous checking of pupils' academic progress
to determine when they are ready for more demanding work, what kind of

remedial action may be necessary, etc. Pupils' learning is of intrinsic concern to teachers, and an important guide to them in their work. Expressing the extent, depth and nature of that learning through assessment and its valorization in marks, grades and scores is of secondary interest.

As a result of these distinctions, attempts to prefer extrinsic values to intrinsic in education meet a wide range of resistances. In particular, attempts to find extrinsic values which provide measures of worth of schools, pupils, teachers to the end of creating quasi-markets are met with scepticism. This is not simply because teachers are historically predisposed to resist such moves. It is because the growing preoccupation with the extrinsic poses direct threats to teachers' own judgements and to their concerns with intrinsic worth. At a quite practical level, for example, if the bureaucracy and machinery of testing to provide league tables of school performance either begin to stand in the way of teaching itself, or to produce very slowly and inefficiently information about pupils' performances already known to teachers (both charges levied against early manifestations of the testing regime) they are rejected as anti-educational.

Such attempts to valorize the extrinsic in contexts where the intrinsic has historically provided the key points of reference will rarely achieve the *essential* indisputable worth of profit, for no consensus has yet been able to accumulate about the functional worth of such measures as test results, truancy rates, or leavers' destinations. To start with basic considerations, the content of each curricular subject is contested in some measure; the overall conception of the National Curriculum as a whole is viewed sceptically in some quarters because of its traditionalist conceptions of knowledge and subject divisions, its conservative cultural orientation and its consonance with dominant ideology (Halpin and Whitty, 1992; Whitty, 1992), for example. In both these senses, the subject matter achieves no absolute endorsement as an incontrovertible reference point for judging value in its own right, so extrinsic values cannot flow easily from it. Yet without such values, neither the reform process nor the establishment of a system in which managers have unassailable but circumscribed powers to control can be completed. So long as the importance of intrinsic value is acknowledged, the power of professional judgement of individuals remains strong, and the power of managers to direct the actions of staff necessarily remains curtailed.

A second and linked set of flaws in the reforms is their dependence upon reconstruction of teachers' and heads' occupational or professional identities. Professional autonomy, a considerable measure of self-determination, and reference to intrinsic values are essential to both. It was noted in the previous section that efforts towards the deliberate reconstruction of roles were being concentrated in initial teacher formation. This leaves out of account the majority of teachers who will remain in post over the next forty years, and whose professional formation pre-dated these revisions. However many of these may already adopt an approach to teaching which finds little conflict with either the reforms or a managerialist system *per se*, there remain many who resist the change of professional identity required. No comparable measures are in place to achieve their resocialization and reconstruction. While the continuing processes of incorporation, from habituation to retraining, will no doubt continue to erode resistance, there are signs that there are clear limits to teachers' adaptability and flexibility, and that their commitment to trainability may be nearing exhaustion. The imposition in 1988 of contracted hours alienated many teachers who knew that they worked many more than the 1265 hours stipulated. This, and the suspension of independent pay negotiating machinery, were read by many as the beginning of an onslaught on the standing of teachers which paralleled similar moves in respect of medical professionals, social workers, and is being attempted for crime-related professionals. When this was combined with testing procedures which rejected teachers' own judgement of pupils' attainments, but imposed workloads in excess of contracted requirements, the loss of support and sympathy was sufficient to bring about the first major act of united resistance among teachers in decades, in the shape of the 1993 testing boycott. There are also signs of united union resistance to the introduction of school-based initial training, and to the admission of non-graduate entrants into teaching. Particularly significant is that in all these resistances, headteachers have more often led than joined their classroom colleagues, not remained on the sidelines as apparatchik managers. On the training front, many teachers prefer to foot the cost of their own continuing professional development through substantial university courses with a sound academic element befitting their postgraduate status, rather than enrol for courses funded by the school or LEA designed with more short-term and instrumental aims in mind.

As regards consumers of education, it remains to be demonstrated whether parents are inclined to treat education as a commodity which they purchase in the same way as any other, taking advantage of such free competitive markets as exist. It is not yet evident that they have the means or inclination to make considered and rational use of published information about schools in the way the architects of reform intended. Indeed there are some findings which suggest that choice consolidates social class segregation (Willms and Echols, 1992), that parents are already disillusioned with consumer choice and that schools, including GM schools, are failing to provide wider choices for parents (Fitz, Power and Halpin, 1993; Bartlett, 1993). It is also unclear whether parents are willing to treat at face value league tables which obscure critical differences in the circumstances and objectives of individual schools. The failure of consumers to behave rationally and predictably has long placed limits on the credibility of neo-classical economics. One reason for it is recognized as being the limited capacities (time, resources, information and knowledge) available to consumers choosing between products which are sometimes only marginally differentiated in a complex and extensive market. Consumers socialized in a world which regarded health, education, etc. as part of an umbrella of equitable service provision to meet need in a state welfare system are not likely to be more inclined to become informed rational exploiters of their alleged sovereignty as consumers, provided they continue to trust the judgements of professionals, if not the equitability of the system, in such complex, specialist areas of practice. The rate at which schools opted out slowed after the initial enthusiasms; the City Technology College programme was quietly superseded long before it came anywhere near to the target number of schools. The ideology of choice in a diverse market place may be faltering before it has become established.

Paradoxically, the increasing involvement of parents in the governance, funding and running of schools promises to do more to reaffirm their faith in and dependence on professionals, as they become more familiar with the complexities of what teaching involves. Alliances between teachers, heads and governors arise in some schools as parents become fully aware of the impact of the National Curriculum and testing on teachers and pupils alike, and of the effects in funding shortfalls, staff shortages or the sheer weight of the bureaucracy which accretes around centralist managerial systems. In these circumstances, heads are less likely to exploit the nature of their relations with governors to assume maximum managerial power along the lines discussed above. The potential for parent-governors armed with insider knowledge to invoke their rights under a so-far-untested *Parents' Charter* is considerable, and could yet become a solidary and organized form of resistance locally or even nationally. Parent power is entirely ambivalent, and may prove antithetical to managerial delivery of centralist objectives. It may also disincline heads to exploit and develop their managerial powers. Governing bodies have the potential to be associations for popular resistance, not the local watch committee for government in a managerial system.

One conclusion which begins to emerge is that it is not just the future of the reform project in education which is hinging on the outcome of struggles over and revisions of the National Curriculum and testing, but also the likely future grasp of managerialism. If extrinsic values and their expression as measures of performance cannot take their hold alongside intrinsic values; if professional identity cannot be altered sufficiently to circumscribe the autonomy of teachers; and if consumers cannot be persuaded as well as enabled to exercise their market powers, then managerialism will not have the scope it needs to shape teachers and parents in the pursuit of centrally determined objectives. The mutual interdependence of reform and managerialism is reaffirmed by the centrality of the struggle over the National Curriculum and testing. It is not just the powers of managers but the conditions of managerialism which will be pushed back if these cornerstones of reform are substantially weakened.

The perceived flaws in the National Curriculum are that it is too prescriptive and grossly overloaded, bringing unacceptable pressure not only on the National Curriculum subjects themselves but also upon other aspects of the school curriculum, most of which are now marginalized almost out of existence. Co-ordinated protests led to the National Curriculum being scaled down following the 1993 testing boycott. The more this and other review processes push back the boundaries of prescription, the less secure will be the basis for control of the curriculum, and the management of teachers. The erosion of uniformity will further inhibit fair comparisons between schools and thus inhibit the exercise of consumer choice (though neo-liberals would view the deregulation and the resultant diversity as a move in the direction of purifying a state-controlled quasi-market, Sexton, 1988). Hence there is a continuing struggle which is sure to be replayed many times during the life of the National Curriculum over what balance should be struck between regulation and professional discretion.

Far less publicly, there is evidence that teachers, faced with what they consider to be an unachievable coverage of attainment targets, continue to use the same kinds of discretion they used before the reforms in selecting what topics to cover, which are essential and which to exclude. The test will almost certainly be whether teachers are ready to continue to use discretion in defiance of direct interventions from managers keen to secure the delivery of a slimmed down National Curriculum. The balance is indeed delicate. Can the majority of heads be more easily satisfied than the majority of teachers that a reasonable compromise on content, extent and prescription has been struck? Will they be more easily satisfied because of their new managerial positions, or less? Will they use their managerial powers to ensure implementation or collude in dilutions? Will this weaken the reforms and managerial authority in tandem? The inter-relation of the two is an apparently powerful one.

Much the same goes for testing. The simplification of tests, their substantial reduction or even elimination for younger pupils, the use of external marking, the incorporation of teachers' own assessments are the terrain on which the struggle is fought. For some in a highly heterogeneous occupational group, it is a politicized battle of principle, for others a rejection of the hypocrisies and contradictions brought to a head by excessive workload, for others still a pragmatic response to what is possible and reasonable. Once again, it may be on the exercise of managerial powers that the extent and nature of resistance turns. The alliance of heads with classroom teachers during the 1993 boycott suggests that all will not be obediently delivered. And here the potential for direct conflict with government is greater than in the case of the National Curriculum. The manipulation of the National Curriculum in the everyday life of schools may be concealed; the conduct of assessments whose results are published cannot. Much hangs on the outcome of these struggles, and how readily and how regularly they will be revisited over the next few years.

The capacity of the system to continue to be able to exercise some of the centrally assumed powers on which managerialism is premised, legally, constitutionally and practically, has already been brought into question (Bogdanor, 1992). The prospect of increasing numbers of financially induced opt-outs being run from London may eventually presage the collapse of centralism, and the creation of local agencies. At that point, the prospect arises of a renewed battle for their democratic control, especially if a rump of LEAs has survived long enough to demonstrate the anomaly of two parallel local controlling and funding bodies; or if the burgeoning regionalism identified in other political spheres is capable of creating area authorities (Benn and Benn, 1993); or if tolerance of unaccountable quangos becomes exhausted.

The conversion effected by the overt reform process of the last six years is provisional and far from complete. The lags and resistances in its achievement are considerable. Long-established conceptions of roles, duties, rights and responsibilities are deconstructed in the face of resentment, resistance, low morale and scepticism. The least amenable leave or retire, the most mouldable enter at the bottom of the profession. The process of reconstruction is only as strong and resilient as the overt reforms which drag it in their wake. As sceptical teachers submit to *force majeure* and comply with the National Curriculum programmes of study, test their pupils, accept appraisal, as reluctant heads sit on sub-committees of governing bodies to apportion the schools' budgets, etc., they come gradually to live and be imbued by the logic of new roles, new tasks, new functions and, in the end, to absorb partial redefinitions of their professional selves, first inhabiting them, eventually becoming them. Alongside the reluctant reconstructees, of course, are sections for whom the process is less disturbing, from a few ideologues completely committed to the reform process, through the ideologically indifferent to the aspiring managers already predisposed to find benefit and advantage in both the reforms and the reconstructions they entail. As redefinition takes hold, though, it is likely to be deep-seated and long-lived. The greatest sources of resistance will have departed, redefinitions will not be easily undone, and as young recruits who never knew any different move up the hierarchy the consolidation of the new regime can bed in. Once a shift in world-view of this profundity has been effected, only an equal and opposite force will achieve a reversal. Improbable as this is in a period of political convergence, managerialism may turn out to be the most enduring legacy of the reforms. The combination of an occupational group unconfident of how far it can take its resistance without fragmenting, and a government too weakened to achieve its more radical political objectives leaves open the way for dilute reforms and creeping managerialism capable of surviving any seriously envisageable political-ideological swings. Cautious managerialism in the service of cautious centralism may emerge as the legacy of an exhausted new right to produce an educational landscape which would, nevertheless, have been unimaginable a decade ago.

References

Audit Commission for Local Authorities and the National Health Service in England and Wales (1993a) *Report and Accounts for Year Ended 31st March 1993*. London: HMSO.

Audit Commission for Local Authorities and the National Health Service in England and Wales (1993b) *Adding up the Sums: Schools' Management of their Finances*. London: HMSO.

Ball, S. and Bowe, R. (1990) 'The spirit is willing but the flesh is weak: an exploration of LMS in one secondary school', unpublished conference paper quoted in D. Halpin and G. Whitty (1992).

Banting, K. (1985) 'Poverty and educational priority', in I. McNay and J. Ozga (eds), *Policy-making in Education*. Oxford: Pergamon Press. (First published 1979.)

Bartlett, W. (1993) 'Quasi-markets and educational reforms' in J. Le Grande and W. Bartlett (eds), *Quasi-markets and Social Policy*. Basingstoke: Macmillan.

Benn, C. and Benn, H. (1993) 'Local government and education: tackling the tasks of the future', *Local Government Policy Making*, 19(5): 67–72.

Bogdanor, V. (1992) 'Heading for square one?' *Times Educational Supplement*, 6 November.

Buswell, C. (1988) 'Pedagogic change and social change', in J. Ozga (ed.), *Schoolwork*. Milton Keynes: Open University Press. (First published 1980.)

Central Statistical Office (1993) *Annual Abstract of Statistics, 1993*, No. 129. London: HMSO.

Dean, C. (1992) 'Opt-out schools deny "back door selection"', *Times Educational Supplement*, 10 April.

Deem, R. (1990) 'The reform of school governing bodies: the power of the consumer over the producer?', in M. Flude and M. Hammer (eds), *The Education Reform Act 1988: Its Origins and Implications*. Lewes: Falmer Press.

Deem, R. and Brehoney, K. (1994, forthcoming) *Active Citizenship and the Governing of Schools*. Milton Keynes: Open University Press. (Quoted in *Times Educational Supplement*, 23 March 1993.)

Diamond, J. (1993) 'The experience of parent governors', *Local Government Policy Making*, 19(5): 21–4.

Fitz, J., Power, S. and Halpin, D. (1993) 'Opting for grant maintained status', *Policy Studies*, 14(1): 4–20.

Great Britain, Department of Education and Science (1991) *The Parents' Charter*, London: DES.

Green, A. (1990) *Education and State Formation*. London: Macmillan.

Halpin, D. and Whitty, G. (1992) *Secondary Education after the Reform Act*, Unit S1/2 of Course EP228, 'Frameworks for Teaching'. Milton Keynes: Open University Press.

Halsey, J. (1993) 'The impact of local management on school management style', *Local Government Policy Making*, 19(5): 49–56.

Inglis, F. (1985) *The Management of Ignorance*. Oxford: Basil Blackwell.

Inglis, F. (1989) 'Managerialism and morality', in W. Carr (ed.), *Quality in Teaching: Arguments for a Reflective Profession*. Lewes: Falmer Press.

Keohane, K. (1991) 'Ignorance', *Social Policy and Administration*, 25(1): 39–48.

Lawn, M. (1988) 'Skill in schoolwork: work relations in the primary school', in J. Ozga (ed.), *Schoolwork*. Milton Keynes: Open University Press. (First published 1986.)

Lawn, M. and Ozga, J. (1981) 'The educational worker', in L. Barton and S. Walker (eds), *Schools, Teachers and Teaching*. Lewes: Falmer Press.

Lawson, J. and Silver, H. (1985) 'Education and social policy', in I. McNay and J. Ozga (eds), *Policy-making in Education*. Oxford: Pergamon Press. (First published 1973.)

Mac An Ghaill, M. (1992) 'Teachers' work: curriculum restructuring, culture, power and comprehensive schooling', *British Journal of Sociology of Education*, 13(2): 177–200.

Ozga, J. (ed.) (1988) *Schoolwork*. Milton Keynes: Open University Press.

Ozga, J. (1992) 'Education management', *British Journal of Sociology of Education*, 13(2): 279–80.

Price, C. (1993) 'Training to be a servant of learning', *Times Educational Supplement*, 15 January.

Sexton, S. (1988), 'No nationalised curriculum', *The Times*, 9 May.

Simon, B. and Chitty, C. (1993) *SOS: Save Our Schools*. London: Lawrence & Wishart.

Statham, J. and Mackinnon, D. with Cathcart, H. and Hales, M. (1991) *The Education Fact File*, 2nd edn. Milton Keynes: Open University Press.

Ward, D. (1993) 'Daggers are out in Penrith', *Education Guardian*, 27 April.

Willms, D. and Echols, F. (1992) 'Alert and inert clients: the Scottish experience of parental choice of schools', *Economics of Education Review*. 11(4): 399–450.

Whitty, G. (1992) 'Education, economy and national culture', in R. Bocock and K. Thompson (eds), *Social and Cultural Forms of Modernity*. Cambridge: Polity Press.

6

Managing the Criminal Justice System

Eugene McLaughlin and John Muncie

'We will spend more on fighting crime, whilst we economize elsewhere.'

(Conservative Party Manifesto, 1979)

'All of us in the criminal justice system now live in a world of measurement, comparison, effectiveness and efficiency.'

(Osler, 1992)

A strong commitment to increasing resources for the 'fight against crime' has been an axiomatic feature of successive Conservative administrations in Britain during the 1980s. There is no doubt that the election pledge of 1979 has been honoured in full. The Thatcherite ideology that elsewhere stipulated that state intervention in the public sphere (for example, in housing, health and welfare) was misguided, because it acted to deny self-responsibility and violated individual rights, remained absent from public debates about criminal justice for much of the 1980s. There is considerable evidence to give substance to the claim that law and order was the hallowed no-go area for public expenditure cuts. Between 1982 and 1990 total expenditure on police, prisons, probation and the courts increased by over 70 percent, an increase without parallel elsewhere in the public sector. Total spending on law and order rose from 2.7 to 4.5 percent of GNP and by 1993–4 cost the taxpayer in England and Wales approximately £9 billion (Fowles, 1990; Reiner, 1992; NACRO, 1992; *Guardian*, 21 May 1993). A sector-by-sector expenditure breakdown discloses that between the late 1970s and early 1990s the number of police officers increased by 17 percent, probation officers by 39 percent and prison officers by over 50 percent.

Systematic empowerment was also forthcoming under Conservative patronage. The police were equipped with contentious powers under the Police and Criminal Evidence Act 1984 and the Public Order Act 1986. Magisterial powers, in determining type and length of custodial sentence (particularly for juveniles), were increased by the Criminal Justice Acts of 1982 and 1988. The courts were encouraged to hand out longer sentences and in 1988 the adult prison population in England and Wales peaked at 50,000, representing the highest rate of imprisonment per capita in Europe. In tandem, a commitment to the largest prison building programme this century was initiated, which by 1995 will see twenty-one new establishments added to the penal estate.

It was because of such developments and Mrs Thatcher's personal promise that the strong state would erect a barrier of steel to protect the honest citizen from the nefarious enemies within, that the 1980s have been characterized by the left as ones of increasing authoritarianism, coercion and repression (Scraton, 1987; Hillyard and Percy-Smith, 1988; Ewing and Gearty, 1990).

The failures of law and order

However, despite the emphasis on law and order, it is difficult to regard the outcome of Conservative rule as a success. The Conservatives' rhetoric and policies of 'discipline and punishment' failed to halt the rising tide of criminality and lawlessness. The crime rate escalated to an unprecedented level during the past decade. Notifiable offences recorded by the police in 1979 stood at 2.4 million, whereas by 1991 the figure was 5.5 million – an increase of almost 125 percent. The police clear-up rate fell from 41 percent in 1978 to 29 percent in 1992, with the rate for some crimes falling below 20 percent. The inability of the Conservatives' criminal justice policies to impact positively on the crime rate is also highlighted if one looks at the 'deterrent' value of the punitive prison system. Despite tougher sentences – epitomized by 'short, sharp shock' regimes for young offenders – serious overcrowding and insanitary conditions, just under a half of adult prisoners and two-thirds of young prisoners are reconvicted within two years of release. Home Office research also indicated that in order to reduce the crime rate by only 1 percent, the prison population would have to increase by 25 percent, or more than 12,000 people (*Independent*, 25 October 1993).

British society has become painfully aware of the economic costs of the crime wave. Legitimate businesses have complained about the impact of a flourishing illegal economy in stolen goods. Hospitals, GPs and employers have protested about the costs of supporting victims of crime, particularly the unacceptable drain of resources on 'patching up' numerous young men who go looking for trouble in pubs and clubs every weekend. Local authorities have had to divert scarce resources to combating vandalism on public housing estates. And house and car owners in the Conservatives' property-owning democracy have been confronted with spiralling insurance premiums to cover escalating theft and burglary. In 1992, for example, the cost of household burglaries for insurance companies reached a record £749 millions – a 27 percent increase over 1991.

Far from guaranteeing a sense of personal security and giving individuals peace of mind (as promised in every Conservative manifesto) successive British crime surveys have revealed that the public's fear of crime – rational or not – is as great a problem as crime itself. The period also witnessed outbreaks of disorder which, although not unprecedented, have underlined the depth of social division of British society. Clashes between the police and urban rioters, industrial pickets, new age travellers and poll tax demonstrators, an ongoing war with Irish republicans, along with recurrent moral panics concerning acid house raves, ram raiders and joy riders, have continued to conjure up images of a society out of control rather than a nation at ease with itself; divided rather than consensual.

There has been a corresponding 'loss of faith' in the fairness and impartiality of the criminal justice system, particularly in the aftermath of the Guildford Four, Maguire Seven, Birmingham Six, Tottenham Three and Cardiff Three acquittals. In a public survey carried out in 1992, 48 percent of respondents said that such cases had made them lose confidence in the police (*Guardian*, 23 November 1992). The same survey revealed that 65 percent believed that the judiciary was out of touch with society. The manner in which the miscarriages of justice were handled, for example, called the independence and credibility of the Court of Appeal into question. Despite increasing public disquiet, both Lord Lane, the then Lord Chief Justice, and Lord Denning, former Master of the Rolls, repeatedly stated that, as far as they were concerned, it was 'impossible' for the finest system of justice in the world to produce such 'grotesque' outcomes. At a more 'everyday' level, concern has also been expressed about the lack of sentencing consistency in the courts with a Liberty survey pointing out that offenders in Devon and Cornwall were 2.5 times more likely to receive immediate imprisonment than those in Dyfed and Powys for similar offences. The report also shows that during the 1980s, 121,700 people were jailed by magistrates in England and Wales, but if all had adopted the sentencing practice of mid-Worcestershire the total would have been only 24,340 (Wynne and Priestman, 1992). By the beginning of the 1990s, with the appointment of a Royal Commission, it was the criminal justice system itself that was on trial.

The managerial solution

The political reverberations of this ignominious 'failure to deliver' and the accompanying legitimation crisis has compelled the Conservatives to rethink both their law and order policies and the uncritical support traditionally given to the criminal justice system. As a result, a strategy has been unveiled which will redefine the *ownership* of the crime problem and promote managerialist solutions. Given the nature of this strategy, it looked initially as if the criminal justice agencies would remain immune from public demands that they be held to account for their inadequate performance and self-evident failures. However, by the late 1980s the seeming incapability or unwillingness of the various agencies to respond to increasing criticism and to put their own houses in order persuaded the Conservatives to open up the criminal justice system to the investigations of the Public Accounts Committee, the National Audit Office and the Audit Commission. As a consequence, law and order is no longer exempt from the processes of fiscal accountability, performance measurements and strict controls on expenditure which feature prominently in the other chapters in this book. It is now apparent to criminal justice professionals that the price of failure is high – they have two choices: either jump or be pushed into the reform process.

The management of risk

Part of the Conservatives' response to the failure of their tough law and order stance has been the gradual withdrawal from wider philosophical debates about the causes of crime and the purpose of criminal justice policies. Home Office officials now inform the public at every opportunity that extreme caution is needed in 'reading' crime statistics because, despite media representations, most crime is petty in nature and Britain remains a relatively crime-free society. In addition, as Jock Young has noted, certain Home Office statements even suggest, in classic Durkheimian fashion, that a certain level of crime is normal and inevitable and that it is therefore unrealistic to expect any set of policies to drastically reduce the crime rate (Young, 1992: 104). All that governments can do, according to the new 'normalization of crime' orthodoxy, is to work with the community in order to reduce both the opportunistic crime rate and the fear of crime to manageable and acceptable levels. As a consequence, the message for the 1990s is that the public and other social agencies will have to 'join up' in the war against preventable crime.

The public is being told that it must recognize that the sources of crime and its control lie, first and foremost, in the actions of individual citizens and local communities. Shared responsibility and individual self-discipline are stressed through the 'target hardening' of homes and businesses and the presumed greater security offered by membership of Neighbourhood Watch. With the coming of age of community safety, police community liaison and community punishment, the Conservatives have effectively relocated to the realm of private citizenship primary responsibility for the failure of its law and order packages. The blame lies with victims who are lax in their efforts to prevent crime, whether it be a failure to adequately protect their property, or learn to avoid dangerous situations, or to meet their moral obligations as parents and citizens.

Private self-help efforts are also being supplemented and augmented by inter-agency approaches to crime and prevention. The Home Office has redoubled its efforts to devolve front-line obligation for the management of crime to other social agencies. Safer Cities and Crime Concern projects have as their common aim, for example, the creation of partnerships between local authorities, local businesses, voluntary organizations and statutory agencies which will prepare effective policies and localized strategies to design out crime and reduce the fear of crime. In the late 1980s the Home Office sponsored a series of high-level conferences entitled 'Inter-Agency Linking in the Criminal Justice System', which stressed the importance of managing the criminal justice system as a *system* and stressing the need for agencies to develop common objectives. It is also hoped that these inter-professional partnerships will be cost effective through the identification of unwarranted duplication of effort (Locke, 1990).

We would argue that these shifts in Conservative rhetoric and practice should be seen as constituting both a diminution of state responsibility for crime control matters and the removal of questions of crime, criminality and punishment from the political and moral arena. In theory, such shifts should have benefited the professional standing of the criminal justice agencies. However, as Pearson et al. (1992) argue, the outcome has been much more contradictory because the agendas of those agencies with a core law and order mandate have been prioritized at the expense of others. Additionally, this shift to inter-agency co-operation has taken place in the context of an overall institutional restructuring of the criminal justice system.

Managing the criminal justice system

A series of managerial and legislative reviews and directives have been implemented, signalling the government's commitment to addressing the problems of the criminal justice system. By the end of 1992 eleven Audit Commission reports had been made on various aspects of police practice, three on the probation service, one on the magistrates courts, one on the Crown Prosecution Service, one on Legal Aid schemes and numerous reports on the prison service by a combination of the Audit Commission, the National Audit Office and the Public Accounts Committee. The recommendations emanating from these sector-by-sector reviews have acted as a stimulus for further inquiries because they have uncovered the need for ever deeper change. Reform is to be achieved within an overall framework of organizational restructuring, fiscal accountability and rationalization. The different agencies are increasingly having to justify their existence and reimagine themselves in terms of market competitiveness, managerial resource control and certifiable cost effectiveness. As a consequence, certain activities and tasks are being centralized, others being devolved and, since the requirement for market testing and innovation is ever present, others are being contracted out or privatized. Such changes have considerable implications for working practices and, perhaps more significantly, the conditions of service of the workforce in core criminal justice agencies, because they necessitate the displacement of the old quasi-military model of administration. Instead, transparent management systems are being put in place and strenuous efforts are being made to managerialize both the different agencies and the overall system. This transformatory process involves introducing more explicitly neo-Taylorist conceptions of control of the workforce and new managerial ideas about how to produce and manage organizational and cultural change.

Taken collectively, these policy responses herald a series of potentially more radical reforms of the criminal justice system than has been witnessed this century. It is increasingly apparent that sections of the Conservative government have a vision of a mixed economy of criminal justice which necessitates the state absolving itself of its traditional role as the natural provider of law and order. We believe that the government's chosen pathway to reform is resulting in a complex unravelling, one which, as we will see in the rest of this chapter, is generating as many contradictions and tensions as it is resolving. The manner in which change is being implemented is provoking considerable institutional opposition as criminal justice professionals and occupational groups, like their counterparts in the health service and education system, find their professional expertise and judgement effectively excluded from the reform process. They and their 'special pleading' are increasingly seen as being part of the problem rather than as part of the solution. However, the government faces particular difficulty in challenging and attempting to curb the discretion and autonomy of groups that were empowered during the 1980s. It remains to be seen what impact the ever-penetrating logic of efficiency and cost effectiveness has on such opposition. On this point, it is important to note from the outset that new sectional interests and divisions are surfacing within institutions. The new managerial strata who have benefited directly from the redistribution of power and resources have a vested interest in ensuring the successful transition to the new order. These new social divisions make long-term professional and occupational opposition much more problematic. Questions must also be raised about the limitations imposed on the reform process by the core coercive function of the criminal justice system, the most fundamental ones being first, what are the implications of reconceptualizing users of this very sensitive public service as 'customers' exercising 'choice' and, second, can these reforms resolve the hyper-crisis of the criminal justice system? Keeping these contradictions and questions in mind we will now examine in detail how the processes of the new managerialism, privatization and the construction of a market-oriented consumer approach to delivering criminal justice have impacted on the probation, prison, police and court services.

Value for money in probation

In the past decade the probation service in England and Wales has had to assimilate a range of economic, managerial and legislative developments which, during the 1990s, are likely to culminate in a radical reappraisal of its fundamental purpose and defining practices.

The first of these was the Home Office's (1984) *Statement of National Objectives and Priorities* (*SNOP*). In the aftermath of the 'crisis of purpose' generated by the collapse of probation's traditional role of offering rehabilitation via treatment, the service found itself facing a vacuum in both philosophy and policy. The Home Office attempted to fill this vacuum by setting out a series of objectives in which the functions of probation were redefined as diverting high-risk offenders away from prison, reducing the incidence of crime and deploying resources in the most cost-effective fashion to meet these ends. The service's traditional role was denied as an expensive and unaccountable ideal. Its social work based tasks of providing through-care and after-care for offenders released from custody were subordinated to the more utilitarian role of controlling and containing offenders in the community. The key to this shift in purpose lay primarily in the new-found resolve to evaluate 'successful' probation practice in terms of resources employed and quantifiable outcomes. It also dovetailed with the emergent political climate of scrutinizing all welfare programmes in terms of their respective costs and benefits. As such, the probation service has become increasingly subject to the prevailing doctrine that public money should only be spent on activities whose purposes could be clearly defined, whose procedures were quantifiable and whose outcomes would then be predictable.

The concept of 'management by objectives' has now become widely employed as the basis for evaluating the success or otherwise of probation practice (Statham and Whitehead, 1992). In turn, this has tended to shift the purpose of the service away from achieving the wider (and by their nature less readily quantifiable) aims of 'advise, assist and befriend' and towards meeting tangible targets based on performance indicators. Result achievement, cost effectiveness and the measurement of outcome from resources employed have become the new principles by which the traditionally diverse and varied practices of probation are to be assessed. As Mair put it: 'with the probation service accounting for more than £200 million a year there was a good deal of pressure on Chief Probation Officers to exercise good resource management and to provide evidence of the economy, efficiency and effectiveness achieved' (Mair, 1989: 37).

During the 1980s probation (along with all other public sector services) was thus required to work to plans with targets, to develop clear lines of responsibility for resources, to set and agree budgets and targets, to monitor costs and work done and to assess outcomes (Garrett, 1986: 430). However, whilst intended to facilitate cohesion and unity in probation practice, the ensuing response to *SNOP* from individual probation areas revealed a notable diversity in perceived objectives and priorities, reflecting a miscellany of particular pressures, dependant on such local and variable factors as degree or urbanization, unemployment and poverty. Moreover, different probation areas came to no consensus on the level of desired involvement in participation in 'alternatives to custody' schemes as the prime focus of their work (Lloyd, 1986). In opposition to the central directive they chose to support their continuing role in after-care, providing support for families of prisoners and developing conciliation schemes. It was notable that these latter duties had indeed been ignored by *SNOP*. This disjuncture between government policy and local practice was eventually addressed not, as might have been expected in the past, by a fundamental reappraisal of policy, but by seeking to find further managerial solutions. In 1986 a financial management consultancy firm was appointed to develop information systems which would allow local areas to compare their practice and performance ratings with others. In other words, the problems of probation were defined as undue professional autonomy and a lack of shared information. By the late 1980s the impact of this initiative was most marked on middle management, necessitating a shift in their role away from a traditional supportive capacity and towards a more administrative and monitoring function. It appeared at that time to have had less bearing on main grade staff practice, with a commitment to social and civil work remaining a key priority, particularly in inner-city areas where the ability to command resources was believed to be less under pressure (Parry-Khan, 1988: 17).

Above all, the major stumbling block remained of how to apply accounting techniques to a complex reality of diverse practice (as in other areas of criminal justice). Nevertheless, the government kept faith with the ethos of FMIS and particularly the need to develop cost-effective, as distinct from welfare-effective services. In 1986 the Audit Commission had already included probation in its review of the administration of justice and by 1988 was suggesting that the value of each probation area could be assessed by comparing gross expenditure per 1000 of the population aged 15–29 and per triable case. To further this exercise it also advocated the gathering of information regarding caseloads, re-offending rates and the proportion of convicted offenders who were being dealt with under supervision in the community (Audit Commission, 1988: 54–5). The 1989 report *Promoting Value for Money* dutifully reported wide variations in probation area expenditure and spending patterns: 'some of which are more the result of past opportunism of former chief officers than of any rational assessment of current local need' (Audit Commission, 1989: 14). In attempting to overcome such diversity, the report asserted that probation had already changed its focus from social casework to the more pragmatic role of dealing with offenders at risk of custody. Taking the Green Paper, *Punishment, Custody and the Community* (Home Office, 1988), as the yardstick of what might constitute effective and useful probation practice, the Audit Commission maintained that the service should concentrate its efforts on developing more stringent forms of community supervision (intensive probation programmes) so that the courts might be persuaded to use non-custodial options in the sentencing of high-risk offender groups (such as recidivist burglars and thieves) who might otherwise be given a prison sentence. The driving force behind this initiative, in turn, lay in the government's wish to to reduce prison overcrowding and overcome the financial and political embarrassment of having the highest level of imprisonment in the European Community. A changing role for the probation service is thus pivotal in implementing radical reform in other sectors of the criminal justice system. As the Audit Commission argued,

> to do this effectively and give value for money the service must target its activities, co-ordinating them with other agencies within the criminal justice system and it must develop and apply new ways of working with more difficult offenders. These changes in turn require it to be managed differently. (1989: 2)

It was particularly critical of the discernible trend since the 1970s for probation's 'market share' to have grown at the expense of fines rather than immediate custody (1989: 30) and recommended a devaluation of social casework practices in favour of skills which emphasize intensive supervision, direct responses to offenders' immediate circumstances and challenges to offending behaviour. Above all, the Audit Commission argued that the probation service was at a critical stage in its development. In what ominously sounded like an ultimatum: it can either adopt a more controlling function in line with government policy or it 'could find that another agency is given responsibility for new community options and perhaps part of its existing workload' (1989: 6). In effect this statement implied that probation could either continue with its old ways but would become increasingly marginalized and find many of its functions put out to competitive tender with the private sector, or it could incorporate the central directives and augment its position as a key criminal justice agency. This *fait accompli* clearly had an effect.

The 1989 report was followed up by local audits of 50 of the 56 probation areas in 1990. Their conclusions were slightly more optimistic. Noting the incorporation of the principle of 'punishment in the community' in the 1991 Criminal Justice Act, the 1991 Audit Commission report *Going Straight* argued that the major task now facing probation was to 'manage a period of significant growth as it implements the government's policy' (1991: 1). Whilst it continued to lament little 'improvement' in some probation areas in realizing a fall in prison receptions or an increase in community service orders (as a direct alternative to prison) and stipulated that more effort be made in developing measures of effectiveness, in disseminating instances of 'good' practice; in responding to the national objectives, rather than local contingencies; and in introducing time recording systems to facilitate cost-effective resource management (1991: 13–14), it was clear that the Audit Commission presumed that the key issue of what constituted probation's core role had been resolved. As a result, certain reforms such as the proposal to establish a national service (*vis-à-vis SNOP*) were dropped in favour of inter-regional collaboration.

Pressure on the service to comply with the government's vision had indeed been maintained by persistent proposals to involve private companies and voluntary organizations in supervising offenders in the community. For example, when three trials were introduced in 1989–90 to assess the viability of electronic monitoring schemes, responsibility for the supervision of tagees was, in the face of the service's reluctance, initially given to Securicor. But this reorganization of responsibility also clearly relied on other sectors taking on probation's traditional welfare functions. The 1992 consultative paper *Partnership in Dealing with Offenders in the Community*, for example, signalled the beginning of competition in some areas of offender supervision by opening up tendering for private bail hostels and suggesting that voluntary organizations should take a more active role in victim support, bail accommodation, skills training, literacy, countering drug addiction and prisoner welfare (Home Office, 1992). The intention was to enable the probation service to concentrate on its new core functions of court work and the policing of supervision orders. The social work aspects of its role, due to their unquantifiable nature, were considered to be less important and could be carried out by a less skilled voluntary sector. This latter function has thus come to be considered as peripheral to central government responsibility. In order to facilitate such a shift the subsequent 1992 decision paper, bearing the same name as its 1990 predecessor, stipulated that the probation service be required to initiate work with the 'independent sector' and that 5 percent of the budget of each probation area be allocated to developing partnership schemes with voluntary and commercial organizations (Home Office, 1992).

With hindsight, it is clear how the efforts to quantify probation practice, the subjugation of professional skills to management ideals, the concern to be seen to be offering value for money, the requirement to comply with the philosophy of the 1991 Act and the move to privatization or partnership, all form part of a long-term strategy to transform probation into a community correctional service. The advantage of this ongoing process, as Pitts (1992) concludes in his review of related developments in juvenile justice, is that at least the 'nothing works' doctrine of the 1970s is being replaced by an ethos of 'something can work' – albeit that the goal of practice is now reduced to one of meeting tangible managerial 'targets' (see also Pratt, 1989). The key issue for probation officers, however, remains that their professional discretion and innovation are being curtailed whilst the quality of their service is guaranteed only to a minimum – albeit consistent – standard. For many the wholesale adoption of the conceptual frameworks of trade and commerce into probation practice remains problematic. McWilliams (1990: 64), for example, has argued,

> In trade transactions the concern is with a product. In a professional transaction the concern is with a person. A tradeable product and the outcome of a professional encounter are two different things. The first is objective and reproducible, the second is specific to the person concerned and thus unique.

It is this ability to relate to uniqueness and deal with local specificities which is at risk in the current desire to reduce probation to a technical exercise which is solely concerned with the batch-processing and cost-effective management of delinquent bodies. Similarly Matthews (1990: 55) concludes that probation is moving towards an increasingly restricted, centralized and administrative organization. Its role is now no longer welfare inspired but driven by court advocacy and the co-ordination of voluntary and private agencies. This shift coalesces in tandem with government resolve to distance itself from broad philosophical or moral debates about the purpose of imprisonment or supervision. The redefining of probation's core tasks has now helped to place such issues in 'a depoliticised and hence uncontentious, scientific/technical realm' (Pitts, 1992: 142).

Paying for imprisonment

Until 1993, the prison service was unique amongst all agencies of criminal justice, because it was financed and administered solely by a central government department. However in April 1993 it was redesignated as a semi-privatized Whitehall agency in which the role of policy making was taken out of the hands of the Home Office. Its first business plan set targets and performance indicators such as reducing escapes, assaults and over-crowding, and setting standards for the average cost per prisoner place and time spent out of cells. In tandem, the appointment of the former chief executive of Granada Group and UK Gold Television as the new director general of the prison service was widely conceived as marking the first step in turning over all 133 prisons to private operators.

Much of the ground to support the privatization of prison construction and management was laid in the 1980s. Initially given serious attention in a 1988 Green Paper on private sector involvement in the remand system, the first privately run prison in Britain (The Wolds) was opened in 1992 and operated by Group 4 Security Services. A second contracted-out prison for remand *and* sentenced prisoners (Blakenhurst) was opened in 1993 and operated by UK Detention Services. Similarly, the longstanding issue of excessive prison officer time being taken up by escorting prisoners to courts (and thus, as argued by some, preventing the development of enhanced regimes inside prisons), was addressed by allowing the private sector to compete with the prison department in providing escort duties. In 1992 the Home Office awarded Group 4 Court Services Ltd a contract to escort prisoners from remand centres and guard them at court in Humberside and the East Midlands. Other candidates for market testing and possible contracting out included the prison education service, dog service, fleet management and the refurbished Strangeways prison (following the disturb-ances of 1990). Whilst an in-house bid was eventually successful in keeping Strangeways within the prison service, twelve other prisons remained listed for privatization (*Independent*, 3 September 1993). If this goes ahead Britain will have a higher proportion of prisoners in private jails than any other country, including the United States. The principle of market testing now compels the prison service to systematically analyse the work that needs to be done for the service to meet its objectives, to open up its tasks to competitive tender and to compare in-house bids with external bids in terms of best value for money in return for a required quality. Under the terms of the 1991 Criminal Justice Act any new or existing prison can be contracted out following a successful vote in parliament.

The process of privatization, contracting out and market testing has rapidly gathered pace since first proposed by the right-wing Adam Smith Institute in 1984; its supporters confidently asserting the success of such initiatives in the USA. The evidence from overseas, however, remains ambiguous (Ryan and Ward, 1989). Around 20,000 prison places are currently managed by corporate interests in the USA, but the numbers are relatively small given an overall 1,250,000 prison population. The largest profits in the USA (and thus private sector involvement) are not to be made in prison management, but in construction and in the supply of goods and services (Lilly and Knepper, 1992). The process of privatization has also not been smooth in the UK. The largest private operator, Group 4, has been publicly ridiculed by the media for nine escapes in the first month of its prisoner escort service, and for allegations of drink and drugs scandals at the Wolds. The Prison Officers Association (POA) has threatened industrial action over 'deskilling' and job losses and in September 1993 walked out of a meeting with Home Office officials because no compromise could be reached over the government's future privatization and marketization plans. The contracting out of certain services and management (for example, prison education; prison service stores) has been delayed or has collapsed for failure to comply with EC legislation which requires private operators to offer the same terms and conditions of employment for workers transferred from the public sector. At one time, the directors of Group 4 seriously considered pulling out of the escort service because of the damage caused to its reputation. Nevertheless, it is clear that the government is intent on pressing ahead. Whilst in-house bids from prison service management were accepted for the rebuilt Strangeways prison, they are explicitly excluded from the new prison at Doncaster to be opened in 1994. Equally, a new generation of six secure training institutions for 12- to 15-year-olds is to be placed with the voluntary and private sectors, rather than local authorities. The privatization debate, however, remains double edged. On the one hand, a danger clearly lies in the rapid expansion of a corrections-commercial complex with the power to influence penal policy through its vested interest in maintaining high levels of imprisonment. On the other hand, to date, private companies have been enforced to provide better conditions for prisoners (for example, time out of cells; a prisoner charter) than those in the public system (consistently described by the Council of Europe and Prison Inspectorate Reports as 'inhumane and degrading'). In this context, a case against privatization is harder to sustain. But a key issue remains of how far the current attention given to the issue is merely acting to divert attention away from the pressing problems and urgent need to improve the state system. A two-tiered system of a well-resourced private sector and an under-resourced public sector may well be the end result.

And what of the issue of cost effectiveness? The contracts offered to the private sector are shrouded in secrecy and so no direct comparisons are possible. The key savings to be made via privatization appear to lie in the areas of staff contracts of service and salaries. Reducing costs thus significantly rests with the government's and the prison service's ability to 'break' the power of the POA.

Attempts to reduce staffing costs have been made consistently through the 1980s. A key factor has traditionally been prison officer overtime. The May Report (Home Office, 1979), for example, noted that the average was 12 hours per week and was particularly concerned that some officers ('overtime bandits') appeared to be manipulating the timing of their duties purely so that high levels of overtime could be maintained. Working weeks of 60 and 70 hours were not uncommon. In tandem the report noted that prison managers appeared to have no control over the situation, did not record precise levels of dependence on overtime and had no policy by which it might be overcome. In 1985 the government finally called in a team of management consultants which concluded that new pay systems and reorganized work systems should be introduced in order to help managers to manage. This was the basis of the 'Fresh Start' system in which prison officers became salaried employees with a standard working week of 39 hours, overtime was abolished, line management within establishments was rationalized, tasks and activities reorganized into 'functional blocks' and regime monitoring introduced to assist the quantification and evaluation of service delivery. The introduction of 'Fresh Start' was also justified on the grounds that, with more efficient deployment of staff and resources, it would result in a much needed enhancement of regimes for prisoners. In order to put these initiatives into effect, a radical reorganization of Prison Service Management was promoted in 1990. Based on a report prepared by PA Consultants, prison governors were to be made more accountable to the Home Office, through introducing greater supervision and checks on their autonomy. Prison management was to be overseen by area managers – generalist civil servants rather than individuals with operational experience of governing establishments. The logic that the prison service simply needed to be managed better in order to be more effective and overcome the myriad of problems which it faced, indeed culminated in it being semi-privatized in 1993, and in the appointment of a new director general who had no specialist knowledge of, or background in, the prison service.

The implementation of new management structures is, however, unlikely to achieve the sought-after goals of cohesion and increased efficiency. Almost immediately prison officers lodged a number of complaints against 'Fresh Start' for its primary intention of cutting costs rather than benefiting staff; and because the Home Office had failed to provide adequate staffing levels to make the new arrangements work safely and efficiently. McDermott and King's (1989) research on the delivery of regime activities following 'Fresh Start' also concluded that, if anything, the quality of regimes for prisoners had declined rather than improved. The over-riding reaction from prison officers was that their interpersonal skills in making life tenable in prisons were unacknowledged in the new emphasis on quantifiable tasks. The same logic of reducing professional skills to measurable practices that have so radically transformed probation is thus being applied to the prison service. Whilst tackling the vested interests of such unionized and professional bodies may hold no fears for central government, a more serious problem may arise with prison governors. They have also almost unanimously rejected the notion that prison management can be organized solely by the same criteria as those employed in the business and commercial sectors.

Management restructuring and privatization aside, the most marked development in current penal policy in England has been the implementation of the largest prison-building programme this century. Faced with severe overcrowding, insanitary conditions and projections that the prison population will increase by 25 percent between 1991 and 2000, fourteen new prisons have been built since 1985 and seven more are due to open before 1995. Collectively, over 20,000 additional prison places will be added to the system at an estimated cost of £1.3 billion (NACRO, 1990). (The precise cost is subject to continual revision due to fluctuations in present and projected numbers of prisoners.) These costs have also been subject to inquiry from the National Audit Office and the Public Accounts Committee. The first report, received in 1985, was concerned not only with costs, but with the wider objectives of the building programme, and also the extent to which prison construction appears to have been a purely technical problem for architects with little consideration given to implications for staffing levels. A further report in 1988 was similarly concerned with cost escalation (increases varying between 20 percent and 82 percent were found) and delays in construction undermining the Home Office's strategy (Fowles, 1990: 95).

The troubled prison service places the problems and contradictions of implementing new management structures in the public sector at their starkest. On the one hand, the government is encouraging privatization of prison establishments and semi-privatization of the service itself, but on the other it wants more direct control over how that service should be managed. It is intent on reducing costs, particularly those associated with staffing, but it is also prepared to finance a major expansion of the system. It is prepared to devolve responsibility for policy making (and thus also criticism for policy failure?), but maintains it has a duty to ensure that accommodation exists for all those whom the courts decide to send to prison. It promotes an ethos of rationality and uniformity, yet has put in motion a series of reforms which are more likely to result in division and confrontation. Faced with a system that is beset with problems of overcrowding, insanitary conditions, riots and self-violence, it is not at all clear how managerial reform, on its own, can be expected to achieve their resolution.

Counting the coppers

During the 1980s the police negotiated a considerable degree of autonomy from the rest of the public sector in Britain. In 1979 the Conservatives implemented in full the Edmund-Davies pay accord linking police pay to average, as opposed to basic, earnings. As a consequence, the police moved well ahead of other public sector workers in the course of the decade – in the period between 1979 and 1982 a constable's pay increased by 41 percent in real terms. In 1990 the police received a 9.25 percent pay rise and in 1992 a rise of 7.2 percent. Necessary funding was also made available to facilitate a 23 percent increase in the number of uniformed officers and a 15 percent increase in the number of civilians. The police were also able to depend on the Conservative government to defend them when questions were raised about controversial police tactics in Britain's inner cities, during the industrial disputes of the 1980s, and about their legal empowerment under PACE and the 1986 Public Order Act. It is not surprising, given the degree of government patronage the police seemingly enjoyed in the ongoing 'war against crime', that many police officers perceived themselves to be safe from the restrictions and cutbacks that were being inflicted on the rest of the public sector.

However, official research findings which were highly critical of police effectiveness and efficiency were published in the 1980s. Home Office reports (Clarke and Mayhew, 1980; Morris and Heal, 1981; Clarke and Hough, 1984) effectively debunked the 'reality' of policing, presenting a picture of police work which differed considerably from the public image. For example, it revealed, contrary to police and media characterization, that crime-related work accounted for a relatively small proportion of police work and that most calls were related to the 24-hour 'social service' side of policing. More specifically, research indicated that patrolling levels had little or no effect on crime rates; that there was no obvious link between particular detective methods and the solving of crimes; that detection rates were an inadequate measure of police effectiveness and that there were many other social influences affecting the crime rate which were just as important as policing styles. These conclusions, as Horton and Smith (1988) have argued, when combined with rising crime rates and falling detection rates, raised fundamental questions about the effectiveness of the police and demolished the idea that increased expenditure on policing had a significant impact on levels of crime and disorder.

In 1985 a report commissioned by the Metropolitan Police presented a damning picture of the organization's management structure. The researchers concluded that a highly centralized and inflexible force structure with an overly long chain of command and an authoritarian management style encouraged deleterious working practices, especially 'Spanish practices', evasion of responsibility and 'enormous inertia' at all levels of the organization (Smith and Gray, 1985: 559). The report, drawing upon positive management theory, argued for: simplified and devolved management arrangements; clearly defined force tasks, objectives and responsibilities; indicators for assessing the performance of officers; incentives for good officers and effective sanctions to deal with the 'rotten apples'.

The major problem was translating these research findings into policing practices. Traditionally, chief police officers deflected 'uncomfortable' research findings by arguing that they interfered with the sacred principle of operational independence. This is, by and large, what happened in the case of the above-mentioned Home Office and PSI findings. However, the force was to find it much more difficult to ignore the fiscal scrutinies of the evaluative state. The Home Office response to the Financial Management Initiative (FMI), declared the need for a period of consolidation rather than continued growth in police expenditure. In its call for the more efficient and effective use of existing resources, Circular 114/83 also introduced 'a highly specific language of rational management into the process of determining policy priorities (Weatheritt, 1986: 111). In future, forces requesting more personnel would have to demonstrate that existing resources were being used and managed to best advantage, that they had the means of assessing the extent to which objectives and priorities were being achieved and that there was a specified reason for the requested increase. It also advocated a more questioning style of management, and encouraged thinking about what constituted 'good practice'.

Weatheritt (1986) argues that the need to account for itself *vis-à-vis* policing forced the Home Office to realize that it needed accurate information concerning what expenditure on the police delivered in terms of results and how the forty-three forces compared. Resultant 'focused inspections' by a revamped HM Inspectorate of Constabulary compelled the different forces, for the first time, to think about their activities and to produce evidence of their effectiveness. Because of the requirement that information had to be broken down into nationally agreed functional categories, as opposed to administrative ones, these inspections provided the Home Office with more detailed information about the activities, costs, resource use and performance of different forces.

In the late 1980s, the effectiveness and efficiency of policing once more came under intense official scrutiny when the Audit Commission finally gazed upon this most sensitive of local government functions, producing eleven reports with suggestions as to how private sector management practices, philosophies and work practices could be injected into policing. Since the Commission was clearly managerialist in orientation, the government had found a means of scrutinizing the organization of policing without trespassing on the sensitive matter of operational independence. The reports discussed the need for rethinking how policing was financed; how budgets were allocated; the manner in which police activities were costed and the organization, rank structure and salary scales of provincial policing. The Commission upfronted the need for decentralized, flexible and streamlined managerial structures; clearly stated priorities and objectives and output-based, quantifiable performance indicators covering key operational functions in order to facilitate inter-force comparisons. The language of the market was also introduced as the Commission discussed the needs of 'customers' and the methods of delivering a 'value for money service'.

Alongside the Audit Commission's findings the 1989 Home Affairs Select Committee's deliberations on policing began to enter the public domain. It shared with the Commission the belief that although policing was 'big business', in terms of budget and personnel, it was insufficiently business-like. However, unlike the Commission, it touched on the constitutional position of the police with Sir John Wheeler, chair of the committee, arguing that the policing needs of the 1990s and beyond, including European union and the transnationalization of crime, necessitated rationalization. In order to compensate for 'glaring deficiencies, incompetent use of resources and blinding incompetence', forces should be merged and police authorities should be replaced by a small board of appointed directors and a national policing policy committee consisting of regional chief officers and Home Office representatives (*Independent*, 26 July 1990).

These findings and deliberations, in the context of embarrassing miscarriages of justice, ongoing allegations of corruption and malpractice, record crime figures, and increasing ministerial disillusionment precipitated the setting up in 1992 of the Sheehy inquiry to examine the organization and working practices of the force and in 1993 an internal Home Office examination of the structure of policing in England and Wales. The resultant reports, which were published in June 1993, envision new managerialism as the means of securing cost-effective policing. The Home Office White Paper (1993) aims to clarify the roles of the different components of the policing structure. Central government will provide key objectives which will constitute the strategic framework within which streamlined and uniform police authorities and managerially empowered chief constables operate. Police authorities will set their own budgets and be responsible for devising costed local strategies. They will also have standard spending assessments from the government and be liable for capping. Chief constables will manage their own budgets, have greater control over the workforce and working patterns and be held to account for achieving clearly defined targets. The Sheehy report (1993) augments the White Paper's 'enhancement of management' approach by starting from the neo-Taylorist premise that all internal barriers to effective managerial control must be removed if police reform is to be realized. To that end the inquiry recommended a radical flattening of the managerial structure, the introduction of flexible localized pay structures and working patterns and the overhauling of the disciplinary powers of managers. To the consternation of police officers Sheehy also recommended that there should be an end to the 'job-for-life' principle with all officers being placed on fixed-term contracts and performance-related pay schedules. Also under consideration was the contracting out of certain police functions – traffic control, court security, registration of firearms – to private security firms.

The growing realization, from the late 1980s onwards, that the status quo was no longer going to be an option has spurred certain forces into responding to this reform agenda. Senior officers were well aware that they enjoyed little managerial control over the rank and file and were not adverse to organizational changes that would enable them to manage more effectively and indeed give formal recognition to their managerial role. Sir Peter Imbert, Commissioner of the Metropolitan Police, and the HMI constabulary took the lead in advocating radical change in order to preserve the organization. In 1989, in the aftermath of the Wolff Olins inquiry (1988), the Plus Programme – the prototype police 'mission statement' – was unveiled, stressing the need for devolved responsibility to divisional level, the setting and monitoring of identifiable standards of service, efficient and cost-effective service delivery systems, indicators to measure customer satisfaction, identifying and disseminating good practice and specified managerial responsibility. Through the encouragement of a classic 'new managerialist' philosophy every effort was made to carry the rank and file with the changes and to ensure their active participation.

In 1989 an internal operational review of policing resulted in the first 'quality of service' corporate statement which acknowledged that there was public concern about 'poor performance and failures that range from incivility and aggressiveness to corruption' (ACPO, 1990). In order to counter this concern the review committed the organization to moving from a police force to a police service and producing a strategic management framework. A matrix of performance indicators would be developed to facilitate implementing and monitoring the quality of service and improve service delivery. Managerial roles and responsibilities would be specified at every level to deliver the new service. There would be clearly identified mechanisms for monitoring and evaluating organizational performance; more consultation and opinion surveys to identify different customer needs and priorities. The attitudes and standards of behaviour of officers would also be monitored more tightly and in the context of a Statement of Ethical Principles.

Senior management also began to indicate to the rank and file that there would have to be changes to the archaic shift system, the inflexible rank structure and the promotion system. Management made it clear that it wanted the freedom to introduce incentives and the power to remove corrupt and ineffective officers. There were also shifts in policing strategies. ACPO has sanctioned the nationalization of certain functions whilst encouraging devolved sectoral problem-solving policing to improve the efficiency and effectiveness of service delivery and community relations (Grange, 1993). In March 1993, soon after his appointment, Paul Condon, Commissioner of the Metropolitan Police, announced plans to downsize the force into five relatively autonomous areas. There are even indications that certain forces are willing to contract out and hive off non-operational functions and to respond to the challenge of private security firms. In 1993 the South Wales and West Yorkshire police announced, for example, that they were giving serious consideration to setting up their own private security firms (*Guardian*, 27 April 1993).

However, despite this commitment to change the organization is involved in a difficult balancing act with police representatives, also attempting to defend themselves against the possibility of a radical privatization programme such as that proposed by the influential Adam Smith Institute. The government has been reminded about the constitutional imperative of operational independence and Sir Peter Imbert warned that a 'non-profit making, caring public service could not be judged by the economic criteria used by ICI and Marks & Spencer (*Independent*, 5 October 1990). In October 1990 Alan Eastwood of the Police Federation complained about the government's restrictions on law and order expenditure which since 1983 had resulted in 'no-growth' budgets: 'it is our view that a policy of putting financial considerations above all others now threatens the ability of the police service to play its fundamental and unique role to the full' (*Guardian*, 5 October 1990). Police representatives have also complained bitterly that they are being scapegoated for the failure of the government's law and order policies and about not being fully consulted about the reform agenda unveiled in 1993. Particularly ironic, given the attitude of the police to police authorities in the 1980s, is the complaint of senior officers that many of the proposals detailed in the 1993 White Paper will undermine the principle of local democratic accountability.

By 1994 it still remained unclear what the final audit on policing would look like. Senior officers argue that they have already demonstrated their commitment to change and that there has to be a limit to the reform process. Hence, their public opposition to the Sheehy inquiry. However, there are indications that the pressures on the police are set to increase as the government looks towards more market-based approaches to resolve the problems of policing. If this does happen it will constitute the most systematic sea change in policing since the formation of the 'new police' in the early nineteenth century.

Controlling the Home Office and the courts

Critics have argued that the criminal justice system is not really a system because it has no coherent planning apparatus (see Harrison and Gretton, 1986). And the Home Office, as the officially designated government department responsible for overseeing criminal justice policy, has been traditionally blamed for this state of affairs. It was one of the few government departments that steadfastly refused to publish an annual report, set targets or construct benchmarks against which its performance could be measured. The traditional response of the Home Office was to point out that the degree of professional autonomy enjoyed by the different agencies and their 'law and order' mandate made it virtually impossible to raise questions of effectiveness and efficiency (Moxon, 1985; Tuck, 1992).

However, in the latter part of the 1980s, as an outcome of the investigations of the Audit Commission and other evaluative bodies, this situation changed. *Tackling Crime* (Home Office, 1989a) made explicit for the first time that the primary role of the Home Office was to 'lead and co-ordinate the effort against crime'. The Home Secretary is now required under the 1991 Criminal Justice Act to collate and publish detailed information about the precise cost and exact functioning of the criminal justice system. Thus, the Home Office has been repositioned to take on the role of managing 'crime' and advancing the development of a rationally integrated, cost-conscious criminal justice system.

If the new Home Office creed of 'economy and justice' is to succeed, the autonomy and powers of the courts (and the legal system) have to be curbed and the 'through flow' regulated because of the financial and organizational implications for the rest of the system. As Harrison and Morgan have noted: 'in the absence of a mechanism for controlling effectively the flow of prisoners from the courts, where the decisions are made, the strain has to be absorbed by the prison system' (1988: 44). The government was forced to confront this problem when, prior to the 1992 election, Home Office officials pointed out that the biggest prison-building programme for a century (costing over £1 billion) which was supposed to 'settle' the problem of overcrowding would have little effect because of the projected numbers of offenders who would receive custodial sentences in the early 1990s. The stark reality of the costs of unregulated sentencing becomes clear when it is remembered that in 1990 the police charged the Home Office £53.5 million for keeping prisoners in police cells – an average cost of £220 per prisoner per night.

In order to exercise control over court business considerable attention has been paid to the framing of recent criminal justice legislation so that the sentencing discretion of the judiciary is more tightly controlled. Hence, the 1991 Criminal Justice Act, which provides a legislative framework for sentencing all offenders, obliges magistrates and judges to structure decision making in a more methodical, consistent and accountable manner and upfronts, for the first time, the need to 'take some account of the costs of implementing their decisions when they sentence, especially when they have a choice of suitable penalties' (para. 2.22).

It has been made clear to magistrates that approximately 60 percent of the cases they sent to the Crown Court in 1991 could and should have been dealt with by the lower courts and they have been reminded that the 1.6 million offences dealt with by their courts in 1992 cost £67 per defendant whereas the 146,000 sent to Crown Court cost £494 per defendant (*Guardian*, 1 April 1993). A Home Office researcher, David Moxon, informed magistrates of the official rationale behind recent moves to curtail the proportion of cases sent to Crown Courts: 'a reversal of the trend towards more cases being dealt with in the Crown Court would speed up justice, save substantial funds in legal aid, reduce the burden on the probation service and cut the costs of implementing court sentences' (1992: 180). Hence the aim is to change 'the culture of sentencing', especially with regard to making criminal justice professionals aware of the consequences of utilizing expensive options.

It is also argued that cost effectiveness can be enhanced by improving rationality, consistency and predictability, and ensuring that criminal justice professionals know what to expect from the court system, and indeed each other. To this end a Criminal Justice Consultative Council, consisting of representatives from all the relevant agencies, was set up in late 1991 to secure maximum co-operation in the management of the system.

Initiatives to transform working practices have been supplemented with strategies to exercise control of court business. The Crown Prosecution Service (CPS), a central government department, has a crucial 'gatekeeping' role to play in furthering the government's reform programme. When the police were responsible for deciding whether to prosecute, other criminal justice agencies were never sure of the basis on which decisions were being made. However, with the CPS there is a code and policy manuals which set out the guidelines for decision making. As a consequence, decisions, in theory, should be more consistent and open to other agencies because they are being made on clearly articulated sentencing principles. The CPS also regulates the flow of cases to the courts more tightly than the police because they use stricter provability guidelines. It is also argued by its critics that the CPS gives overarching consideration to the costs of bringing a prosecution.

There have also been efforts to redefine the rights of 'customers' of the criminal justice system. The CPS has voiced a desire to introduce plea bargaining with incentives for offenders to plead guilty at an earlier stage of proceedings and abolish the right to trial by jury. The right to legal aid has also been curbed in the aftermath of an Audit Commission report which expressed concern about the spiralling costs of a demand-led service. After changes to eligibility criteria in April 1993 legal aid is now only available to those on income support with the upper limit for aid being reduced in civil court cases.

The internal structure of the courts and attendant legal services are also being reorganized. In February 1992 the government's *New Framework for Local Justice* unveiled proposals for the modernization of the management and structure of the magistrates' courts (see also Home Office, 1989b). The intention is to produce a more business-like magistracy that will be more efficient and effective, as measured in the 'through-put' time taken to complete cases coming before the courts, the unit costs of cases, the collection of fines and compensation and the quality of service provided to the courts' users. In order to secure these changes, area services are to be merged and restructured and magistrates courts' committees will have a more clearly defined managerial role. Senior managers on fixed-term contracts will have clearer personal accountability for performance standards and a magistrates' court inspectorate is being established to disseminate best practice and to regulate standards. Although the government maintains that there is to be no change to the funding of the service, 'funding by performance' has begun to take hold in the new business-oriented environment. Legal commentators argue that cash-limited magistrates' courts are becoming aware that certain lines of crime are more profitable than others. Court managers now have financial incentives to crack down on fine defaulters and to get cases to and through courts more quickly. There is also increasing evidence that certain courts are giving priority to uncomplicated income-generating 'cash earners' such as motoring offences and television licence cases rather than serious criminal cases which are unpredictable in terms of outcome, time consuming and therefore expensive (Northam, 1993). Court committees will also be free, under the new arrangements, to put support services – including security services – out to competitive tender. In order to complete the initial reform process the courts service, which maintains the High Court, Crown Courts and County Courts, will become an executive agency in 1995.

The delivery of legal aid is also being redesigned to secure value for money. In order to prompt improvements in the productivity of legal aid lawyers, the Legal Aid Board has introduced performance targets. As part of its 'Smoother Path to Justice' initiative the Board is planning to award franchises, subject to satisfactory audit, to law and advice firms which would grant them the power to make decisions and incur costs. The government is also seeking to reduce the costs of the service by replacing hourly rates of criminal legal aid work in magistrates courts with a system of standard fees.

Predictably, the response of criminal justice professionals to the proposed changes has been mixed. Opposition has been forthcoming in relation to changes which interfere with the discretion of the legal profession and the government has been forced, in certain notable instances, to compromise. A vociferous campaign, launched in the aftermath of the James Bulger murder, against those sections of the Criminal Justice Act 1991 that obstructed the judiciary in dealing with persistent offenders, resulted in the

Home Secretary promising to amend the offending clauses. The issue of judicial independence also had to be resolved before judges would participate in the Criminal Justice Consultative Council. The senior judiciary was also successful, despite Treasury protests, in its campaign for the appointment of ten to thirteen new judges to help clear the backlogs in the High Courts. Senior members of the legal profession have also warned the government against tampering with the right to trial by jury, and in 1993 solicitors attempted to take legal action to challenge the legality of the government's changes to the legal aid system. There have also been complaints that the outcome of letting market forces loose in the courts is a weakening of the right to justice. Anthony Scrivener QC, former Chair of the Bar, argues that as a result of the changes to the ethos, functioning and management of the court system there is, for example, 'a great temptation by a very cost oriented court to do entirely the wrong thing' (quoted in Northam, 1993).

Nevertheless, what is striking is the overall success of the government in pursuing its reform agenda to the very heart of the criminal justice system. The lack of real opposition can only be explained by the fact that key figures in the judiciary, most notably the Lord Chief Justice, Lord Taylor and the Lord Chancellor, Lord Mackay, have been persuaded to take the lead in 'selling' the need for reform and to warn 'reactionaries' that the cost of confrontation could be a statutory sentencing council, a paid magistracy and formally trained judiciary. It remains to be seen, however, whether senior members of the judiciary will sanction an ongoing reform process which by definition will continue to challenge their discretionary powers and demand quantifiable cost effectiveness.

Conclusion

What will the landscape of criminal justice look like as a result of this restructuring? From the vantage point of 1993–4 it is clear that the Conservatives have shown themselves to be more radical in their approach to criminal justice than anyone would have countenanced in 1979. Given their traditional position on law and order issues, criminal justice agencies and professionals could have expected to remain relatively immune from attacks on the public sector. Overall, as the lavish expenditure on law and order of the 1980s indicates, this had been the case. However, the government, smarting under record crime rates and public disorder, has, in a relatively compressed time-scale, confronted the cumbersome organizational structures and restrictive working practices of a malfunctioning and politically contentious set of public services.

The overall purpose of this sea change in policy is to create a cost-effective, efficient 'seamless' criminal justice system which will be suitably motivated to work with the community to reduce the crime rate and the fear of crime to acceptable levels. Within this overarching 'task environment' the professional remit of the agencies is to work together within nationally agreed sets of guidelines and standards to deliver a specific product – 'justice' – for their customers, whilst also ensuring that demands for the product are kept within economically manageable levels. Hence, the police, CPS and the courts have the role of ensuring the detection and conviction of the guilty by meeting strict procedural rules of evidence; the post-Woolf private and public prison service should treat prisoners with humanity and decency; and the probation service should deliver tough and effective non-custodial sentences. Throughout, managerialism has been identified as the 'tailored pathway' to 'economy and justice'.

As a result of placing managerial imperatives at the heart of this reconfigured system, reports emanating from the probation, prison, police and court services are now prefaced by mission statements which discuss the success or otherwise of operational and strategic managerial initiatives in achieving flexible service delivery systems. Also included in the reports are indicators, measurements and targets relating to the comparative performance of individual cost centres as well as the stage of development of performance review and appraisal systems.

The managerialist discourse is also depoliticizing a highly sensitive political issue. Carol Jones (1993), drawing upon the authoritarian state thesis, has argued that talk of 'consumer responsiveness' and 'devolved decision-making' constitutes a linguistic 'false front' behind which a concerted centralization of state control over the criminal justice system is taking place. We would argue that the new managerialist approach entails a much more radical redefinition of the relationship between the state and the criminal justice complex. It is undoubtedly the case that the regulatory powers of the state and policy parameters have been much more clearly defined and strengthened in order to oversee the system. However, we would argue that centralization and devolution, are complementary processes. There has been a redistribution of decision-making powers to the new managerial strata that are now firmly in place within the criminal justice agencies. It is the local managers of the system, not the state, who have maximum responsibility for delivering law and order through their new 'hands on' control of resources and this reconceptualization constitutes the replacement of political accountability with managerial accountability. Clarification of responsibility is being accompanied by managerial empowerment through the assertion of the right to manage all facets of the organizational configuration, and this includes the right, after establishing the essential core of their work, to 'externalize' large areas of their work through market testing. This inculturation of the 'right to manage' has serious implications for the workforce because, if the organizations are to deliver a customer-focused service, there has to be a shift from rigid bureaucratic working practice and contracts to much more flexible and localized arrangements. Thus, it would be a mistake to misread the complex political repositioning embedded in the centralization–devolution nexus as being just a 'false front'.

The promise of the managerialist discourse to cure the ills of a particularly discredited public service is also producing a new political consensus on law and order. Although there has been political opposition to privatization and contracting-out initiatives, no such opposition has been forthcoming to the actual managerialization process. Indeed, given that many of the government's ideas seem to have been borrowed from progressive centre-left criminal justice pressure groups, it is not surprising that they, rather than the workforce, have entered into an enthusiastic alliance to establish and extend the government's supposedly apolitical technocratic approach. And the good news for criminal justice managers is that the Labour Party's new realist 'tough on crime, tough on the causes of crime' approach will arguably result in more of the same if the party is ever re-elected.

However, we would not wish to understate the, as yet, unresolved problems with this new 'economy and justice' mapping of criminal justice. As we have indicated, there is considerable internal resistance to certain reforms, especially privatization and the attempts to limit certain forms of occupational and professional discretion. And, because crime and fear of crime remain highly emotive issues there remains the opportunity for critics to contest the reform process. In late 1993, for example, increasing public and party political concern about 'lawless Britain', forced the Conservatives to announce 'the most coercive law and order package for a decade' (*Guardian*, 7 October 1993). New offences, new police powers, more prisons, secure units (for persistent child offenders), curbing bail and cautioning and limitations on the rights of suspects were welcomed by the 'law and order' lobby. This caused much consternation among officials and pressure groups concerned about the impact of such an 'arrest, conviction and custody' policy on both rationalist approaches to crime management and attempts to extract 'value for money' from the substantial financial investment in the criminal justice system. We shall have to wait and see what impact this apparent U-turn has on the managerialization process.

In addition, even if the public can be persuaded that managerialism can produce 'leaner and meaner' organizations and internal opposition is overcome, it is not clear that this agenda for change will resolve the hyper-crisis of law and order. As we argued earlier, under Conservative governance there has been a persistent denial of any causal connection between wider economic and social processes and crime. However, if increasing unemployment, social disinvestment and deprivation are generating escalating crime rates, the restructured criminal justice agencies will continue to have little lasting impact on the levels of detected and undetected crime or the causes of crime. And, in a sense, this is why managerialist solutions are geared much more towards resolving the immediate problems of organizations working in an impossible 'task environment'. However, this sets limits to the capability of the system to meet the needs of its customers and it is not certain that they will accept the message that all we can hope to do is manage crime as effectively and as efficiently as possible.

References

Association of Chief Police Officers (ACPO) (1990) *Setting the Standards: Meeting Community Expectation*. London: ACPO.

Audit Commission (1988) *Performance Review in Local Government: Action Guide*. London: HMSO.

Audit Commission (1989) *The Probation Service: Promoting Value for Money*. London: HMSO.

Audit Commission (1991) *Going Straight: Developing Good Practice in the Probation Service*, Occasional Papers No. 16. London: HMSO.

Clarke, R.V.G. and Hough, M. (1984) *The Effectiveness of Policing*. Aldershot: Gower.

Clarke, R.V.G. and Mayhew, P. (1980) *Designing Out Crime*. London: HMSO.

Ewing, K. and Gearty, C. (1990) *Freedom under Thatcher: Civil Liberties in Modern Britain*. Oxford: Oxford University Press.

Fowles, A. (1990) 'Monitoring expenditure in the criminal justice system', *Howard Journal*, 29(2): 82–100.

Garrett, J. (1986) 'Developing state audit in Britain', *Public Administration*, 64 (Winter): 421–32.

Grange, T. (1993) 'Police: changing management', in L. Willcocks and J. Harrow (eds), *Rediscovering Public Services Management*. London: McGraw-Hill.

Harrison, A. and Gretton, J. (1986) 'Accounting for crime', *Crime UK, 1986, Policy Journals*: 5–7.

Harrison, A. and Morgan, J. (1988) 'Efficiency and offloading in the criminal justice system', *Crime UK, 1988, Policy Journals*: 43–8.

Hillyard, P. and Percy-Smith, J. (1988) *The Coercive State*. London: Fontana.

Home Office (1979) *Report of the Commission of Inquiry into UK Prison Services*. Cmnd 7673. London: HMSO.

Home Office (1984) *Probation Service in England and Wales: Statement of National Objectives and Priorities*. London: HMSO.

Home Office (1988) *Punishment, Custody and the Community* (Green Paper). London: HMSO.

Home Office (1989a) *Tackling Crime*. London: HMSO.

Home Office (1989b) *Magistrates Courts: Report of a Scrutiny 1989*. London: HMSO.

Home Office (1992) *Partnership in Dealing with Offenders in the Community: A Decision Document*. London: HMSO.

Home Office (1993) *White Paper on Police Reform*. London: HMSO.

Horton, C. and Smith, D. (1988) *Evaluating Police Work*. London: Policy Studies Institute.

Jones, C. (1993) 'Auditing criminal justice', *British Journal of Criminology*, 33(3): 187–202.

Lilly, J.R. and Knepper, P. (1992) 'The corrections–commercial complex', *Prison Service Journal*, 87: 43–52.

Lloyd, C. (1986) *Response to SNOP*. Cambridge: Cambridge University Press.

Locke, T. (1990) *New Approaches to Crime in the 1990s*. London: Longman.

Mair, G. (1989) 'Some developments in probation in the 1980s', *Home Office Research Bulletin*, 27: 33–6.

Matthews, R. (1990) 'New directions in the privatisation debate?' *Probation Journal*, 37(2): 50–61.

McDermott, K. and King, R. (1989) 'A Fresh Start: the enhancement of prison regimes', *Howard Journal*, 28(3): 161–76.

McWilliams, B. (1990) 'Probation practice and the management ideal', *Probation Journal*, 37(2).

Morris, P. and Heal K. (1981) *Crime Control and the Police: A Review of the Research*. London: HMSO.

Moxon, D. (ed.) (1985) *Managing Criminal Justice*. London: HMSO.

Moxon, D. (1992) 'Magistrates court or crown court: mode of trial decisions by magistrates and defendants', *The Magistrate*, 48(9): 185–6.

NACRO (1990) *The Prison Building Programme*, NACRO Briefing No. 9. London: NACRO.

NACRO (1992) 'Expenditure on the criminal justice system', *Criminal Justice Digest*, 73: 21.

Northam, G. (1993) 'Justice on trial', BBC Radio 4, 29 June.

Osler, A. (1992) 'The Criminal Justice Act 1991 – a probation viewpoint', *The Magistrate*, 48(8): 155–6.

Parry-Khan, L. (1988) 'Management by objectives in probation', *Social Work Monographs*, University of East Anglia: Social Work Today.

Pearson, G., Blagg, H., Smith, D., Sampson, A. and Stubbs, P. (1992) 'Crime community and conflict: the multi-agency approach', in D. Downes (ed.), *Unravelling Criminal Justice*. London: Macmillan.

Pitts, J. (1992) 'The end of an era', *Howard Journal*, 31(2): 133–49.

Pratt, J. (1989) 'Corporatism: the third model of juvenile justice', *British Journal of Criminology*, 29(3): 236–54.

Reiner, G. (1992) 'Beaten by the big stick', *Times Higher Education Supplement*, 20 March.

Ryan, M. and Ward, T. (1989) *Privatisation and the Penal System*. Milton Keynes: Open University Press.

Scraton, P. (ed.) (1987) *Law, Order and the Authoritarian State*. Milton Keynes: Open University Press.

Sheehy, Sir P. (1993) *Inquiry into Police Responsibilities and Rewards*, vol. 1. London: HMSO.

Smith, D.J. and Gray, J. (1985) *Police and People in London: The PSI Report*. Aldershot: Gower.

Statham, R. and Whitehead, P. (eds) (1992) *Managing the Probation Service*. London: Longman.

Tuck, M. (1992) 'Community and criminal justice system', *Policy Studies*, 12(3): 22–38.

Weatheritt, M. (1986) *Innovations in Policing*. London: Croom Helm.

Wolff Olins (1988) *A Force for Change: a Report on the Corporate Identity of the Metropolitan Police*. London: Wolff Olins.

Wynne, A. and Priestman, P. (1992) *Unequal Before the Law*. London: Liberty.

Young, J. (1992) 'The rising demand for law and order and our maginot lines of defence against crime', in N. Abercrombie and A. Warde (eds) *Social Change in Contemporary Britain*. Cambridge: Polity.

7

Managing Change in Local Government

Allan Cochrane

Local government has been at the centre of the process of political restructuring which has been sweeping across Britain since the mid-1970s. Some aspects of this have been reflected in changing institutional relations, with the rise of new forms of local state organizations such as public–private partnerships, community care, training and enterprise councils, family health service authorities, inter-agency working, the increased importance of school governing bodies and the removal of further education and what was the polytechnic sector from local government control. Other chapters have looked at the changing forms of management associated with some of these arrangements. Intuitively, at least, the new arrangements seem to imply a declining role for elected councils as local expression of the welfare state. Yet – paradoxically – just as decline seems inevitable, extensive new claims about the importance of local government have begun to emerge from within the beleaguered local government community. Some have begun to argue that, far from becoming residual or marginalized, councils will take on a pivotal role in the new world of fragmented and decentralized service delivery through multiple agencies.

These arguments have drawn on some of the changes being imposed from above to suggest that they offer new possibilities, particularly in redefining local government, moving away from seeing it as delivery system towards viewing it as 'enabling authority'. In more developed and confident form these arguments have moved beyond 'enabling' to talk of 'community government'. At the same time – coming together to create a formidable and almost unchallengeable ideology which inevitably tends to strengthen the position of senior managers – there has been an increasingly explicit borrowing from the language of private (corporate) sector management, in the context of wider moves towards a new public sector management. At the core of these arguments is the ambition to develop devolved (or post-bureaucratic) delivery systems managed at arm's length through processes of strategic management, based at the centre of a spider's web of overlapping networks, linking the voluntary, private and public sectors.

In a sense, of course, there has always been 'management' in local government as there has in other large organizations, but each generation seems cursed in turn to explore the concept once more and to give it new meaning. Each successive interpretation is required to supplant and dismiss those of the past, emphasizing how only the new approach can solve the problems which beset the organization or those areas of society for which it is responsible. 'Management' means different things at different times and in different places. It is not simply an objective tool which can be pulled down from the shelf to be utilized as required, but is rather a historically variable discourse which is the product of conflict and controversy. In order to be clear about the claims being made today, it is helpful to explore their roots in the past. As a result, this chapter will set the new claims for strategic management in a wider historical context, before looking more closely at their contemporary significance.

The pre-history of management in local government

The historical view of local government management bears little relationship to present-day understandings. The legacy of the nineteenth century was one which emphasized legal and financial rectitude and links to the traditional middle-class professions. As late as 1933 the Local Government Act required a County Council to appoint a Clerk, Treasurer, Medical Officer of Health and Surveyor, and it required Borough and District Councils to appoint these and Sanitary Inspectors (Collinge, 1992: 64). The leading officers were treasurers and town clerks, both of whom drew their legitimacy from professional roots in private practice – accountancy and the law. Until quite recently, the dominant role of local authority treasurers was to act as efficient book-keepers, balancing the books and resisting the incurring of unwarranted expenditure, while the role of town clerks was to ensure that councils did not exceed the legal powers which they had been delegated. In many authorities (particularly the smaller ones) the position of town clerk was still a part-time appointment as late as the 1950s and 1960s (Keith-Lucas and Richards, 1978: 103).

The expansion of welfare state activities undertaken by local government between 1918 and 1945 as well as in the years after 1945 was accompanied by a gradual growth in the number of specialist departments responsible for different aspects of provision. According to Finer (1950: 242) the instinctive response to a growth in functions was 'to establish new Departments and divisions of departments, and to set up for each of these divisions a specialist committee of management'. 'Management' was still discussed in terms which focused on the role of individual specialist committees, each responsible for particular aspects of a council's work. The assumption was that each department was headed by a 'small directing professional group' responsible for a 'large clerical or administrative non-professional subordinate staff' (Robson, 1954: 321).

> The local authorities still demanded the accepted professional qualifications . . . solicitors held a practical monopoly of the town clerkships; other departments were headed by professional men – architects, doctors etc. There was no place for the general administrator, nor ladder for the university graduate unless he had a professional qualification. (Keith-Lucas and Richards, 1978: 105)

Collinge (1992: 63–6) notes that concerns were being expressed about this fragmentation and lack of overall responsibility even in the inter-war period. As early as 1934 the Hadow Committee on the qualification, recruitment, training and promotion of local government officers argued that the town clerk should be a co-ordinator and therefore an administrator rather than a lawyer. 'He should be a person of broad and constructive outlook, interested in the wider issues of local government, skilled in negotiation. And he should ordinarily have had experience of administrative work' (para. 98, quoted in Robson, 1954: 350). Explicit contrast was frequently drawn between the administrative grade of the civil service, which drew on university graduates and was based on notions of generalist administration, and the narrower focus of local government with its large tail of poorly qualified clerks. Particularly in the years after 1945, stress began to be placed on the need for town clerks to move towards 'considering the large administrative questions relating to the work of the authority as a whole, the coordination of the separate departments, negotiations with central government, new and ambitious schemes of municipal development, and the intelligent anticipation of future problems and difficulties' (Robson, 1954: 340). Although the language is different (and the civil service model has, as Tom Ling notes in Chapter 2, itself faced sustained criticism in recent years) these broad concerns have continued to run through debates about the management of local government.

The expansion of local government after 1945 as the main local expression of a growing welfare state brought substantial changes, but retained and even extended existing divisions. Local authorities lost their old responsibilities for aspects of the health service, the supply of gas and electricity and the domestic provision of water, but saw their responsibilities for key aspects of welfare provision increase (such as education, children's and personal welfare services and low-cost rental housing). Coventry in the mid-1960s was if anything less fragmented than many other urban authorities yet it had twenty full council committees at that time, without taking into account all the sub-committees and joint committees. The committees were responsible for overseeing the work of a total of twenty-three separate departments ranging in size from 14 to 7735 employees (for full list, see Friend and Jessop, 1969). Of course, some of these functions (such as Waterworks) have now been removed from local government responsibility but, even so, the most striking feature of the list is simply the fragmentation of responsibilities between departments. Each was basically left to be run by its own professionals, within apparently non-controversial financial guidelines laid down by the Finance Department and legal constraints set by the Town Clerk's Department.

The growth of the welfare state brought with it the formation of an identifiable category of welfare professionals whose activities in turn helped to shape dominant interpretations of the local state. Emphasis was placed on professional expertise, with the employees of the new departments setting out to identify their positions with those of the older professions, even if they were rarely accorded the status their members felt they deserved, Traditionally professionals (for example, in law or medicine) were defined (or defined themselves) by their independence or autonomy from the state and other private interests – their ability to control the terms on which their services were offered, their ability to control entry into their profession and their ability to regulate the professional behaviour of their members. Certainly the state often had an important part to play in this – for example by licensing certain professions to operate in particular areas. But the professions themselves always resisted direct state influence on their behaviour – to the extent that, for example, general practitioners successfully managed to avoid becoming direct employees of the National Health Service when it was set up.

The growth of the welfare state, on the other hand (as Janet Newman and John Clarke have argued in Chapter 1), and of local government within it, encouraged the rise of a quite different set of professions – what Mintzberg (1983) calls 'bureau-professions' whose existence was dependent on the rise of the public sector 'bureaux' by which they were employed. The 'new' professions remained 'new' and their professionalism was frequently called into question, because of their dependence on the state:

> The new bureaucratic professions . . . have no choice but to be public employees . . . they generally welcome the extension of state power, for it is the only source of such power as they themselves possess; indeed these occupational groups owe their very existence to the extension of the power of the state. (Reade, 1987: 126)

These professions were also different because many of their members were women, particularly in education (and particularly in junior schools) and in children's and welfare departments, although senior officials (and head-teachers) still tended to be men. This helped to confirm the uneasy status of the 'new' professions because the dominant image of the old (and by definition legitimate) ones was overwhelmingly male.

The new world was uneasily grafted on to the old, so that departmentalism survived (indeed flourished) and new departments emerged while others declined in importance. Within individual councils, departments tended to remain insulated from each other, each jealously guarding its own specialist responsibilities while professionals within the departments were (as Rhodes, 1988, explains) linked into their own separate, if not quite autonomous, national policy networks. In practice, in the first twenty years or so after 1945 the professional approaches associated with particular service areas, rather than the old (generalizing) expertise of the law and finance, tended to take the lead in local policy making. It was the overall programmes of the new professionals which were implemented and the emphasis was placed on 'needs-led' (or 'demand-led') initiatives, even if those needs were generally defined by the professionals themselves. Until the mid-1960s there was little serious attempt to impose any form of council-wide management on the various departments and the professional leaderships within them. Management was the responsibility of professional experts and administrators, rather than a set of managers with specifically managerial skills, training or expertise. Whatever management skills were acquired were learned 'on the job'.

The rise of corporate management

In the 1960s and early 1970s, a new set of arguments emerged which began to criticize the power of departmentalism and the dominance of professional prejudice. These focused on the inability of those who should have been 'managers' to raise their sights above the fragmented visions of their own professions and their own departments. Lessons were explicitly drawn from developments taking place within the private sector and local government was compared to 'big business' (Benington, 1976) rather than the smaller businesses that were more characteristic of the private sector professionalism which local government and lawyers had traditionally tried to emulate. The underlying assumptions incorporated a view of strategic planning borrowed from the corporate sector of the economy, dominated by large monopolistic companies (or alliances between a limited number of oligopolistic firms) able to shape the markets within which they found themselves. Emphasis was placed on the need to construct long-term stable plans (usually subject to a process of rolling remake), within which departments could develop their own more detailed plans, but – above all – which would make it possible to construct programme-based initiatives capable of mobilizing contributions from across a range of departments.

Attempts were being made to modernize local government, as part of a more extensive strategy of state-backed social and economic modernization, fostered first by the Wilson governments of 1964–70, and then by the Heath government of 1970–74. A clutch of official reports and Royal Commissions at the end of the 1960s and the beginning of the 1970s focused on ways of improving managerial efficiency and 'streamlining' decision making, within larger (more business-like) authorities (Dearlove, 1979: Part 2 provides a valuable summary of debates current in the late 1960s and early 1970s). Local government boundaries were redrawn and new councils created, first in England and Wales and later in Scotland (in Northern Ireland local government had already effectively been replaced by wider regional agencies). Stress was placed on the perceived inefficiencies of local government and the low calibre of its councillors and officers (incidentally concerns already expressed by Robson, 1954: 320). It was argued strongly that the old structures bequeathed from the nineteenth century were inadequate for the mid-twentieth century.

Modernization meant not only that larger units were required but also that new forms of management had to be introduced. In the most 'progressive' authorities, there was a move away from departments to much larger directorates, and everywhere new chief officer management teams were set up and chief executives appointed. Setting up the new councils was expected to make it easier to break away from petty interdepartmental rivalries and to encourage the development of organizational forms more suited to strategic – or corporate – policy making. The Bains Report (1972) on management structures combined detailed advice on appropriate management models with broad claims about an expanded role for local government. No longer were councils to be defined solely in terms of the services they delivered directly. Instead they were to be the managers of social and economic change in their communities. Local government, said the report, was 'not limited to the provision of services. It is concerned with the overall economic, cultural and physical well-being of the community' (Baines, 1972: 122). Councils were to be the local strategic agencies of the welfare state in the business of what Cockburn (1977) described as the management of cities and people.

The clearest explicit expression of the new regime was the way in which the post of chief executive – rather than town clerk – became an almost universal feature of organizational life. Every council seemed to have a policy and resources committee and a management team or chief officers' group. Many of them had corporate planning or corporate management units. Attempts were made to set up interlocking sets of cross-departmental sub-groups, frequently based around notions of activity or programme-based planning and serviced by the new corporate units. Reforms in town planning which introduced a nested system of structure plans and local plans, apparently offering a more rational framework for development control, also encouraged some planners to see themselves as having a leading (corporate) role in the development of council policies (see, for example, Reade, 1987: 59–62). Documents setting out corporate objectives were published by councils up and down the country (see, for example, Greenwood and Stewart, 1974). Councils commissioned management consultants to tell them how they should reorganize themselves in line with best (private sector) management practice (see, for example, Cockburn, 1977, who notes the role of Urwick Orr in Lambeth, p. 24, Booz Allen in Stockport, p. 130, and McKinsey more generally, p. 21).

The rise of explicit 'managerialism' in its corporate management form, however, was a relatively short-lived one. In part this simply reflected some of the over-ambitious claims made for the new arrangements which tended to underestimate the continued (and in some cases growing) power of the specialist service delivery departments and their positions within more extensive policy networks connecting groups in local and central government. Education departments in metropolitan districts and shire counties, for example, still accounted for by far the largest single element of local authority budgets – at around 60 percent of overall council spending. Their key relationships were with officials within the Department of Education and Science and Her Majesty's Inspectors of Schools as much as (and possibly more than) with other parts of local government. As a result, directors of education were generally reluctant to participate in corporate arrangements which undermined their power base (see, for example, Kogan and van der Eyken, 1973, particularly the rather dismissive comments of chief education officers about central – administrative – departments within their authorities on pp. 48–51). The new social services departments were at this time principally concerned with claiming their position within local government, while housing departments saw themselves as engaged in a clearly identifiable and specialist activity: managing housing stock and allocating it to tenants. They, too, relied on relationships with departments of central government as much as other departments of local government. As a result, the best that could be hoped for was, as Stewart noted, 'the control and co-ordination of policies that remain separate in origin rather than on the co-ordination of the processes which lead up to those policies, on the efficiency of policy implementation rather than on the effectiveness of policy formulation' (Stewart, 1974: 13). This meant, in practice, that most chief officers' groups operated as forums within which negotiation could take place between senior managers, rather than as sources of managerial – corporate – direction.

Arguably, just bringing the service departments together and suggesting that it was necessary to develop a council-wide approach might in itself be seen as a significant step, not least because it implied that decisions taken within particular departments were open for discussion by other senior officers, and by the chief executive in particular. Moves in this direction, however, were also substantially undermined by events taking place outside the local government system. Just as local government seemed ready for a managerial revolution reflecting and reinforcing its high status in the organization and management of urban change, the rules of the game changed in ways which undermined its claims. Greater policy claims were being made just at the time (in the early 1970s) when the British economy was facing major problems and governments were responding by seeking to restrict public spending, and particularly spending by local government. Although some argued that the new spending reductions had themselves opened up new opportunities for the 'comprehensive rational analysis' of budgets (Greenwood and Lomer, 1980: 57) with the creation of 'structures and procedures that would facilitate a central review of service expenditures', partly as a 'product of managerial and organisational impulse to secure effective and balanced contractions in services' (Greenwood, 1983: 166; see also Greenwood et al., 1976), the accumulating evidence suggested that the main result was, rather, more fragmented and unpredictable decision making. Clapham has shown how in some authorities it fostered a move away from medium and long-term planning towards a more short-term focus on the demands of the immediate situation, which tended to be interpreted through a set of cash indicators (Clapham, 1983, 1984, 1985). Not surprisingly, the main result was that departments set out to defend their own budgets, engaging in a range of more or less successful budgetary strategies to do so (see, for example, Jordan, 1987; Rosenberg 1989) while at the same time appealing to those parts of their own professional policy networks that had influence at other levels of the state system for political and financial support (see, for example, Rhodes, 1988). Instead of 'rational' corporate planning at national or local level, the policy process looked more like the 'mess' identified by Rhodes (1985).

The return of financial control

If there was an increased role for central departments within local government in the late 1970s and 1980s it was expressed in the higher status given to the finance function. The model of budgetary formation which dominated in local government clearly changed at this time. Traditionally, budgets had been constructed by putting together the separate proposals made by different service departments, possibly shaving growth proposals here and there to meet broader financial targets, in a 'contest over the allocation of growth' (Rosenberg, 1989: 130). At first similar methods were used to deal with the fiscal austerity imposed by central government – instead of incremental budgeting, it was possibly to identify a process of 'decrementalism', as departments were encouraged to adjust to the new financial atmosphere. But the workings of professional politics were too deeply ingrained for this approach to work effectively: departments were reluctant to make cuts in practice and were more likely to use the negotiating process to strengthen their own positions relative to others, using by-now-familiar techniques such as 'shroud waving', offering to make cuts in the most politically sensitive areas (see Jordan, 1987). More important perhaps, the extent of the external pressures and unpredictability of changes from year to year also made it an unconvincing response.

As a result there was a gradual move towards a budgetary style which was resource- rather than departmentally (or 'demand-') led. It was, in other words, heavily influenced by the outcomes of central government's annual grant-setting exercise and by attempts to predict in advance what global budgets were likely to be (Elcock et al., 1989: 13–14). If the reorganization of local government at the start of the 1970s was accompanied by the growth of various forms of 'corporate' institution within councils, the pressures on public sector spending and local welfare state spending within that led to a mushroom-like growth of 'sweat boxes' or 'star chambers' within which senior officers and councillors scrutinized proposals for spending and proposals for spending reductions (see, for example, Game, 1987). Although chief executives were generally involved in these new structures, their role was subordinated to that of financial control and, if anything, a form of financial control which had more to do with book-keeping than financial management (see, for example, Pendlebury, 1985).

The dominant expression of managerial orthodoxy found its expression in the notion of 'value for money', which was often associated with new forms of accounting practice (as expressed, for example, in Butt and Palmer, 1985). At this time:

> The accounting ideology of the private sector, with its emphasis on individual financial responsibility and its apparently systematic and ordered approach to management . . . had considerable appeal. By offering to bring intangible, intractable matters under managerial control and giving contentious issues a technical appearance, any opposition seemed illogical and irrational. (Humphrey and Scapens, 1992: 142–3)

Where notions of corporate management had focused on wide claims to manage processes of change at local level and had emphasized the need to develop broad sets of 'objectives', the new approach assumed that the objectives were clear (because handed down from the centre) and that it was possible to be more or less efficient in achieving them. The language, therefore, was one which emphasized the bland and the technical over the political, even if the outcomes might be politically significant, with some groups losing while others gained. This was the underlying justification for setting up the Audit Commission in the early 1980s, with its focus on monitoring and advising on the 'economy, efficiency and effectiveness' of local government and the health service (McSweeney, 1988). It was at this time, too, that suggestions were first made which implied a move away from elected local *government* to forms of community trust which would be able to deliver specified services (Adam Smith Institute, 1989). It was argued that new methods should be developed that would allow consumers to judge the relative efficiency of different local governments. The ultimate expression of this approach was the introduction of the community charge or poll tax whose purpose was to develop a clear relationship between the costs of services and levels of local taxation. It was hoped that forcing consumers/ electors to pay for the inefficiencies of their local councils through higher taxes would lead to increased electoral pressure for greater efficiency (and lower taxes).

The same external pressures encouraged rather different – and potentially inconsistent – responses within the management of local government. The emphasis on overall budgets, largely determined by the allocation of central government grant, also encouraged the process of what came to be called 'creative accounting' (again, of course, a notion borrowed from practice in the private sector). At its most basic this simply required senior council managers – above all finance officers – to understand the grant system and the rules on the raising of capital in ways which enabled councils to take full advantage of available sources of finance. But it could also be (and was) developed in ways which sought to maximize grant by the manipulation of financial information – shifting spending from one budget head to another or from one financial year to another – or sought new sources of funding which lay outside the grant limits, for example by intervening in the financial markets or by a whole range of schemes involving deferred purchase or the translation of current into capital spending. In other words the very people who were expected to utilize 'value for money' as their watchword were at the same time engaged in activity which made the financial information on which 'value for money' was supposed to be judged virtually meaningless.

It is not clear, therefore, that an increased role for central structures of financial management necessarily implies a greater 'rationality' for the organization as a whole. On the contrary, the experience of the 1980s suggests that it may serve to mask a rather more confused and uncertain set of responses. The attempts to impose a new rationality from above, through the departments of central government and the development of increasingly complex financial rules, do not seem to have been very successful – and since current spending by local authorities actually rose across the decade it is clear that more modest ambitions to reduce levels of public spending in this sphere were not achieved either.

The rise of strategic management

It was in this context that a different set of pressures for change began to emerge. In part they reflected a widespread recognition of the severe limitations of dominant approaches to financial control within local government. Efficient book-keeping might ensure that spending was kept within agreed budgets (although 'creative accounting' always meant that even that could not be guaranteed) but it left existing state structures largely unaffected. As a result the rise of finance is best understood as a transitional phenomenon – as a first step in questioning the position of service departments. It helped to undermine claims for the importance of professional expertise by suggesting that it was possible to scrutinize their operations with the help of a superior (somehow more 'rational') set of tools provided by 'value for money' accounting. Within this new discourse, welfare (bureau) professionalism itself could even be dismissed as little more than a self-serving means of defending entrenched positions.

The regular production of service-based reports and local authority profiles by the Audit Commission helped to reinforce the position of finance professionals within local government, and to bolster their claims to objectivity. But the ideology of 'value for money' and the centralization of financial scrutiny which followed from it could not deliver all that was needed or expected, because, in a sense, it took the existing structures of the local welfare state for granted, with delivery still determined from above and accountancy being left to determine whether agreed packages were being delivered with more or less 'economy' or 'efficiency' (see, for example, Cochrane, 1993a). In other words it was possible to monitor existing delivery systems (and possibly to make them more 'efficient', or at least less costly), but it was less easy to see how they might be transformed. The frustration of the auditor's role soon found expression in the production of reports which moved beyond it and began to suggest more fundamental organizational changes, in the shape of what was called the 'competitive council' (see, for example, Audit Commission, 1988, 1989).

These suggestions also fitted in with changing interpretations of the welfare state and of local government within it, which emphasized the need to move away from approaches based on hierarchical and centralized delivery systems. In part this reflected an understanding that the old centralized hierarchies never worked, because – as Rhodes has emphasized – the organization of the British welfare state has always been characterized by having multiple centres and dispersed delivery systems. If this was true of the system as a whole, it was equally true within the local welfare state, where fragmentation between departments reflected national fragmentation, with members of local policy élites linking into different specialized regional and national policy networks. At local level, too, each department managed its own set of interest groups, with even local political parties rarely being able to produce programmes or manifestos which were much more than the accumulation of departmentally based briefs. There were also often major divisions within local government departments, with different sections fitting into rather different national and local policy networks, so that – for example – higher, further and secondary education related to different sections of (the same) central government department as well as relating to rather different political (and policy) communities at local level. Although the language of general local government acts and constitutional discussion tended to define local authorities as unitary multi-functional agencies, the closer one moved to the practice of individual departments the less appropriate such a construction appeared.

But the emphasis on the need to move away from hierarchical models increased in 1980s, where it fitted in with wider shifts in the organization of the welfare state (see, for example, Loader and Burrows, 1994). Although the moves within the welfare state across the decade were often masked in the language of 'markets', 'customers' and 'citizens', in practice they were leading towards a fragmentaliz of responsibilities, forms of decentralization and an increased recognition of the importance of working across organizations through policy networks. The main characteristics of the new world of the local welfare state at the start of the 1990s can be summarized relatively briefly. There has been a fragmentation of responsibility between a range of agencies in the public, private and not-for-profit or voluntary sectors. This has been achieved largely through legislative changes coupled with tight financial controls from Whitehall, but an increased interest in encouraging economic growth and in civic boosterism through culture has also encouraged the development of public–private partnerships of various sorts at local level. New institutions, such as Training and Enterprise Councils and Local Enterprise Companies, have been created, while others (such as further education and the new universities) have moved outside local government control, and privatization and contracting out have brought a whole new set of private (and quasi-private) organizations into existence as well as encouraging the growth of others (see Cochrane, 1993b, for more extensive discussion of these changes).

As so often in the past, the changes within local government and its organization also reflected and were justified by evidence of shifts in approach within the private as well as the public sector. In attempting to respond to the perceived failure of US business in the face of challenges from overseas (particularly from Japan, but also from some parts of Europe) the US management literature began to question traditional forms of organization and their inflexibility. The old managerial styles associated with major corporations (such as General Motors, IBM and Ford) were contrasted with the successes of more dynamic (and generally smaller) firms in the service as well as manufacturing sectors. Many of the arguments cut across the public and private sectors, with managerialism working to legitimate changes, and moving away from the narrow disciplines of Taylorism (Pollit, 1990; Osborne and Gaebler, 1992). Although slightly different conclusions were drawn by the different authors who, in developing market niches for their work, presented their own particular solutions to the problems, they did – at least – all seem to agree that attempting to run business centrally through hierarchical systems of managerial control was doomed to failure (see, for example, Peters and Waterman, 1982; Moss Kanter, 1984; Piore and Sabel, 1984; Peters, 1988; Handy, 1989).

There was no longer a belief in the possibility of centralized and comprehensive 'rational' planning within corporate organizations. Instead, it was argued that strategic managers had the task of identifying key issues on which their organizations should focus, while ensuring that their decentralized divisions were able to respond flexibly to and create demand for their products. They needed to be in touch with the demands of consumers. This found an expression in what Hoggett describes as a 'paradoxical development through which radical forms of operational decentralisation become combined with the further centralisation of strategic command' (1991: 249). There was an increased emphasis on notions of quality rather than value for money, with the argument that successful business organizations were run in ways which ensured quality, rather than in ways which emphasized retrospective scrutiny of the extent to which they achieved their financial targets. Success might, after all, be reflected in the need to reassess those targets. There was, of course, in all this no suggestion that costs were unimportant or that balance sheets did not matter – on the contrary the emphasis was placed on ways of ensuring that value added through quality assurance was paid for at premium rates.

The extent to which the 'new management' has spread through the private sector in anything more than rhetorical flourishes remains open to question, but there can be little doubt that it has had a substantial impact on debates within the public sector, and particularly within local government, where its arguments have been reinterpreted and used to underpin and justify many of those changes. In the US context, for example, Osborne and Gaebler argue that government should take responsibility for 'steering' (that is determining policy direction) but that 'rowing' (that is service provision) should be delegated to a range of other agencies (private, public and not-for-profit) (Osborne and Gaebler, 1992: Chapter 1). There has been an explicit and clear-cut attempt within local government to borrow from the business sector and from what has been called the 'discourse of enterprise' (du Gay and Salaman, 1992). One of the aims is, in a sense, to become more 'business-like', in part to make it easier for agencies in the public and private sectors to work more closely together (Bennett and Krebs, 1991). As in the late 1960s and early 1970s, the involvement of private sector consultants is often an important aspect of this as they offer to import the insights of the private sector and to give their imprimatur to new organizational arrangements (Humphrey and Pease, 1991). At a time when idealized visions of markets and the private sector have become the measures against which the local welfare state is tested, so that local government itself appears under threat and has been the subject of extensive (government supported) criticism as a home of unfeeling and wasteful bureaucracy, managerialism offers a powerful means both of claiming a greater role for local government and of legitimating the position of senior managers within it. The move away from direct responsibility for service delivery in many areas becomes translated into an opportunity, instead of a threat. Whatever the precise model being proposed, each consultants' report inevitably concludes on an upbeat note with the model proposed by the consultants making it possible for the authority to take advantage of new opportunities (see, for example, Isaac-Henry and Painter 1991: 77).

Emphasis is increasingly put on the need to work in an inter-organizational context and across the public, private and not-for-profit (or voluntary) sectors. This is a wider point frequently made in the context of public sector management:

> Management is not just an intra-organizational process. Management means taking responsibility for the performance of a system. In public management, more often than not, systems are interorganizational. . . . Effectiveness depends on managing the whole, including the relationships between component organizations, not just on tightening up internal systems. (Metcalfe and Richards, 1990: 217)

In the case of local government this insight provides the rationale for making more extensive claims for strategic management. As a leading proponent of the new world argues – incidentally starting with an echo of the claims made in the Bains Report

> [councils] will have as a main concern the overall welfare of their areas. They will seek practical ways of influencing other agencies to achieve a desirable result. . . . The managerial consequences on the local authority will be profound. Key to its success will be the way in which it can establish relationships with the external agencies which provide services, the way in which it can establish networks with other bodies. (Brooke, 1989b: 10–11)

The new role identified for the local authority (here described as 'enabling') also leads inexorably into the identification of a new and dynamic role for senior managers (or chief officers). The enabling authority opens the possibility of operating beyond the narrow statutory responsibilities traditionally granted to councils in ways which mean it will be more entrepreneurial (another borrowing from the language of business) as a 'catalyst in presenting opportunities to others' (Brooke, 1989b: 161).[1]

The managerial implication here is that, 'The cadre of officers who serve the policy-making process will be recruited more for their strategic and political abilities than for their ability to run a vast professional bureaucracy' (Brooke, 1989b: 21). There will be a split between the different parts of a traditional local authority structure, so that there will be 'a central core of strategic planners and regulators. . . . Such a core would of necessity embrace officers of different professional disciplines.' But alongside this central core there will be, 'A second cadre of managerially inclined or entrepreneurial officers [who] will run services either as independent agencies, private sector companies, voluntary bodies or direct service organisations' (Brooke, 1989a: 60). Following the logic of the 'purchaser'/ 'provider' division discussed elsewhere by Langan and Clarke (Chapter 4, this volume), the core group will largely be responsible for the 'purchasing' of services provided by others, but members of the group will also be responsible for maintaining a strategic overview within which the guidelines on which purchasing takes place are developed. As Janet Newman argues

(Chapter 9, this volume, this division is also implicitly a gendered one, so that the core will be overwhelmingly male, while the second cadre will include more women and those employed at lower levels in the second category of organizations (and incidentally in a third category of part-time employment and informal work) are overwhelmingly likely to be women. Halford (1993) effectively shows how the old structures of local government helped to sustain resistance to equal opportunities and access to career progression by women. But instead of opening up new opportunities for organizational advancement, the changed world seems likely to generate new forms of gender-based division.

A key aspect of the new management is the way in which it promises a transformed culture to fit with the changed world. On the basis of their survey Isaac-Henry and Painter (1991: 86) conclude that 'what is now almost universally accepted are the arguments for a managerial practice on sound management principles'. The precise interpretation of what constitute 'sound management principles' may vary, but whatever they are, their ability to act as means of transforming existing organizational cultures does not seem to be in question in the increasingly evangelical statements of visions and missions being produced throughout the country. Sabin (1990: 26) places great stress on the task of developing an organizational vision and style, and encouraging the ownership of a shared set of values throughout the authority. Similar points are made in the discussion of changes in Nottingham after the appointment of a new chief executive at the start of the 1990s, which found their expression in the publication of 'Nottingham into the Nineties – a New Management Style'. Here the aim was to change the council's organizational culture with senior officers and members 'united in a vision of a City Council which is geared up to meeting the demands and need of its customers into the 1990s' (Buckland and Joshua, 1992: 25). It is increasingly apparent that strategic managers are expected to be the local government equivalent of the 'movers' and 'shakers' often identified in the business literature as necessary change-makers (see, for example, Fogarty and Christie, 1990).

An increasingly powerful argument has been developed that points towards the need for effective leadership within local government, and is often expressed in calls for the development of convincing organizational visions and the identification of achievable missions. In practice this argument helps to undermine traditional divisions between the officer and member sides of local government, with an internal élite (sometimes involving elected as well as appointed officials) being defined as having strategic responsibility. In more general terms Metcalfe and Richards argue that, 'Management is not just an executive process separate from policy-making: effective public management requires strong links between policy-making and implementation. In the real world, there is no clear division between management and politics' (1990: 216–17). Although there are frequently still nods in the direction of the formal constitutional position which suggests that officers implement decisions made by councillors, in practice strategic management soon encourages rather different interpretations. One survey reported by

Isaac-Henry and Painter (1991) highlights the initiative taken by central officers in all the cases reviewed, and looking at particular cases reinforces this point. In the case of Kent, for example, it is clear that Sabin, as a new chief executive, played a major part in initiating change in the 1980s, deciding on strategic issues while allowing other chief officers to get on with their responsibility for the operational management of services (Sabin, 1990: 25; see also Holliday, 1991). Although Sabin's own formulation of the new relationship successfully retains a role for the leadership of elected local politicians, it is hard to escape the feeling that his own role is rather greater than to implement the decisions of his political masters. It is, he says, to help 'members to articulate their values and priorities and translate the leadership's perspective into the language of management' (Sabin, 1990: 27).

The arguments of the new strategic management are also arguments for a different notion of local government. Instead of a focus on democratic accountability through elections there is a shift to other forms of accountability through contracts and charters, which emphasizes a role for monitoring and regulation (see, for example, Alexander, 1991). Many councils have issued guarantees of service quality to those they variously describe as consumers, users or customers, often explicitly drawing on the arguments of popular management theorists such as Tom Peters to justify this focus (see, for example, the debate between Kerley, 1990, and Passmore, 1991). Some have been eager to take up the potential of citizen's charters by developing them at local level (Sellgren, 1992) and indeed a similar approach (with compensation being paid when agreed standards were not reached) was used by many councils even before the term was taken up by John Major and the Conservative government at national level. Others have placed stress on notions of quality assurance (see, for example, Hambleton and Hoggett, 1990; Davies and Hinton, 1993). At the same time there have been forms of decentralization, whether expressed in budgets or offices, bringing front-line workers closer to consumers in practice or rhetoric. As an alternative to democratic control through elections – or possibly in addition – use is increasingly made of the language of 'empowerment', as part of a process of encouraging communities and individuals to take an independent stance, giving a share of power to the public (Clarke and Stewart, 1992).

All of these approaches fit in with new managerial styles, because they imply a fragmentation of responsibility. Councils and their departments become responsible to different 'consumer' or 'user' groups and individuals in different ways, so that the same person may have multiple relationships with them. It is the task of strategic managers (and only them) to provide a framework within which those relationships can flourish, so that, although it is not their task to carry out the strategy, it is their task to build an organization capable of carrying it out (Stewart, 1992: 63). 'Strategic management', says Stewart (1992: 64), 'is best defined as changing the organization to enable it to meet changing need and to express changing values'. To a large extent, of course, such formulations continue to beg the question of who it is that will actually implement the strategy and how they will be expected to do so. There often seems to be a gap between the grand ambitions of the strategists and the rather narrower necessities (and priorities) of those with small or non-existent budgets who are responsible for delivering services in practice.

Conclusion

It is tempting simply to see the arguments of the late 1980s and the early 1990s as little more than a re-run of the debates over corporate management twenty years earlier. Doing so would have the great advantage of allowing us to dismiss all the academic and practitioner 'froth' about the new management, with the comment that we (or at any rate those of us over the age of 40) had seen it all before. The sound and fury which followed the Bains Report and was reflected in collections of case studies identifying best corporate practice, as well as in critical writing which saw corporate management as an attack on local democracy, ultimately amounted to nothing, or next to nothing. What makes it so different this time?

The key difference is that the emphasis on strategic management represents a response to significant changes in the organization and scope of local government that have been taking place alongside the emergence of new political arrangements at local level. It also represents a recognition that the possibility of stable long-term planning has gone; it has become a commonplace of the new world that the only thing which is predictable is that nothing is predictable. Strategic management offers a means of claiming a powerful place – or at any rate some role – in the enclosed network of relationships which is increasingly defining local politics. At best it suggests that strategic managers will be able to manage change, leading other agencies through networks in a complex process of negotiation; at worst it allows them a place at the table when powerful agencies are involved in determining how their communities will develop or how welfare services will be delivered.

The grander claims made for the new management cannot be taken at face value. Nor can it even be taken for granted that the agenda set by the strategic managers will dominate in any straightforward way, since the organizational world of the local welfare state includes a wide range of actors with different ideological starting points. The old professionals may be facing substantial challenges, but they retain a powerful position, still able to appeal to an alternative set of understandings and to negotiate settlements in a continuing war of position (as Langan and Clarke illustrate in their discussion of changes within social work, Chapter 4, this volume). Nor are all agencies within the voluntary sector transforming themselves into contracting organizations with quite the alacrity that might have been expected: many of them have distinctive self-images which cannot easily be subverted. Within the new approaches, too, the process of change is incomplete. The world of strategic management itself is in contention. What counts as 'strategic' is under debate everywhere, even before the nature of the strategy is open for discussion. Although it sometimes appears as if only the élite identified by Brooke has the right to influence strategy, there is still some scope for others to become involved because (possibly for the first time) strategies have to made explicit and may also, therefore, be challenged. This possibility is emphasized by the other side of the management rhetoric, because of the way in which it seeks to involve 'consumers', 'customers', 'users' and even 'citizens', as well as by the recognition that strategic management means working with and through others (who need to be persuaded or negotiated with).

The strongest expression of this tension between centrally determined strategy and the need to work with others probably emerges in discussions of 'empowerment'. This notion has a rather confused political and intellectual heritage. In the early 1980s, it was quite clearly associated with the 'left' and in local government with those authorities which came to be identified as 'loony left' or 'local socialist' (Gyford, 1985). The argument was that the old structures of the welfare state had been bureaucratic and hierarchical and had marginalized those who were defined as its clients (as part of a process of managing the poor in an increasingly unequal capitalism). 'Empowerment' was presented as a radical challenge to the status quo which would allow the previously marginalized to determine their own needs and to make their own claims to resources, no longer mediated through the rationing systems run by the welfare professionals. More recently the notion has been taken up within managerial discourse as a means of involving the new consumers in processes of service delivery or networks of influence, with less powerful groups licensed by more powerful ones to achieve particular ends. Jacobs, for example, looks to forms of corporate social responsibility as the base for the future, stressing the value of community empowerment as part of the 'social vision of the free market' (Jacobs, 1992: 217) alongside the rise of non-profit organizations. In exploring what he calls 'initiatives beyond charity' Jacobs looks to the possibility of private sector based agencies negotiating with local – neighbourhood level – communities. This focus on politics below the level of the city implies the breaking up of existing institutions of local (city) government, to the extent that Jacobs concludes with the warning that they may 'be seen as an obsolete way of organising human activity' (1992: 263).

Clarke and Stewart take a rather different approach, from within local government, but also emphasize that there may be different models of empowerment, depending on whether the person being 'empowered' is defined as 'customer' (in which case the emphasis will be on individual choice through quasi-markets); 'citizen' (in which case the emphasis will be on rights); or 'community' (in which case the emphasis will be on new forms of democratic arrangement). Although their sympathies seem to lie with the notion of self-governing communities, since a 'local authority as the community governing itself empowers the community and those who live and work within it' (1992: 22), Clarke and Stewart argue that a balance between the different models is required in practice, in what they describe as a pluralistic approach, not least because 'actions which empower some may disempower others' (1992: 24). In this context it becomes necessary to move beyond managerialism, to emphasize the role of local government as that of community government, in ways which are not merely strategic in the usual sense, but recognized as political so that they involve campaigning as well as managing and – above all – set out to rediscover (or build) a representative role for local governments which allows them to build on notions of democratic accountability, instead of encouraging it to be lost in the increasingly confusing networks of inter-agency working, pragmatic bargaining, partnerships and appointed boards.

Sometimes in reading the literature on strategic management in local government it is easy to forget the constraints under which councils are operating and easy to believe that they are the only agencies with any local legitimacy. It is easy to forget that budgets are declining alongside direct service responsibility. But it can no longer be taken for granted that elected authorities will retain a leading role at local level. Other agencies – ranging from training and enterprise councils and public–private partnerships to housing associations and health authorities of various sorts – are already making claims to strategic responsibility. And one consequence of declining budgets (and the increased earmarking of budgets for particular uses, such as housing benefit or locally managed schools) is that councils do not always have the financial leverage to influence others effectively. Even the issuing of contracts to other bodies for the delivery of specified services may be a double-edged process, with councils trapped in longer-term contracts required to pay substantial sums to escape or modify them. The rise of nationally based and multinational organizations in some areas of service delivery is already making the negotiation of contracts less of a 'competitive' activity, since contractors will only submit bids on terms which they are prepared to accept. At the other end of the scale, management buy-outs and direct service organizations imply continued close relationships which may sometimes even slip into corruption (Paddon, 1991: 43–4). There is a danger that instead of a new 'pluralism' based on a vibrant voluntary sector, with which partnerships can be developed, there will be a growth of large not-for-profit organizations which are effectively indistinguishable from large private sector bureaucracies (see, for example, Gutch, 1992).

In this context, therefore, the need to move beyond the private sector model becomes increasingly clear. Stewart argues strongly that public sector management needs to be more explicitly grounded in values (including a commitment to equity) and to recognize the possibility of conflicting values. He argues for approaches to management which clarify political choices and are able to learn from political protest, particularly because managers have the task of rationing scarce resources. Stewart emphasizes that it is difficult to get adequate accounting measures of success or failure and instead suggests that it is necessary to take a broader view which seeks to assess costs and benefits to communities (Stewart, 1992: 38; see also Flynn, 1990: 181–6). A more realistic understanding of the scope for strategic management in local government implies the acknowledgement that councils have to bargain and negotiate with others to achieve their ends, and that the agenda on which they have to negotiate will not always be under their control. At local level individual councils will not always even be first among equals in terms of policy development.

They still, however, have a role unlike that of the other agencies with which they have to work, because they alone can make claims to representing local communities through the process of electoral account-ability. The issue of accountability is one which runs through the changes we have been discussing in this chapter, because the new forms of management also suggest changing forms of accountability. Unfortunately, from the point of view of a democratic polity, the complex pattern which is emerging often makes it more difficult to follow through the strands of accountability for particular decisions. It is increasingly difficult to determine quite who (or which organization) is responsible for taking which decisions. One way of dealing with this has been to transform the notion of accountability into a technical or financial process, in which effective auditing ensures that accusations of corruption can be avoided and provider agencies can point to their success in meeting their contractual obligations. But this is a narrow and unhelpful way of considering the choices which have to be made within the local welfare state. It is here that local government may continue to have an important role if it is prepared to take it on, as political lightning conductor for local communities, ready to speak on their behalf and to ensure that the increasing opacity of decision making is opened up to scrutiny and political debate. The new world is one which emphasizes diversity among groups, consumers, users and customers and sets out to manage this. An alternative vision might give local government the role of encouraging groups to come together in ways which make *managing* them more difficult, but empower them to build on their particular ambitions to clarify shared objectives at community level.

Note

1. This is a particularly forceful expression of the argument for an enabling authority. It is, perhaps, worth pointing out that the role accorded to elected local government using apparently similar terms may be quite varied. Some would define it in relatively passive terms (in that councils simply 'enable' other agencies to do the work through market-style arrangements and contracting), while others may use it to make claims to 'strategic' responsibility wherever no other agency has explicitly defined responsibility. Even in a world in which the language used is similar, the precise interpretation may remain in contention and outcomes may vary significantly between authorities, organizations and places.

References

Adam Smith Institute (1989) *Wiser Counsels. The Reform of Local Government*. London: Adam Smith Institute.

Alexander, A. (1991) 'Managing fragmentation – democracy, accountability and the future of local government', *Local Government Studies*, 17(6): 63–76.

Audit Commission (1988) *The Competitive Council*, Management Paper No. 1. London: HMSO.

Audit Commission (1989) *Losing an Empire, Finding a Role*. London: HMSO.

Bains Report (1972) *The New Local Authorities: Management and Structure. Report of the Study Group on Local Authority Management Structures*. London: HMSO.

Benington, J. (1976) *Local Government Becomes Big Business*. London: Community Development Project.

Bennett, R.J. and Krebs, G. (1991) *Local Economic Development: Public–Private Partnership Initiation in Britain and Germany*. London: Belhaven Press.

Brooke, R. (1989a) 'The enabling authority – practical consequences', *Local Government Studies*, 15(5): 55–63.

Brooke, R. (1989b) *Managing the Enabling Authority*. Harlow: Longman.

Buckland, Y. and Joshua, H. (1992) 'Nottingham into the 1990s – managing change in a District Council', *Public Money and Management*, 12(3): 21–5.

Bulpitt, J. (1989) 'Walking back to happiness? Conservative Party governments and elected local authorities in the 1980s', in C. Crouch and D. Marquand (eds), *The New Centralism. Britain out of Step in Europe?* Oxford: The Political Quarterly/Blackwell.

Butt, H. and Palmer, R. (1985) *Value for Money in the Public Sector. The Decision Maker's Guide*. Oxford: Basil Blackwell.

Clapham, D. (1983) 'Corporate planning and the cuts', *Local Government Policy-Making*, July: 28–33.'

Clapham, D. (1984) 'Rational planning of politics: the example of local authority corporate planning', *Policy and Politics*, 12(1): 31–52.

Clapham, D. (1985) 'Management of the local state: the example of corporate planning', *Critical Social Policy*, 14: 27–42.

Clarke, M. and Stewart, J. (1992) 'Empowerment: a theme for the 1990s', *Local Government Studies*, 18(2): 18–26.

Cochrane, A. (1993a) 'From financial control to strategic management: the changing faces of accountability in British local government', *Accounting, Auditing and Accountability Journal*, 6(3): 31–52.

Cochrane, A. (1993b) *Whatever Happened to Local Government?* Buckingham: Open University Press.

Cockburn, C. (1977) *The Local State. The Management of Cities and People*. London: Pluto.

Collinge, C. (1992) *The Development of State Systems. Accumulation, Territory and Organisational Form*. Cranfield: Dissertation submitted for the award of M. Phil in the School of Management, Cranfield Institute of Technology.

Davies, K. and Hinton, P. (1993) 'Managing quality in local government and the health service', *Public Money and Management*, 13(1): 51–4.

Dearlove, J. (1979) *The Reorganisation of Local Government: Old Orthodoxies and a Political Perspective*. Cambridge: Cambridge University Press.

du Gay, P. and Salaman, G. (1992) 'The cult[ure] of the customer', *Journal of Management Studies*, 29(5): 615–33.

Elcock, H. and Jordan, G. (eds) (1987) *Learning from Local Authority Budgeting*. Aldershot: Avebury.

Elcock, H., Jordan, G., Midwinter, A. with Boyne, G. (1989) *Budgeting in Local Government Managing the Margins*. Harlow: Longman.

Finer, H. (1950) *English Local Government*, 4th edn. London: Methuen.

Flynn, N. (1990) *Public Sector Management*. Hemel Hempstead: Harvester Wheatsheaf.

Fogarty, M. and Christie, I. (1990) *Companies and Communities Promoting Business Involvement in the City*. London: Policy Studies Institute.

Friend, J. and Jessop, W. (1960) *Local Government and Strategic Choice. An Operational Research Approach to the Processes of Public Planning*. London: Tavistock.

Game, C. (1987) 'Birmingham City Council', in H. Elcock and G. Jordan (eds), *Learning from Local Authority Budgeting*. Aldershot: Avebury.

Greenwood, R. (1983) 'Changing patterns of budgeting in English local government', *Public Administration*, 61(2): 149–68.

Greenwood, R. and Lomer, M. (1980) *The Local Impact of Central Financial Institutions*. London: End of Award Report to Social Science Research Council. HR 5600.

Greenwood, R. and Stewart, J. (1974) *Corporate Planning in English Local Government*. London: Charles Knight.

Greenwood, R., Hinings, C., Ranson, S. and Walsh, K. (1976) *Pursuit of Corporate Rationality: Organisational Developments in the Post Reorganisation Period*. Birmingham: INLOGOV, University of Birmingham.

Gutch, R. (1992) *Contracting: Lessons from the US*. London: NCVO Publications.

Gyford, J. (1985) *The Politics of Local Socialism*. London: Allen & Unwin.

Halford, S. (1993) 'Feminist change in a patriarchal organization: the experience of women's initiatives in local government and implications for feminist perspectives on state institutions', in M. Savage and A. Witz (eds), *Gender and Bureaucracy*. Oxford: Blackwell.

Hambleton, R. and Hoggett, P. (1990) *Beyond Excellence: Quality Local Government in the 1990s*, Working paper 85. Bristol: School for Advanced Urban Studies.

Handy, C. (1989) *The Age of Unreason*. London: Business Books.

Hoggett, P. (1991) A new management in the public sector? *Policy and Politics*, 19(4): 243–56.

Holliday, I. (1991) 'The conditions of local change: Kent County Council since reorganisation', *Public Administration*, 69(4): 441–57.

Humphrey, C. and Pease, K. (1991) 'After the rainbow', *Local Government Studies*, 17(4): 1–5.

Humphrey, C. and Scapens, R. (1992) 'Whatever happened to the liontamers? An examination of accounting change in the public sector', *Local Government Studies*, 18(3): 141–7.

Isaac-Henry, K. and Painter, C. (1991) 'The management challenge in local government – emerging themes and trends', *Local Government Studies*, 17(3): 69–90.

Jacobs, B.D. (1992) *Fractured Cities. Capitalism, Community and Empowerment in Britain and America*. London: Routledge.

Jordan, G. (1987) 'Introduction. Budgeting: changing expectations', in H. Elcock and G. Jordan (eds), *Learning from Local Authority Budgeting*. Aldershot: Avebury.

Keith-Lucas, B. and Richard, P. (1978) *A History of Local Government in the Twentieth Century*. London: Allen & Unwin.

Kerley, R. (1990) 'In search of the customer', *Local Government Policy-Making*, 17(2): 7–13.

Kogan, M. and van der Eyken, W. (1973) *County Hall. The Role of the Chief Education Officer*. Harmondsworth: Penguin.

Loader, B. and Burrows, R. (eds) (1994) *Towards a Post-Fordist Welfare State?* London: Routledge.

McSweeney, B. (1988) 'Accounting for the Audit Commission', *Political Quarterly*, 59(1): 28–43.

Metcalfe, L. and Richards, S. (1990) *Improving Public Management*, 2nd edn. London: Sage.

Mintzberg, H. (1983) *Structure in Fives: Designing Effective Organizations*. Englewood Cliffs, NJ: Prentice-Hall.

Moss Kanter, R. (1984) *The Change Masters: Corporate Entrepreneurs at Work*. London: Unwin Hyman.

Osborne, D. and Gaebler, T. (1992) *Reinventing Government. How the Entrepreneurial Spirit is Transforming the Public Sector*. Reading, MA: Addison Wesley.

Paddon, M. (1991) 'Management buy-outs and compulsory competition in local government', *Local Government Studies*, 17(3): 27–52.

Passmore, J. (1991) 'A passion for customers', *Local Government Policy-Making*, 18(2): 50–5.

Pendelbury, M. (1985) *Management Accounting in Local Government. A Research Study*. London: Institute of Cost and Management Accountants.

Peters, T. (1988) *Thriving on Chaos. Handbook for a Management Revolution*. London: Macmillan.

Peters, T. and Waterman, P. (1982) *In Search of Excellence. Lessons from America's Best-Run Companies*. New York: Harper & Row.

Piore, C. and Sabel, P. (1984) *The Second Industrial Divide*. New York: Basic Books.

162 *Managing social policy*

Pollitt, C. (1990) *Managerialism and the Public Services. The Anglo-American Experience.* Oxford: Blackwell.

Reade, E. (1987) *British Town and Country Planning.* Milton Keynes: Open University Press.

Rhodes, R. (1985) 'A squalid and politically corrupt process'? Intergovernmental relations in the post-war period', *Local Government Studies,* 11(6): 35–57.

Rhodes, R. (1988) *Beyond Westminster and Whitehall: Sub-Central Governments of Britain.* London: Unwin Hyman.

Robson, W. (1954) *The Development of Local Government,* 3rd edn. London: Allen & Unwin.

Rosenberg, D. (1989) *Accounting for Public Policy. Power, Professionals and Politics in Local Government.* Manchester, Manchester University Press.

Sabin, P. (1990) 'The role of the chief executive in Kent County Council', *Local Government Policy-Making.* 17(1): 24–8.

Sellgren, J. (1992) 'The Hertfordshire Citizen's Charter: a charter for a million people', *Local Government Policy-Making,* 19(2): 22–8.

Stewart, J. (1974) *The Responsive Local Authority.* London: Charles Knight.

Stewart, J. (1992) 'Guidelines for public service management: lessons not to be learned from the private sector', in P. Carter, T. Jeffs and M. Smith (eds), *Changing Social Work and Welfare.* Buckingham: Open University Press.

8

Leisure and the New Managerialism

Alan Clarke

Managerialism has become the touchstone of policy change in the 1980s and 1990s with every new challenge and change being warranted by its contribution to the more effective, more streamlined and more responsive delivery of services. This has cut across all areas of leisure but can be well documented in the elaborate process which has transformed the Arts Council into more of an 'organization for the 90s'. We have seen the restructuring of the Arts Council's own committees, the reorganization of its regions and the development of a National Arts and Media Strategy paper with its vision, mission and the performance measures. This process could stand as an allegory for what has been happening to the whole of the leisure services. However, the moral of the allegory is not to be found in any of the tangible phenomena, such as the streamlined organizational flow chart or the plethora of policy papers, but in the fundamental shift in the values which have driven the process. The full impact of managerialism for leisure, as with other services, is in the changes which it has wrought to the value system which informs the leisure services. This chapter will seek to demonstrate the form that those changes have taken and the effect that has been produced through the introduction of this managerialist orthodoxy into leisure.

There is both a mixed economy in the provision of leisure and in the types of leisure provided within the different sectors. This has helped to make leisure a very volatile field and one which is very receptive to new ideas as it seeks to establish itself as a distinct field of operation. The traditional distinctions between public, private and voluntary sectors do help to spell out the different approaches which have guided the development of provision into the 1980s. We are told that the private sector provides services for a market that can create a demand which produces a profit for the provider. The voluntary or non-profit sector is organized around enthusiasms and the mutual supply and demand for activities. The public sector has been far more concerned with the provision of facilities, rather than services and is a major provider of facilities for the other sectors to make use of – either as participants or as providers of the means of participation.[1] This was recognized by the Yates Report into leisure management which observed:

> Many other interests, voluntary, private, commercial and public have played their
> part in the development and management of facilities for sport and outdoor

recreation, but the main burden of capital investment in purpose-built sports facilities for sport and recreation has been borne by local government. (Yates, 1984: 5)

However this sectoral view is far too simplistic to capture the increasing number of partnerships and interlocking interests. Leisure services are often neglected in the accounts of social welfare provision and no doubt there will have been some puzzlement at their inclusion within this collection. There is a popular view that leisure is no more than a marginal set of activities which are not essential to our lives and, as a result, leisure services are regularly dismissed as not being as important as the 'real' social services such as health, housing, education and social care. Evidence of this marginality can even be drawn from the non-statutory nature of the public services provided. Libraries are the only leisure service which local authorities are obliged to provide and this clearly embodies one of the logics which has been used to underpin leisure services. There has been a strong social welfare ethic and an educational logic rather than any form of leisure ethic which helped to establish the nature of the leisure services provided by the public sector. It is also possible to point to the public provision of leisure as a form of compensation, particularly for disadvantaged groups within society.

This is most noticeable if we turn to the historical origins of the public sector's involvement in leisure. Public provision can be traced back to the period of rapid urbanization which brought together large concentrations of people for the first time within towns and cities. It was also this process of urbanization which saw pressure on the amount and use of the open spaces. The public health arguments were reinforced by claims that the popular pastimes of the working classes were demoralizing the population and that they therefore needed to be controlled. The negative controls introduced included the regulation of public space and the licensing of such activities as drinking, music making and gathering on the streets (Clarke and Critcher, 1985).

Alongside such regulation were proposals for more constructive uses of leisure time, where the emphasis was on the production of 'acceptable' leisure forms. It was here that the new local authorities discovered their role and their ability to make use of permissive legislation to develop much of the recreational infrastructure which we know today. This produced a notion of leisure provision which contributes to a sense of improvement, both social and personal. Parks, playing fields, swimming pools and sports halls were developed alongside museums and libraries to provide opportunities for the urban working classes to better themselves. The alternatives of drinking, gambling and brutalizing sports were condemned and either outlawed entirely, as with bare-knuckle fighting, cock fighting and bear baiting for example, or controlled by statutory licence, determining drinking hours and when and where performances of various kinds could take place. The drive behind this was a moral imperative, founded on the desire to avoid the revolutions in France and America and on the notion that the best workers were those who developed themselves away from their place of work with some rational forms of recreation (Bailey, 1979).

The ideals of the rational recreation movement developed beyond the public sector as they were heavily influenced by voluntary groups, by concerned civic elders and by the leaders of the churches. There is an interesting history to be written documenting the many different facets of this drive towards rational recreation. However, there were strong linkages between those who advocated a religious rationale and those who proposed a more earthly concern for the social order. The religious principles were clear. By adapting the Protestant work ethic to leisure time and finding meaningful sporting activities to complement the spiritual development undertaken in church, temple and Sunday school it was thought to be possible to develop the proper values in the whole person. Sometimes referred to as 'muscular Christianity', this ethos echoed throughout the nineteenth century, especially where leisure and young people were brought together. Similar messages came from the playing fields of the public schools, the Boy Scout movement and the employers themselves, who promoted workplace sports and social clubs for their employees.

The development of many forms of leisure provision in the United Kingdom is unusual in many respects as the broad patterns of that development have been led by the public rather than the private sector.[2] It has been based on a rationale which has been appropriately described as 'recreational welfare' (Coalter et al., 1988). Coalter (1990) has usefully summarized the key points which the study identified as the elements in the recreational welfare policy for public leisure:

- Urban deprivation: A belief that recreation provision could contribute to the quality of life in urban environments.
- Physical health: This was related to the problems of urban deprivation and a concern for the health and productivity of the workforce. However on occasions, such as the aftermath of the Boer War, there was a more widespread concern with the 'health of the nation', and its fitness to fight.
- Moral welfare: A concern with the content of working-class leisure, symbolised by the campaigns against the pub and alcohol.
- Social integration, social control and 'community': 'Public' space and 'public' facilities could be used to establish a socially integrative, civic culture transcending social and economic inequalities and counteracting tendencies toward social fragmentation. This was based on an ethos of 'participation' which has remained a constant theme in public policy. Participation is viewed as confirmation of a broader social consensus.
- Self-improvement: The emphasis on physical and moral health and socially integrative recreation, mixed with a strain of puritanism, meant that an ideology of self-improvement dominated public policy and provision.
- Limits of public provision: Despite political rhetoric, there was a marked reluctance to become more directly involved in leisure provision. While the state set the outer limits of leisure behaviour and morality, through prescriptive legislation and licensing, the development of leisure policy

was left to the permissive powers of local government, voluntary effort and the commercial sector. (Coalter, 1990: 8)

The concerns for social order are bound up in the arguments which saw the introduction of policing and the control of public gatherings. Leisure was to be a series of orderly activities, helping the working classes to achieve respectability within a changing society. The linking of health, cleanliness and exercise sums up this desire and can still be seen in areas where the redevelopers have not yet removed the old 'public baths'. These buildings would often contain three separate 'recreational welfare' purposes underneath a single roof – the slipper baths would offer personal cleanliness, the swimming baths exercise, and alongside these the public laundry would offer the promise of external cleanliness to encapsulate the other two (Clarke, 1992).

The development of the public, private and voluntary sectors of the leisure industry has produced a mixed economy which recognizes very sharp differences between specialist interests. This complexity within the industry created an operational divide, sometimes more symbolic than real but nonetheless powerful for all that, between managers in the private sector and managers in the public sector. The value system which developed amongst public sector managers was focused on the local users of the service. John Benington has summarized this view and observed that public sector leisure managers believed that:

> Leisure is an integral part of living a full and rounded life. Leisure must not be seen therefore as an appendage in the context of local authority service – indeed, it is being increasingly regarded as a respectable and essential service. Leisure provision is resource intensive – return is measured not so much at the box office as in the physical and mental well being of the individual user and of the community at large. (Benington, 1988: 259)

There is therefore an odd dualism to be found in the approaches to public sector leisure which combine freedom and facilitation with control and coercion. This can most readily be seen if the leisure services are treated in the same way as other services and set in the wider social context. The local authorities' earliest interventions into leisure promised a veritable cornucopia of opportunities to the urban populations. Museums were created which included treasures not only of local history but of national importance and colonial significance. Libraries were filled with literature which promised the joys of the classical novelists and dramatists alongside the latest information about scientific and technical discoveries. Even such routine offerings as a reading room where the newspapers could be consulted should not be underestimated, given that this was the first major creation of such public access to topical information. It was possible to promenade in the newly landscaped parks or on the piers at the seaside. Games which had recently been codified were made possible by the designation of playing fields with the appropriate goalposts. The early twentieth century was a time for expansion and development. At the same time it was a period of increasing control over the leisure time, habits and occupations of the working classes. Pastimes which had once been popular were now outlawed and the energies channelled towards the new regime of acceptable activities. Nor should it be thought that this is solely a feature of the distant past as one of the Sports Council's major initiatives owes everything to this dualism. Action Sport was conceived as a project to take sports to young people in inner city areas, with mobile sports equipment and peripatetic development workers. This opportunity was modelled on pioneering work in South Yorkshire but only received full support, and a sizeable injection of government funds, when Lord Scarman recommended such schemes in his report on the inner-city riots of 1981.

This is clearly a problematic which affects many forms of social welfare but it is particularly sharply drawn with leisure, given the belief that leisure is the part of people's lives where they can exert the greatest control over their choices. It is the central tension which has guided the development of the leisure professional, coming to see the role of management and planning as being one of meeting the needs of local people and of particular interest groups within a notion of the local population. The people became the beneficiaries of facilities and provision, despite the fact that the range of provision may not have matched what the people would have chosen for themselves if they had not been subject to the controls of their new environment. There are problems for those who would attempt to justify the types of provision which have been developed, for little work has been undertaken on actually discovering the leisure needs of the local populations. We have seen a form of beneficient paternalism produce an epidemic of sports centres and, more recently, leisure pools with flumes and whirlpools, but we have not seen consultation with local people to identify their needs for these facilities. There are other reasons for providing ever-grander leisure pools as they contribute to civic pride and help to recover greater amounts of the subsidy per swim than other pools, but whether they meet leisure needs remains an unanswered question.

The local authorities became major direct providers of leisure facilities. As we have already shown, the original remit did not limit itself only to sporting pastimes but addressed a whole range of leisure activities. By the early 1890s, local authorities were providing a range of services which contained elements of the ideology of social improvement as well as elements of the Fabian discourse of public professionalism. These elements combined in a series of rationales for public sector involvement ranging from the need to control the working classes, through the need to provide avenues for self-improvement, to the need to provide meaningful leisure facilities. The definitions of need play an important part in shaping the role and nature of public sector leisure provision. It was conceived and developed as a response to social need, defined either from the desire for social control by the state or a recognition of the public good created by leisure, but certainly not as a response to demand. The issues of disadvantage and of access were central to the formation of public sector leisure. It was always a targeted service, although the motivation for the targeting obviously requires further exploration.

Services were run on the basis of 'need', as defined by the leisure and recreation officers. It was a classical example of the role of Fabian professionals defining the parameters of the public service. The idea that they were thought to be sheltered from the harsher realities of the commercial sector and the need to produce a 'bottom line' profit continued well into the 1980s. The most dramatic representation of this divided image of leisure managers came with the creation of the two journals which still dominate the field. The *Leisure Manager*, the house journal of the Institute of Leisure and Amenities Management, defined a niche around public service development and issues around the changing roles of local authority leisure officers. It was here, for example, that the debates about single-function departments – such as sport, recreation, arts, museums and libraries – merging into single multi-purpose Leisure Departments was conducted. The other key journal which emerged was *Leisure Management* which saw itself addressing the concerns of the private sector managers, featuring interviews with successful entrepreneurs from the leisure industry thus providing role models and examples of good practice for the new generation of leisure managers. These different approaches were more than just market positioning. They embodied two very different views of the world of leisure service delivery and development. This is still evident in the two journals in the 1990s with the different examples taken to illustrate particular themes, but the themes themselves are growing closer together. The rest of the chapter will consider those themes and the conversion of recreational welfare into leisure managerialism.

Professionalism: the new respectability

The first issue which we need to address is the professionalization of leisure services, as the way in which the profession has been defined has serious consequences for the models of management which have been introduced. The leisure profession has developed along lines very similar to those suggested by Etzioni in the research on emerging professions. The formation of the Institute of Leisure and Amenities Management (ILAM) in 1977 is generally recognized as the foundation of the profession as it brought together many smaller institutes and associations under its more generic umbrella. However, the key factor was not that the terms of reference became more embracing, but that they clearly focused on aspects of professional development of management. The role ILAM defined for itself was to act as a spokesperson for leisure managers and it therefore pulled away from the narrow subject specialisms of the previous institutions. It was, of course, still concerned with horticulture, arboriculture and high culture but it was primarily a lead body for an integrated service. This allowed it to develop as a complement rather than as a rival to the groups within these specialized areas, such as librarians and museum curators.

The basis for the profession was taken to be the common ground which was emerging around leisure and focused on the concept of 'management'.

The skills which were necessary to be a successful librarian, museum keeper, sports centre manager were seen to have a common core, and this point of commonality could bring people together into one organization. However, it was also stressed that the skills were specific to leisure and not simply management skills but leisure management skills, otherwise leisure professionals could join the formal management groupings. It was the beginning of the managerialist revolution in leisure. As Benington observes in his review of the leisure services profession:

> The key aims of the profession were also not totally agreed on. They varied from a desire 'to supply as much leisure provision as possible within the finances of the Council, and to assist and encourage provision by the commercial and voluntary sector' to . . . 'to be cost effective: to ensure value for money and the highest quality of life for *all* sectors of the community. (Benington, 1988: 259)

The survey for the Future of Leisure Services project also gathered comments on management training and 'those who did [reply] were unanimous: managers in the leisure service in the next two decades will have to be more astute, more business minded and far better trained' (Benington, 1989: 260) The training ILAM has provided has been geared to meeting this perceived demand for management skills to fit leisure professionals to their new environment. It is training which is best summed up in the course ILAM run regularly called 'Finances for non-financial managers' as this encapsulates the key concerns for the new managers.

There is more than a semantic difference involved in this shift, for inherent in the development is a redefinition of the rationale for the service. This is most clearly seen if we examine the way the concept of leisure need has been recast. This is not simply as a result of the 'professionalization' of leisure but has emerged as the product of many social forces, not least the introduction of a dominant form of individualism. However, as we shall demonstrate, the profession played a key role in this redefinition. Leisure need has been the subject of much debate but there appear to be three key phases. The first was an imposition of need from expert nutritionists, health specialists and moral guardians. These needs were created by social leaders in order to ensure that the workforce was fit and healthy enough to win the battle against foreign competition, either in times of war or in international trade (Evans, 1974). However, this created an area of operation which was explored by local authority officers subscribing to a Fabian ideology. These people produced initiatives based on their professional definitions of normative and comparative need and much work still continues to fulfil this programme.

What any particular authority actually provided depended on what their formal responsibilities were, with differences being created between County and District councils, the particular characteristics of the local population and the political and professional inclinations of the authorities. In many respects it is precisely this diversity which characterizes the second phase and which produced the calls for greater management of the services across the United Kingdom, as local leisure officers were seen to be serving their own interests and building their own empires rather than meeting the needs of the public or fulfilling the core role of the local authority.

This area of discretion proved to be a fertile ground for the critics of the excesses of local authorities. Within this body of critics, the Audit Commission's role cannot be underestimated in this transformation. The notion of introducing the three Es within the culture of local authorities clearly affected all the services. It was of great relevance to leisure, which was built so firmly on the often forgotten fourth E of equity, because the concepts of economy, efficiency and effectiveness can so easily be applied to leisure in a simplistic and formalistic way. Calculations of economy will vary depending upon the nature of the facility, with, for example, heating costs rising along with the roof space. If you want to provide a multi-purpose sports hall, there is a requirement to provide some head room for badminton and volleyball players. However if you want to provide a competition venue for these sports, the requirements become more explicit and if the competition is going to extend to international challenges then the requirements become mandatory. This then leaves a local authority with an international competition facility which used for the majority of the time as a local sports hall but is uneconomical when compared with a hall that is only ever used for non-competitive games. The Audit Commission remain unconvinced that it was necessary for local authorities to provide international competition venues and this put further pressure on those authorities who had already made such provision (Audit Commission, 1989).

However, the need which drives the current generation of providers, in what can be seen as the third phase of development, is the concern to hold their performance within the financial provision of their bottom line. Service delivery has become cost-centred and cost-driven. Finance has indeed become the concern for all managers, non-financial and financial. Even traditional areas of provision such as parks and open spaces have become subject to these financial calculations, with studies seeking to locate cost centres for aspects of public open space (Henley Centre for Forecasting, 1986). This leads to the technicist's utopia, with a scenario of charging the costs of sports pitches separately from the open space within the park and opening up long technical arguments about how much space is needed alongside the actual pitch before the pitch becomes unplayable. Such space is unproductive but still bears the full costs of maintenance and upkeep (Audit Commission, 1988). What has been forcefully highlighted throughout the Audit Commission's work on leisure is that 'few authorities attempt to examine performance in the ways suggested in the Commission's recent publication on performance review, or to compare net expenditure with usage. . . . Overall many authorities do not therefore know what they are achieving with the money they spend.' They conclude: 'It is disappointing that many of the problems described in this Chapter are identical to those found in 1983. These management deficiencies have to be addressed before authorities can adequately respond to the challenges they face' (Audit Commission, 1989: 11–12).

There is a recognition in some of the Audit Commission's writings that public services do have a role beyond cost efficiency, but their proposals always reduce the monitoring and the evaluation of the service to the readily quantifiable areas of economy and efficiency.

CCT: love me tender

As the position of local authorities as direct providers came under increasing criticism, it may have seemed obvious to address these criticisms to an area of provision which was not only discretionary but dealt with a part of people's lives which they could easily, in individualist terms, take control of for themselves. However, leisure was not so obvious as it was largely overlooked in the early discussions of privatization. This may have been partly due to the number of central government departments which were responsible for some but not all aspects of leisure services. As it was, grounds maintenance was included in the drafting of the 1988 Local Government Act, but sports management was only included as an after-thought and became part of the Act following a separate amendment to the original proposed legislation.

This Act provides for the compulsory competitive tendering (CCT) of the management of sports facilities. The legislation is quite clear that it concerns only the management contracts for the running of the buildings and not the sale or transfer of the facilities themselves. The assets remain with the local authority as do the liabilities for the long-term upkeep of the premises. The Act came at a time when the massive infrastructure building programme had peaked. The increase in the building of sports halls serves as an indicator of the effort which was made to promote the facilities during the 1970s and 1980s. This has now slowed to almost zero, with a few spectacular exceptions to prove the rule.[3] What has emerged as a key concern to leisure providers is the cost of maintaining all the buildings that were constructed in the golden period of expansion but which will become increasingly difficult to maintain in a period when local authority resources are being cut and stretched in other directions (Sports Council, 1992).

What the 1988 Act has done is to focus attention on the management of leisure services and forced local authorities to review their procedures. Some commentators have suggested that the managerial changes are due solely to the introduction of CCT. However, this ignores the other measures that have cut across local service delivery, and therefore across leisure, which presaged the introduction of contracting. Leisure services have been directly affected by changes in the nature and level of funding available to local authorities and to departments within those authorities, the reorganiz-ation of education at both school and college level, specifically the changing responsibility for dual-use centres, and the creation of internal markets within authorities. All have added to the pressures on senior officers to review leisure services.

The process of CCT has been important as it has produced a crystalliz-ation of the managerialism of leisure. The two principal parts of CCT are the contract specification and the bifurcation of functions between a contractor and a client. The specification of the contract has become a highly technicist procedure with the definition of the local authority service being drawn in to a tightly worded and binding definition. This has involved a fundamental review of the services provided by local authorities within the facilities they have developed. There has been a degree of flexibility built into the leisure provision in the UK by the very nature of the buildings which have been designed to house the activities. This multi-functioning within a building has been criticized because it prevents the development of specialist facilities, but it does promote usage of the building by varied groups of the public. The buildings do not become the possession of one particular group of enthusiasts, they remain truly public (Clarke, 1991). However, there is a cost to be borne for this diversity of programming as the flexibility of programming necessarily means that some activities will be more and some less popular than others, attract different social groupings and take different amounts of time. Some will remain popular over a long number of years whilst others may fade. This means that local authorities are not maximizing the benefits of the space. They are forced by their belief in meeting local need to act in a sub-optimal way when the use of the space is judged in terms of income generation and through-put.

The mission

CCT has forced local authorities to address the issue of what their leisure services have been attempting to do and to clarify more precisely the aims and objectives of the service. What facilities should they provide, who should be using those facilities and what services do they want when they are there? What are the target groups the authority is trying to reach and, having decided that, how should they be reached? There was also a need to think through the pricing policies adopted by the local authorities. This thinking process looks familiar to those who have studied any of the new managerial texts because we are in search of a mission, a statement of strategy and clear objectives. The challenge is that the review process is not a neutral review. The terminology, the criteria and the tests are alien to the conception of recreational welfare, being more concerned with the strategic management of the business organization rather than the equity of the process involved in the development of the services. The sense of missionary zeal which inspired many early developments has been excommunicated from the body of the new leisure orthodoxy.

What is being offered as the new vision for leisure departments owes more to the study of Victorian entrepreneurship than to the recognition of social need. Leisure services are identifying themselves through a new language of niche markets, customer-centred responsiveness and income generation. The missionary zeal now produces messages aimed at obtaining corporate sponsorship and benefits are expressed in itemized lists of personal advantages. The vision is now focused on individual cost centres and individual users with the result that the horizon of the quality of life has been lost in the mists of commercial targets.

Many observers have described how the formal process of auditing has been helpful to local authorities in forcing them to formalize the aims and objectives of their service delivery (Tomlinson and Parker, 1992). There can certainly be great benefit in a review process but this implies that the review is neutral, whereas the CCT process imposes a review which is value laden. It is also worth noting that those values are not those of the local authority leisure professional. They have been put in place by following the Audit Commission guidelines on addressing management problems and a central government committed to demonstrating that local services have been unwieldy, over-paid and inefficient. It has therefore been claimed that the first round of CCT will save money (Knox, 1992). This prospect can hardly be disputed as the tenders will only be let to the lowest priced tender.

It may be thought that this is an overly cynical view of the tendering process as there are opportunities to write social clauses into the contract and make rigorous specifications which remain within the legal definitions of not being anti-competitive. Contracts will only be let to those contractors demonstrating that they can meet all the requirements of the tender but it is clear that different authorities have taken different views on what the term 'meeting the terms of the contract' actually means. There are authorities who have let contracts on a minimal agreement basis, whilst others have been accused of anti-competitive behaviour because they have sought to guarantee the existing service. It was also argued that the contractors had the right to specify opening times, programming policy and pricing but the CELTS research showed that almost half of all the authorities had not specified fixed criteria in this social policy area (CELTS, 1992). The lack of such criteria means that the monitoring process becomes less rigorous as there are few standards against which to monitor.

One of the greatest concerns is that the contracts will deny the space which has been created for work with disadvantaged groups within the local areas. This is often criticized as tokenism, but development officers have contributed a great deal to the opportunities of such groups. The Sports Council and the Arts Council have both worked with the notion of target groups throughout the 1980s. These were sections of the population who had been identified as participating in various sporting or artistic forms at levels which were lower than the national average.[4] These groups had been identified for social reasons and programming was encouraged which allowed them to develop their potential for participation. It is clear that the groups selected – ethnic groupings, the young, women, the over-50s – were chosen for a reason and this process of targeting demonstrated the lasting effectiveness of a Fabian approach to recreational welfare.

However, these target groups contain those social groups who are least able to enter any economic market and who are least able to pay. What we have seen with the introduction of CCT is a concern for the bottom line of the contract and the reduction of the level of subsidy as far as possible. The militates against the provision of non-profitable or loss-making activities and can already be seen to be squeezing some of the target group activities from the programmes. Social services and sport development workers are finding it increasingly difficult to find convenient times to hold events for groups such as the elderly when the centres can find more profitable uses for the hall space. This conflict between social provision geared to increase the well-being and quality of life of individuals within society and the market provision for those who can pay to play seriously threatens the values which were at the core of the development of the leisure services.

Performance indicators

Leisure services are being circumscribed by the new managers' desire to establish measures for the performance of public services. Leisure is no exception and the local authorities have been told that:

> In much of the public sector the bottom line of profit does not exist. Financial performance and the impact of services are difficult to assess. Nevertheless it is essential to ensure that resources are being allocated effectively to the public sector and within the public sector. Evaluation of this kind relies upon a range of performance measures. Without the information provided by these, public sector managers are in danger of allocating resources in the dark. They will have little or no idea about how their activities are contributing to economy, efficiency or effectiveness; they will not know how their performance compares with that of similar departments elsewhere in the public sector or indeed how their own performance has changed over time. (Jackson and Palmer, 1989: 1)

It is important to know how performances are changing and there have been working groups of practitioners, managers and consultants helping some local arts groups to develop measures and indicators which reflect their concerns for their performance rather than using ones which have been imposed from a general view of what is important to management rather than what is important within leisure. Beeton (1988: 99) has argued that: 'Performance is measured largely in terms of how productivity inputs are turned into outputs, and how successful producers are in providing the mix of outputs that consumers want'. This covers both 'technical efficiency', relating to the process of turning inputs into outputs, and 'allocative efficiency', concerned with the mixture of outputs and the match with the demands of the consumers. However, it appears to have become popular to think in terms of three types of measure for public services: prescriptive measures (which can be tested against specific policy statements and objectives); proscriptive measures (which clearly outline standards which are not acceptable); and descriptive measures (accounts of the activities and through-puts). The Audit Commission has produced suggested perform-ance indicators for all local authority services following the Local Govern-ment Act 1992, using these categories, and making some suggestions that will become compulsory and others that will be advisory indicators. The document includes recommendations for recreation and leisure and libraries, with the promise of more to come for theatres, arts, tourist attractions, children's play schemes and availability of facilities. They suggest proxy indicators for accessibility and usage, and actual figures for net costs for total visits to facilities. The libraries similarly suffer from this concentration on cost factors. The comments from the Audit Commission actually state that the measure of issues per head 'does not measure the quality of the service per se, or the quality of the items borrowed . . .' (Audit Commission, 1992: 70). In fact the responses from the local authority associations (AMA, ACC and ADC) demonstrated the complete lack of indicators for the qualitative evaluation of performance in the process being proposed. This again drags the managerial regime further away from one of the original reasons for the provision of leisure with its contribution to the quality of life of all in society.

This system has tended to concentrate on the three Es which we first saw in the work of the Audit Commission. It could be argued that there has emerged a hierarchy within the Es, with economy and efficiency being the focus of the greatest activity because of the ease with which they appear to be measurable. Effectiveness is often left trailing behind as its definition, and therefore its measurement, proves more difficult to establish. What is also noticeable is that the lists of performance indicators for leisure and the arts which have been proposed have focused on the economy of the use of inputs rather than attempting to find ways of accounting for the outputs of leisure services. These are the ones which are being offered as the compulsory indicators of the service. It is also noticeable that a fourth E is not included in the lists as there is no concern to take equity into the debate about the performance of the services. Definitions of equity revolve around notions of social justice and the fairness of the distribution of resources. It also raises the questions of who should benefit and why from the resources and, as we have seen, much of the leisure provision has been constituted on redistributive and remedial criteria not on the market criteria of ability to pay. Removing this fourth E is therefore a significant omission.

As Head (1990: 5) has argued 'Performance indicators are an aid to and not a substitute for judgement in decision taking. Performance indicators cannot in themselves provide a means of evaluating the effectiveness of provision, rather they provide signposts or guides to aid judgement.' This advice has often been forgotten in the formulation of performance indicators and their subsequent use in ranking service delivery, both within a local authority and between local authorities. One recent study of two London boroughs criticized the low library visiting rates in one borough when compared to the other, but failed to note that the lower borough allowed readers to take out seven books for three weeks as compared to the neighbouring borough's policy of five books for two weeks. If the two services had been compared on the number of issues per thousand of the local population, the picture would have been reversed.

For the indicators adequately to describe and improve service delivery they must originate within the service plans of the Leisure Services departments and not be imported from a managerialist desire to monitor performance. They must also attempt to register the nature of the work being undertaken and not simply measure the costs of the service delivery. They will have to be located within the specific contexts of the local authority and the local population. This necessitates a review of performance which builds from the bottom of the organization to the top, rather than imposing a top-down definition on the organization. There are benefits to be obtained from working through this exercise, as it allows the organization to obtain a clearly focused idea of its objectives. However, just as there was this possibility with CCT, so too are there dangers of this process not being undertaken properly or simply being imposed on the workforce. Another danger is that it provides, with the writing of the specification by management experts, the justification for the introduction of 'quality' into the organization.

There is little evidence that fundamental measures of performance, let alone intermediate indicators of intermediate outputs, suggest that the quality of services is actually improving. In fact it is possible that, despite all the rhetoric and activity, things may actually be getting worse. This then feeds into another concern for the leisure manager, the concept of total quality management. Quality in its various guises is the key to the new manager's heart, as it has been granted a special place at the centre of the managerialist revolution. Whether we take quality to be the hallmark offered by BS 5750 or, for those with European aspirations, ECO 45000 and, for international operations, ISO 9000; or whether we consider that it is the heart of the listening, customer-centred organization in its quality assurance systems (which do not have to be assessed by an external auditor to be effective) we must still address the central notion seriously. Many contract specifications insisted that the tender adopt the principles of BS 5750 without there being too much understanding of what those standards meant on either side of the contract. It is still an area of major concern, as managers are now producing manuals which fit their practice into the quality system framework and allow themselves to obtain the hallmark for the status quo. There is a potential in quality assessment which is being lost in the logic which drives it, forcing the process to become ever more introspective and static rather than a dynamic agent of change within the organizations.

This was noted in the review of quality systems carried out by Ziethaml et al. (1990: 74) when they observed:

> Many companies believe they are committed to service quality but their commitment is to quality from the company's own internal, technical perspective. Service quality in many firms means meeting the company's self-defined pro- ductivity or efficiency standards, many of which the customers do not notice or desire. In other firms, quality is defined in terms of advanced technology – meeting standards required to keep pace with competitors on things for which customers will not pay and do not want.

What is being proposed within total quality is service delivery focused on the customer and the customer's level of satisfaction, but many local authorities are seeking this within the BS 5750 framework which is significantly different. Again, there is potential here to shift the focus of service delivery from the traditional notion of 'citizen' to the market-based definition of 'customer', with a different set of rights and no noticeable responsibilities. As we can see with the citizen's charter initiatives what is being offered is not citizenship but customer rights.

Quality systems embrace everyone in the organization and hence are the epitome of the managerialist desire to unite the workforce into one harmonious team working to fulfil the corporate mission. They are more than an inspection of service delivery so transcend descriptive measures. They are also never completed and therefore become the subject of prescriptive measures which will be built into the *Quality Assurance Manual*, which in turn will be owned and shared by everyone in the organization. Some leisure managers appear to be regarding quality assurance as preventive medicine: it will reduce the number of complaints and reduce the number of dissatisfied customers which in turn will increase the number of satisfied customers and the number of repeat visits. As one training consultant put it: 'One can see BS 5750 as systematic common sense, nothing new is revealed, it is simply a list of those things that you know you should be doing in any event' (Integra, 1989).

The introduction of this common sense involves formulating transparent monitoring systems, where systems are not only in place but can be seen, by employees and customers alike, to be in place. The monitoring process is also 'total', all aspects of the service are included and this again includes the customers. They (we) are experiencing a changing environment for their leisure, they (we) are playing in a more managed space. During one research exercise, our researchers saw an attendant suggest to four badminton players, who were chatting between points, that they could do that in the bar. This was all the more pressing because he had other customers waiting for the court who could make better use of it. This calculation of benefit ignores the sociability factors involved in leisure and, whilst not being the official policy of that centre, was a logical development of its concern to meet its contract targets, generate income and provide quality sporting facilities. The attendant had merely extended the 'quality loop' to the activities of the badminton players.

The introduction of even the straightforward quantifiable indicators has implications for the leisure organizations, requiring systems for the collection and collation of information. These demands can in turn transform the organizations themselves. It is noticeable that the 'contract culture' has already made significant impacts on the voluntary groups involved and the smaller arts organizations, which are having to regard grant applications in a new light. The grant relationship, with both the local council and the funding councils, has moved from endowment to a contractual relationship with specified outcomes required as a necessary part of the application. They will be the next organizations to seek the quality grail. This, then, furthers the role of the monitoring of services by extending that monitoring to a new layer of organizations.

There are already small-scale organizations being forced to 'appoint' marketing officers because their expenditure plans, submitted for grant support, contain a budget heading for marketing costs. The managerialist logic insists that if there is a cost centre there has to be someone responsible for that centre. This logic drives the argument on and forces a bureaucratic split on to organizations which have tended to work along divisions of enthusiasm. Similarly, producing business plans requires time and expertise and involves setting financial targets for the organization. These then have to be monitored and explained – does the increase in income come from increased attendances, increased bar sales, increased sales from the souvenir shop and does it offset the increased expenditure, which in turn should be itemized by category? This is a long way from collecting money at the door and keeping it safe in a coffee tin which was, and maybe still is, the stage many small arts groups are at. The coffee tins were being used in a northern town to collect the revenues from three theatres as recently as 1989. Their request for a computerized management information system came from the need to produce 'reliable' figures for a grant application when the volunteer treasurer decided that the task was impossible given the level of knowledge available to the group. The introduction of these new demands also creates the opportunity for diversionary activities, sometimes referred to as 'gaming', where the effort goes into meeting the performance target rather than into the quality of the service. There is also a danger of short termism affecting the funding of organizations and the development of ideas within those organizations.

Conclusion: the private profit and the public prophet

The basis for this paper was the origins of leisure services within a complex mixed economy which had a distinct and separable role for the provision of public sector leisure. The early missionaries believed in the value of their message for the local people and delivered well-intentioned services in open facilities. The introduction of managerialism has been one of the contributing factors which has eroded this role of providing recreational welfare through the local state. To present a critique of the new managerialism and its interest in the profit, in income generation and in cost centres for all activities, is not to pretend that the old ways were perfect. It addresses the change in the value system which is inherent in the new managerialism and fits more comfortably with the wider political conjunction, not to condemn all the changes which are taking place but to ask whether the new leisure managers are 'managing' the same phenomenon that we started with. Some of the changes are valuable and have contributed to the development of a responsive and progressive service, but others have seen equally important aspects of the work squeezed out to make way for more profitable activities.

In the context of this chapter, the most significant feature of 'demand'-led provision is that it is measurable through the price mechanisms within the market. Hence the 'needs' of disadvantaged groups are met through systems of proxy payment such as Passports to Leisure, discounts for target groups and so on. These mechanisms mean that the local authorities are acting as a secondary market place or quasi-market for leisure, with the combination of real and adapted pricing policies turning the leisure needs of the community into the economics of demand. There is a role still for a public sector with a voice of a prophet speaking for its values, its policies and its programmes. The community leisure schemes, the disabled activities and the programmes for ethnic minorities, women and the elderly are important contributions to the quality of life of those people and of the whole community. The value of providing facilities for major international sporting or cultural events cannot be judged solely on the subsidy per seat for the major concert halls or the cash surpluses generated from the Cup Final. The system has to be designed to include quality and qualitative response – the individual and social appreciation of the event is the outcome, not how many seats were sold. This is revealed in an interesting way in the recent study of public art, undertaken by the Policy Studies Institute (PSI, 1993). Public art is not owned by anyone and some would say not seen by many, but the study has demonstrated that it does have an impact on the quality of life experience of people who use those spaces which contain public art, although those benefits are not tangible in the new managerialist sense.

The public prophet in leisure has to argue for the recognition of leisure need perceived by the local communities not by the local economic market. This is not a plea to return to the old-style paternalisms of welfare. There is still a role for a reconstructed missionary, grounded in the experiences of those communities and reacting to the needs expressed by those communities to argue against the profiteering of the new managerialism. A reliance on meeting demand will stifle service development, disenfranchize disadvantaged groups and create a situation where disparate provision is the norm. This would deny the benefits of access to leisure in its widest sense to large sections of the population and leave local authority leisure services as nothing more than providers of the last resort, filling the gaps left by the failure of the market but not reaching out to extend the provision of leisure throughout the population. The public missionary can still find a large audience for provision which has taken the benefits from but not been submerged by the managerialist revisions of its central rationale. In particular, the missionary vision must continue to inform the policy making of the local authorities as this will then have to be enshrined in the contract specifications for the service deliverers and continue to benefit the local publics.

Notes

1. It is interesting to note that some infrastructure has been provided by the private sector and we can see that significant investment in public houses, music halls, some theatres, and the growth in the number of cinemas and bingo halls have been led by private capital. These areas are more specialized aspects of leisure than those developed by the public sector, where usage can often be multi-purpose. What is important, though, is how these facilities and services are to be managed.

2. It is recognized that some leisure forms have been developed almost exclusively by the private sector, most noticeably the regulation and institutionalization of gambling has led to a very profitable industry which, whilst tightly proscribed, offers a return to the operators. The moral position of guardian of the local people has meant that local authorities have not become involved in such areas. This is further evidenced by the doubts which surround national and local authority lotteries in this country, despite their success elsewhere in Europe and the idea of a national lottery which would help to finance the arts and sports developments in this country. The sale of alcohol has also been controversial, with the introduction of catering areas preceding the sale of alcohol by many years. There are still examples of local authorities which refuse to sell alcohol in sports centres. The cinema may also have been left to the private sector not simply because of the willingness of the film producers to create venues and an audience for their product but because of the moral threat many saw from the cinema.

3. The Olympic bids by Birmingham and Manchester have seen building developments commissioned. The most spectacular building of the early 1990s, however, remains the building of fifteen new facilities undertaken by Sheffield City Council at a cost of over £175 million in order to host the World Student Games in 1991.

4. The problems inherent in this definition of target groups are recognized but it was an important part of the councils' approach to their role to seek to develop this involvement. Target groups are defined against the participation norms for the whole of the population and this takes into account none of the social and cultural factors which can determine the choice of leisure activities. Ethnic differences are ignored in favour of a generalized notion of 'normal' participation rates within the specified and officially recognized range of activities on offer. The work of sports and arts development officers is capable of transcending such formalistic barriers and, from a strong base within the local community, identifying groups who are seeking sporting, cultural and artistic opportunities.

References

Audit Commission (1988) *Competitive Management of Parks and Green Spaces*. London: HMSO.

Audit Commission (1989) *Sport for Whom? Clarifying the Local Authority Role in Sport and Recreation*. London: HMSO.

Audit Commission (1992) *Citizen's Charter – Performance Indicators*. London: HMSO.

Bailey, P. (1978) *Leisure and Class in Victorian Britain*. London: Routledge and Kegan Paul.

Beeton, D. (1988) 'Performance measurement: the state of the art', *Public Money and Management*, 8(1&2) (Spring–Summer): 99–103.

Benington, J.B. (1988) 'The need for a new strategic vision for leisure services', in J.B. Benington and J.W. White (eds), *The Future of Leisure Services*. London: Macmillan.

CELTS (1992) *CCT: A Nationwide Study of the Effects*. London: Centre for Leisure and Tourism Studies, University of North London Press.

Clarke, A. (1991) 'Community, leisure and regeneration: a historic compromise', in D. Botterill and A. Tomlinson (eds), *Ideology, Leisure Policy and Practice*, Leisure Studies Association Conference Papers 45, Brighton.

Clarke, A. (1992) 'Citizens and consumers: leisure after the welfare state', in J. Sugden and A. Tomlinson (eds), *Leisure after the Welfare State*, Leisure Studies Association Conference Papers 46, Brighton.

Clarke, J. and Critcher, C. (1985) *The Devil Makes Work*. London: Macmillan.

Coalter, F. (1990) 'The mixed economy of leisure, in I. Henry (ed.), *Management and Planning in the Leisure Industries*. London: Macmillan.

Coalter, F., Long, J. and Duffield, B. (1988) *Recreational Welfare: The Rationale for Public Sector Investment in Leisure*. London: Avebury/Gower.

Evans, J. (1974) *Service to Sport: The Story of the CCPR 1935–1972*. London: Pelham.

Head, P. (1990) 'Performance indicators quality assurance', unpublished paper, Asper Consultants, London.

Henley Centre for Forecasting (1986) *The Economic Impact and Importance of Sport in the UK*. London: Sports Council.

Integra (1989) 'Practical quality management for contractors to local authorities', Seminar at the Moat House Hotel, Drury Lane, London.

Jackson, P. and Palmer, B. (1989) *First Steps in Measuring Performance in the Public Sector – A Management Guide*. London: Public Finance Foundation/Price Waterhouse.

Knox, C. (1992) 'The effects of CCT in Northern Ireland', in J. Sugden and A. Tomlinson (eds), *Leisure after the Welfare State*, Leisure Studies Association Conference Papers 46.

Policy Studies Institute (1993) *The Public Benefit of Public Art*. London: PSI.

Sports Council (1992) *Sport in the Nineties – New Horizons*. London: Sports Council.

Tomlinson, A. and Parker, S. (1992) 'The introduction of CCT management reactions', in J. Sugden and A. Tomlinson (eds), *Leisure after the Welfare State*, Leisure Studies Association Conference Papers 46.

Yates, R. (1984) *Training for Recreation Management*. London: HMSO.

Zeithaml, V.A., Parasuraman, A. and Berry, L.L. (1990) *Delivering Quality Service*. New York: Free Press.

9

The Limits of Management: Gender and the Politics of Change

Janet Newman

Most of this book has been concerned with the managerialization of politics. In the 1980s a radical policy agenda was matched by a strong political interest in the organizations which were to deliver it. We saw an unprecedented degree of political intervention into how organizations should be run, and Chapters 2–8 have traced the complex interaction between the restructuring of the policy agendas and the organizational restructurings faced by each sector in turn. In this process, management itself has become politicized in new ways. First, it has been the mechanism through which political change is to be delivered. In the late 1980s, and especially evident in the 1991 election campaigns, we can see the emergence of a strong consensus across all three main political parties about the ability of managerial techniques to transform the public sector. But secondly, it has become the focus of change itself. Indeed, it could be argued that recent years have seen an important shift in the discourse of political debate away from the language of goals ('What is to be done?') to the more impoverished language of means ('How should we go about doing it?'). As well as the managerialization of politics, then, we are concerned with the politicization of management.

In this chapter I want to explore the interaction between management and politics by assessing the problems and prospects of the new managerialism as a gendered domain. I approach this in a number of ways. The first section looks at gender and the politics of restructuring by suggesting some key issues arising from the processes of organizational change. The second section considers management as a changing set of discourses and practices which involve shifting relationships of power, and which offer different kinds of organizational and individual identities. The third section considers the interaction between management and women's political agendas as agents of change.

In each, my interest centres around how far change offers new opportunities for women or new spaces within which we might act to reshape organizational cultures and develop new ways of working. For example, in the first section I consider how far 'restructuring' heralds a new flexibility of structures and working patterns which may benefit women. The following section discusses the seemingly promising shift in language and style offered by the 'new managerialism', with its emphasis on people, communication, culture, and empowerment. The final section assesses the prospects offered by a new alignment between 'equal opportunity' agendas and the discourses of human resources management and business efficiency.

The underlying theme of the chapter is the interaction between the depoliticization of gender relations in the 'post-feminist' climate of the 1980s and 1990s, and the emergence of new managerial initiatives which promise to deliver change that will benefit women. During the 1970s and the early 1980s the gender relations within public sector organizations had become increasingly politicized. This occurred as many women who had benefited from the expansion of women's access to Higher Education in the 1960s developed professional careers in the expanding welfare state and in other parts of the public sector. This expansion arose in a social climate which had been profoundly transformed by the feminist movements of the 1960s and the 1970s. New expectations and demands surfaced and became institutionalized and incorporated through the development of equal opportunity policy agendas and initiatives within organizations.

These took very different forms depending on the culture, traditions and (in the case of local authorities) political control of particular organizations, and were often little more than tokenistic. However, they became an important target for direct and indirect governmental interventions in the mid-1980s, and provided a legitimation for intervention in other areas. The Conservative assaults on the power bases of some local authorities (especially the Labour-controlled London boroughs and the GLC itself) were partly conducted through the demonization of their equal opportunity initiatives around gender, race and sexuality. The left was stigmatized as 'loony', partly through a government-led campaign against the presumed 'excesses' of these initiatives. At the same time, local authority power to deliver equality policies was severely weakened through legislation on CCT and through the opting out of schools from local authority control. Similar processes are evident in the removal of hospital trusts from health authority control. The development of localized employment agreements across many parts of the public sector further weakened the power of personnel departments to implement their equality policies, and of trades unions and equalities units to defend them (or even push for their enhancement). As I shall argue, the effects of the erosion of equality policies has been experienced most acutely at the 'sharp end' of public sector work – by women and by black and minority ethnic workers in the contracted-out service roles on which organizations and their users depend.

But while equal opportunities as a strategy for change may have lost much of its legitimacy, managerial strategies are gaining ground. In the 1990s there has been a renewed interest in the debate about increasing women's access to public office and to leadership posts in public and private sector organizations. This interest can be traced to the publication of a series of reports (Hansard Society, 1990; Nevill et al., 1991; Institute of Management, 1992). But, more significantly, it was fuelled by the political furore about Major's early mistakes (in failing to appoint any women to his cabinet following the election in 1991) and his subsequent launch of the Opportunity 2000 initiative. This aims to improve both the 'quality and quantity' of women in the workforce, and encourages organizations to set goals and targets for change. It is oriented around the 'business case' for increasing the numbers of women in management and for seeking a balanced workforce.

These reports and initiatives provide a context for a new managerial orientation to overcoming barriers to women. The emphasis is, however, very different – it is not about the politics of disadvantages and discrimination, but about the effective management of resources. The new Human Resource Management is concerned with 'maximizing' the potential of the total workforce within an organization (and women who are 'blocked' and therefore under-utilized represent a potentially wasted resource). Some organizations are recognizing that a good profile on equality is an important part of their public image, and are appointing women to senior positions. Some are even talking about the need to 'manage diversity' – that is, to ensure that organizations benefit from the particular contributions of women and of black staff.

Before assessing the prospects and possibilities of change which some of these approaches signal, it is necessary to set out some initial concerns about the way in which they constitute notions of 'women' and of 'management'. The focus of much of the new orientation remains limited since it is concerned almost exclusively with increasing the numbers of women at senior levels. It is, then, primarily concerned with enhancing the prospects of women who are middle-class, professional and usually white, and who already possess a considerable degree of social power.

One of the important lessons we have learned from the equality movements of the 1980s is that we can no longer talk about 'women' in the undifferentiated way evident in the reports and initiatives mentioned above. This has consequences both for the knowledge we gather about women's employment, and for how we evaluate initiatives aimed at improving prospects for women. The knowledge we currently have available in this plethora of reports is inadequate since it does not differentiate between the experience of different groups of women. It is clear that the changes we have been experiencing have different kinds of impact on black and white women, working-class and middle-class women, women of different ages. As yet, however, we do not have enough data to say exactly how.

The reports and initiatives cited are also limited in that they present an inadequate conceptualization of change. Change is generally measured in terms of whether things are 'getting better' or 'getting worse' as measured by numbers of women in different kinds of grades. This ignores the complexity of the shifting patterns of employment in the public sector and the consequences for how the kinds of work being done by different groups of women – black and white, young and old – is being restructured. The focus on women in management also has implications for how changes and initiatives are evaluated, and from whose perspective. Initiatives designed to smooth the path of women attempting to combine work and family responsibilities are clearly of value, but are of more value to middle-class white women in managerial or professional grades than for women on the organizational margins for whom pay and basic entitlements are much more urgent concerns.

A further issue raised by the 'women and management' debate is that it problematizes women rather than management. 'Management' is not, of course, a neutral term. It is based on a body of knowledge that developed in the context of male-controlled organizations (the military, factories, the civil service). It was written about and encoded into 'theories' principally by men, and the research which has established the norms of managerial practice has mainly been based on male subjects. Its concepts and images are predominantly drawn from the domains of order, hierarchy and rationality. Its goals are the control of the internal world of the organization and mastery of the external environment. The definition of management itself, then, raises questions about the value placed on different kinds of work, and the changing nature of that work.

Central to the ideas and practices of management over the last fifteen years has been the emergence of a 'new' managerialism, and its widespread adoption by the public sector in Britain. The 'new managerialism' centres around, but is much broader than, the work of Tom Peters and his associates (Wood, 1989). It is based on a new wave of literature aimed at reforming US industry as a response to concerns about the weakening of its competitive position in the international market place, and especially in relation to Japan (Clarke and Newman, 1993). This literature has achieved enormous sales and has entered the 'popular consciousness' of managers on an unprecedented scale, offering a new and positive imagery of the manager as champion and hero. 'Twenty years ago managers and businessmen were either the subject of mimicry or associated with power-game dramas. Now, they occupy a central role in images of modernity, and the leaders of business have become super-heroes' (Wood, 1989: 379). Its significance for the British public sector is twofold. First, it offers a 'liberation' from the sterile and dreary views of public sector bureaucrats, and a new set of identities for managers as the champions of change. It promises a personal liberation and transformation (du Gay, 1991). For managers in the public sector, the promised freedom from the shackles of bureaucracy also offers more concrete benefits: more power over resources; more freedom to take decisions; and more discretion over their own work.

Secondly, the literature offers a set of techniques with which managers can transform organizations. The focus of analysis of the new managerial texts was the big corporation of US industry which, it was argued, had become too bureaucratic, too ossified, too set in their ways. The analogies with the critiques of the British public sector – by politicians, by the public and by managers themselves – are self-evident. The recipe for success which the new managerialism offered was simple. Organizations needed to loosen up, become more concerned with change rather than stability, more concerned with people (the 'human resources' of an organization) than status, more oriented to culture than rules, more externally rather than internally focused. Above all, organizations needed to become more flexible.

The 'new managerialism', then, signals a break with earlier management approaches since it places a greater emphasis on people, relationships, values and culture, and seems to signal a shift from the domains of mastery and control to those of process and transformation. Before trying to assess the gender relations of this shift, I want to explore the implications of 'flexibility' for women in the process of public sector restructuring.

Gender and the politics of restructuring

The restructuring processes set out in successive chapters in this book have had profound consequences for women since many of the public services in Britain are largely delivered through the labour power of women. Women have traditionally occupied the front-line roles through which the interface between the health and welfare services and the users of services (themselves mainly women) has been managed (see Chapters 3 and 4 in this volume, by Walby and Greenwell, Langan and Clarke). Many of the public sector professions have formed traditional career routes for women. And most of the organizational servicing roles (from chief executive's secretary to school cleaner) are occupied by women. We cannot, then, discuss change in the structures, cultures and patterns of work within public sector organizations in gender-neutral terms. In this section I want to suggest some key issues in the changing patterns of women's employment and the ways in which they experience the restructuring process.

Women in the flexible organization

One of the core principles underpinning the restructuring of public sector organizations has been the search for 'flexibility'. We can see the emergence of more flexible patterns of service delivery across the public, private and voluntary sectors in the emerging 'mixed economies' of provision. Flexibility has also been a key principle underpinning a succession of internal restructurings designed to introduce greater levels of devolution and decentralization. While some of this restructuring has been led by a concern with costs (devolving responsibility for the allocation of scarce resources to spending units), such changes have also been presented as a way of delivering greater flexibility and responsiveness to service users. 'Flexibility' takes on a rather different inflection when labour forces, rather than structures or services, are targeted. Public sector change has led to a new flexibility in the use of labour power within the public sector, with the erosion of national pay bargaining agreements and new, more flexible employment contracts. We can also see evidence of the growth of 'functional flexibility', in which employees are expected to deploy a range of skills and a flexible approach to their working roles, for example in nursing (Walby, 1992).

At first sight, flexibility looks like a good thing for women. It seems to provide a means of overcoming the limitations of traditional career routes built on male career patterns, or the intransigence of inflexible hierarchical structures, and the lack of flexibility in working patterns which has made combining work and family responsibilities a major barrier to women's advancement. Change seems to promise to unlock the rigidities of male norms and to create space for alternative values and practices. Women are also thought to have greater flexibility in their working styles and practices, and to be able to transfer skills flexibly across organizational functions.

But we need to look more closely at what is signified by these new 'flexibilities' of public sector organizations, and their real implications for women. It is important to note, however, that the changes are not uniform since women are not a homogeneous group. In particular, change will have a differential impact on white and black or ethnic minority women positioned differently in the labour market. One such source of difference lies in where women are positioned in relation to the increasing split between the 'core' and 'periphery' of organizations. Contracting out, and competitive tendering: the split between purchaser and provider roles; the devolution of power from LEAs to schools, and the development of 'contract cultures' between organizational centres and devolved business units (or departments and agencies within the civil service) can all be seen as aspects of this pattern of restructuring.

This core/periphery model has been widely used in the literature on Fordism and post-Fordism (Pinch, 1992). The changes also resonate with Charles Handy's more populist picture of the organization of the future, the 'shamrock' organization, which has three separate but inter-related parts (Handy, 1989). At the centre is a small core of highly qualified professionals, managers and skilled workers. These are highly paid (and rewarded in other ways) but are expected to have a high degree of commitment, work long hours and put their all into the success of the organization. The 'contractual fringe' consists of self-employed professionals paid fees for delivering specified services as and when the organization needs them. The 'flexible labour force' is the third element of Handy's shamrock, and consists of low-skilled, part-time or temporary workers who occupy the servicing roles of the organization. Handy's analysis is not ungendered – indeed he sees the flexibility of this new kind of organization as a positive advantage for women who may have 'low aspirations' (*sic*) or for women who wish to move in and out of work as family commitments change.

Handy's comments can be seen as part of an ideological gloss on the new flexibilities, stressing their advantages for women. But the emergence of the contractual arm of the new organization is not, in general, good news for many groups of women, since its purpose is to provide flexibility for employers rather than employees. In the climate of devolved budgets and cost constraints, we are seeing an increase in short-term and fixed-term contracts: for example term-time only contracts in schools and short-term teaching contracts in Higher Education. Both predominantly apply to female staff, and both have severe drawbacks in terms of career progression and security of employment. Of course, new forms of contract arrangement apply to men too, especially at the very top of organizations where contracts are linked to pay and performance; but the effects are experienced most acutely by women because of their generally worse position in the labour force and lower rates of pay. The effects are experienced most acutely by black women, who form the backbone of many of the contracted-out services in cleaning, catering and laundry services. Women in the contracted-out sectors have tended to lose their security of employment and the benefits (however slight) of working for a 'good employer' such as a local authority or hospital. Pay and employment conditions, hours of work and so on have generally worsened, and from a lower base than that of male manual workers. Women in the contractual fringe are also less able to make claims under equal value legislation since their work cannot be directly compared to workers remaining in the 'core'.[1]

For black and white women in the 'flexible' arm of the organizational labour force, then, things are getting worse. As the organization is squeezed by economic constraints, it is the most flexible parts that suffer most in terms of pay, choice and employment benefits. The contracting out of services reduces part-time opportunities for women within the core. As part-time workers are increasingly used as a cheaper alternative to filling vacant full-time posts, so, ironically, the 'flexibility' of traditional forms of part-time work is reduced.

Pinch (1992) points to a general process of polarization and segmentation of the public sector workforce in terms of pay rewards, working conditions and employment prospects. This segmentation and polarization has led to improvements in the pay and rewards for senior managers (in return for performance), at the same time as cost savings are driving down pay and leading to 'flexibility' strategies at lower levels, with substantially worsening conditions of service in the contracted-out and flexible sectors. Given that men are more likely to be senior managers and women more likely to find themselves in the flexible or contracted-out sectors, this polarization must be seen as profoundly gendered. It does not, however, affect all women in the same way. There are parallel polarizations taking place around ethnicity, age and class. The flexibility strategies I have been discussing apply differentially to working-class and middle-class women. For example, middle-class women in the professions and in career grades (usually white) are more likely to remain in the organizational 'core' and so be protected from the cost-cutting implications of flexibility strategies. (Ironically these are the very women who call for greater flexibility in the way organizations employ staff in order to enable them to combine childcare with a career). However, we can see variations in degrees of security and protection for middle-class women of different ages. For employers seeking flexibility, older women are seen as more expensive (they may have to be paid at higher points on pay scales) and so less desirable. Older women may be more likely to be subject to redundancies. There is, furthermore, a growing practice of offering short-term contracts to new, younger staff at the lower end of the pay scale (for example, teaching and research contracts in Higher Education), thus reducing opportunities for older women, many of whom want to develop their careers after their childcare responsibilities have lessened.

The effects of flexibility strategies are experienced worst of all by black women, who in many organizations have traditionally propped up the whole edifice through their support roles of cleaning, catering and low-grade clerical and care roles – precisely those areas most likely to be based on part-time or contracted-out labour. For black women who gain entry to the professions or career grades, promotion depends increasingly on the devolved decisions of business unit managers or the governors/managers of schools or trusts, in which they are subject to double processes of discrimination around gender and race.

Life in the 'core' – a suitable job for a woman?

But not all women are located in the periphery. I want to turn now to the changing position of women in the 'core'. Life in the core is hard, demanding and short. Handy sees work in the core as corresponding to the high-energy, peak years of a career after which, rather than a gradual decline, people are expected to move out and take on a new occupation, develop their leisure and charitable activities or contract some of their labour back to the organization. One problem with this view is that it is based on a typically male career path, which peaks in their 30s and 40s – the time at which many women are only beginning to develop the high-energy period of their working lives. Secondly, the high intensity and hours of work expected in the core are only really possible for those without care responsibilities and, indeed, assumes that domestic labour is done by someone else (in the case of men, by a wife; in the case of a woman, by another woman). Senior women in management have traditionally been less likely to be married or have care responsibilities than women at more junior levels; but we are now seeing the emergence of some 'super-super' women, who use increased flexibility in employment (for example, job share or part contracts) to pursue high level careers as well as domestic or care responsibilities at considerable personal cost.

The new organizational forms and structures have been accompanied by changes to traditional hierarchies based on functional or professional specialisms. New posts have been created with corporate responsibilities (for example, posts concerned with resources, performance review, quality, HRM, contracting, PR or marketing). While this has opened up some new areas to women seeking senior posts, it has also led to the erosion of traditional career routes and structures of opportunity for many women in the 'female' professions. For example, in local government, successive restructurings have led to the creation of larger units based on organizational or political rationalities rather than professional specialisms. Generally speaking, the larger the unit, the more likely it is to be managed by a man; and the fewer rungs in a hierarchy, the less chance of women getting into senior management. This is illustrated in work on the impact on career routes for women managers resulting from successive changes within social services departments (Foster, 1987, 1988a, 1988b; Social Services Inspectorate, 1991; Allan et al., 1992; Lupton, 1992). So the transition from professional to managerial cultures means that conventional career routes for women may become closed. Women in nursing, education, social work and so on who might previously have been promoted as 'senior professionals' may find that these jobs no longer exist. Changing structures have also led to increasing male dominance of the new areas of key significance in the core: posts linked to strategy, policy, finance, IT and so on.[2]

Earlier in this section I suggested, following Pinch (1992), that we were witnessing a polarization in the pay and conditions of public sector workers linked to the growing split between core and periphery, and that women and black and ethnic minority workers were disadvantaged in this polarization. However, there may also be other forms of polarization taking place. As more women have gained managerial roles in the professional occupational hierarchies, so we have seen an increasing split between strategic roles and service management roles. This split has always been implicit in traditional hierarchical structures. It is now deepening as other lines of difference open up: between purchasers and providers; between centre and periphery; and between those engaged in 'strategy' (in, for example, the smaller core of the 'enabling' organization) and those engaged in managing the delivery of services. The implications of this split for gender divisions, and for divisions between white, black and ethnic minority workers, is as yet unclear. But we may be seeing the emergence of a gendered split between strategy/policy and operational responsibilities; and between new formulations of 'men's work' and 'women's work'.

At the same time, many of the transformations seem to promise the possibility of changing such expectations and assumptions: for example the opening up of some traditionally male domains (such as the police force) to women, and the increasing numbers of junior or middle management posts held by women. But the way in which women experience managerial power is not straightforward. Many women seemingly have more power, by virtue of increased responsibility, in newly devolved or decentralized structures; by more frequently having jobs with a management title, and sometimes by being able to advance to more senior management posts, previously the preserve of men. Accompanying this, however, is a general sense of increasing powerlessness to effect change. This powerlessness stems from a number of sources. One lies in the general decline in the power of local authorities, schools and so on *vis-à-vis* central government. Another lies in the reduced power of the professions *vis-à-vis* management. Women working in the 'periphery' of the new, flexible organizations, whose jobs are to achieve targets within increasingly tight resource constraints and time deadlines, experience increased powerlessness *vis-à-vis* the 'strategic' centre. Women working in service delivery roles with declining resources and increased demands on those resources experience increasing frustration at their powerlessness to deliver a good service, despite the growing rhetoric about quality.

Restructuring 'women's work'

The restructurings of different sectors which this volume has discussed also have consequences for traditional definitions of 'women's work', and I want to suggest that we are currently witnessing a reconfiguration of the ideas and practices of women's work in new forms to meet changing conditions. The kinds of jobs available to women have traditionally been partly based on assumptions about women's suitability and aptitude for 'caring' roles. These have reflected patterns of women's domestic labour: caring for the sick, the very young, the very old; feeding and servicing workers, both inside the home and in catering, cleaning and secretarial jobs. Such caring roles have been characterized as based not only on meeting physical needs but on supplying the 'emotional labour' inherent in the relational and interpersonal aspects of the job.

The process of change and restructuring, however, is producing new needs for such labour inside organizations themselves.[3] Emotional labour is becoming an increasingly significant part of the work of staff on the front line in direct service delivery. These jobs, largely held by women, are concerned with managing the interface between declining public services and the needs and demands of users, in the context of increased pressures to perform within a 'customer care' culture and increasing focus on the rights and entitlements of service users. But this intensification of emotional labour is not only occurring at lower levels of the organizational hierarchy; it affects women in management posts too. Women are taking on new responsibilities as managers at a time when the delivery of public services becomes more stressful, and as customers or users are being 'empowered' to expect more. The (marginal) increase in numbers of women managers is occurring at a time when the management of change is both becoming more important and is changing in nature. Managing change in the public services is becoming more fraught with difficulty as the services themselves are reduced or curtailed (or 'targeted' to particular groups, leaving other needs unmet). 'Managing change' is no longer merely about the design of new systems and procedures. It is concerned with mediating between organizations and a complex network of stakeholders, and between staff and service users. Managing change increasingly means managing the human dimensions of change: the pain of transition for staff undergoing redefinition of their jobs; responding to the climate of uncertainty about their future; experiencing the pain of loss as whole sections or services are lost from the public domain; and the trauma of making hard choices as staff are required to do more with less in the new lean and mean contexts of public service provision. Managing change, then, means managing stress: that of staff, of users, of communities and of whole organizations undergoing trauma and amputation. This involves emotional labour of a kind in which men have traditionally not been skilled, and which senior women managers are experiencing as a new set of pressures and demands. Whilst change has made it possible for some women to break barriers to reach senior positions, they may do so at an increasing cost.[4]

At the same time, women's experience of change is a greater level of responsibility for management (even if at relatively low levels of the hierarchy) coincident with a general dismay about how organizations are being managed. This dismay centres especially around how change is being introduced, which often shows a lack of attention to the processes and consequences of change for staff and users. Women are quick to criticize the 'techno-fix' approach to managing change – an approach which prioritizes getting the systems designed and the technology up and running. This approach, of course, partly stems from the way in which change has been imposed on public sector organizations by successive governments, which has left little time for careful consideration of how change can best be introduced or for consultation with those who have to deliver it. However, it could be argued that the techno/rational approach to change management also stems from the predominance of men in senior management posts, and the managerial culture and style which has developed over time as part of that pattern. This has been exacerbated by the increasing emphasis on business-oriented management cultures, with an emphasis on costs and competition – an issue which I discuss further in the next section.

Finally, the gender politics of restructuring contains a tension around the division between women as workers in, and as consumers of, public services. Terms such as 'customers' and 'communities' do not really help express the particular impact of change on women as the main users of many public services. The new initiatives to provide managerial opportunities for women have been introduced precisely at the time when the effects of change are impacting on women as service users and as members of communities suffering the impact of successive cuts in public service provision. There is, then, a complex set of inter-relationships between the impact of change on women as services users, as public sector employees, and as members of community or voluntary organizations. These inter-relationships are affected by class and ethnicity – not all women experience reduced public provision in the same way. And not all women have the same needs as employees. For example, much progress has been made in the development of policies regarding women as mothers of young children; but little attention has been paid to continued care responsibilities for the sick, for the elderly or for people with disabilities (an area which will become increasingly significant with the implementation of Community Care legislation).

Women and cultural change: the new managerialism

The new managerialism, together with the changing structures and organizational forms within which it is deployed, seems to contain the promise of new opportunities for women. The reshaping of organizations seems to offer the possibility of opening up the self-replicating and exclusive male clubs of senior management. The flattening of hierarchies offers better career development opportunities (and articulates with equal opportunity prescriptions for change). Undoubtedly some women have been able to take advantage of these changes. But as well as looking at career opportunities for individuals, we also need to explore how changes in managerial regimes give rise to different cultural configurations of male and female identities, and of gender relations. I want to explore the gender implications of three cultural forms: the *traditional* culture (based on a mix of administrative and professional regimes); the *competitive* culture; and the *heroic/transformational* culture.[5] Any organization will, of course, contain a complex mix of such configurations, and a woman must understand the rules of each and act appropriately as she moves between them. I want first to look at the gender relations of the 'traditional' culture.

Women in traditional cultures

The traditional culture is based on a mix of administrative and professional discourses, each delivering its own language, imagery, values, relationships and ways of doing things. Each offers particular identities or subject positions within a hierarchy. Administrative discourses offer functionally specialized identities and a hierarchy of clearly defined roles. Professional identities are based on the application of knowledge and skills to problems, and operate through a hierarchy of expertise and experience. Within the mix of administrative and professional cultures which characterized the public sector up until the last decade, women have tended to occupy the functional specialisms or professions most closely associated with female roles (for example, personnel, nursing, social work). While some have risen to senior positions within these sectors, there has been an invisible hierarchy between sectors. For example, male-dominated professions have generally been accorded more pay and higher status and more than traditionally female professions. The male-dominated function of financial management has been accorded more pay and higher status than the female specialism of personnel management. This is not just a matter of occupations being based on gender stereotyping (number focus for men, people focus for women), but is a matter of the value placed on different kinds of work. As 'people' management has become linked with resource use (HRM), and has become part of larger departments and associated with more strategic roles, so it has tended to become the province of male rather than female managers.

But we need to go beyond an exploration of the kinds of jobs typically held by women and men in order to understand the gender basis of a particular cultural regime. One way of doing this is to attempt to unlock some of the gendered and sexualized meanings operating within the workplace, and the invisible hierarchies which operate through these meanings. Women in traditional regimes are offered quasi-familial roles and identities around a core of male hierarchies and privileges. Women managers can act as mothers (the kindly personnel officer or line manager concerned with staff welfare); as aunts (the older, probably single woman allowed a senior status but little real power); as wives (the supportive secretary or assistant); as daughters (allowed some privileges on the expectation that they would eventually 'leave home' and therefore present little challenge). A few women are admitted to the ranks of the 'lads', and can be seen in more collegial roles: as fun-loving sisters, or as 'tomboys', able to join in and laugh with the lads (even if sometimes at other women's expense). Those who take on any other kind of role (for example those who adopt a more sexualized, un-daughterly presence, or who break the rules of permitted sisterly behaviour by, for example, talking about 'women's issues') are seen as a troubling presence. Many women, of course, exist outside these Anglocentric familial relationships. These are the women occupying the sub-class (perhaps below stairs?), in print rooms, typing pools, canteens and other predominantly female collective spaces – all, of whatever age, consigned to the status of 'girls' and addressed only by first names.

Women in 'competitive' cultures

As these traditional regimes have become the target of change, new kinds of managerial regimes have been developed. The form these take, however, has depended on the ways in which organizations (and units within them) have responded to the restructurings and changes of recent years. An important part of this reshaping has been oriented towards making organizations (or parts of them) more 'competitive'. We can, however, identify different responses to building competitive capability. 'Being competitive' is not an objective set of attributes, but depends on subjective understandings drawn from imagery of how the business world works. The public sector has so far tended to operate on an image of that world as requiring hard, cut-throat, macho or 'cowboy' styles of working. It is as if the unlocking of the shackles of bureaucratic constraints had at last allowed managers to become 'real men', operating in the 'real world' of the market place, and released from the second-class status of public sector functionaries.

The gender relations of the macho/cowboy regime are less familial than the traditional regimes. The old patriarchs and benevolent paternal figures are being de-throned (made redundant) or de-powered (in sideways moves). Power now lies where the action is – where people do business. Informal hierarchies develop around which jobs are seen to be most 'sexy' – those linked to dynamic, thrusting entrepreneurialism, in business-linked jobs such as marketing, or linked to fast changing, exciting and big money techno-cultures of IT. Being an individual or team charged with delivering fast results in an area of major and strategically important change (such as opting out or going for trust status) is also seen as 'sexy', and brings consequent rewards in terms of future career paths.

These cultures are based on internal as well as external competition. Women are allowed to join in if they can prove that they can 'deliver', and are 'tough enough' to stand the pace. Power is more fluid, and there are few rules about how it should be exercised, so women may have a tough time. As men jostle with each other for organizational space, they may be trampled under foot. Cynthia Cockburn's (1991: 156–7) study of men's responses to women in organizations argues that we are seeing the creation of 'new men', with a different kind of management style and apparently more sympathetic to women and equalities issues generally.

> The new men, though certainly different from the old guard, were little better from a woman's point of view. . . . Women had identified this type of male not only in High Street Retail and in the Service but in the Trade Union and the Local Authority. What distinguished him was an overt and confident machismo. Women everywhere made reference to the 'cod-piece wearing jocks' of the policy unit, the 'new men' of the advertising department. This masculinity does not share the women's-place-is-in-the-home mentality of the old guard. These men expect to find women in the public sphere. Nominally at least they welcome women into this exciting new world because their presence adds sexual spice to the working day . . .

This is a heterosexual culture in which, as in modern marriage, there is a notional equivalence between male and female roles. But this equivalence depends on women taking on roles in which they compete with men (and with each other) in the battle for resources and jobs. They also have to compete to gain recognition of their value and performance. Success depends, in large measure, on the cultivation of profile and visibility. Success also depends on access to the informal clubs and networks where the 'real' business goes on, clubs largely controlled by white men jealously guarding their own power base. Exceptional women may be permitted entry, in a similar way that 'sisters' were allowed into the sub-cultures of 'lads' within the traditional culture. But entry does not depend on 'being a good sport', but on showing you understand the rules of the game and proving (and continually re-proving) your worth. So a few women will be able to elbow their way into the 'sexy' jobs or succeed in establishing a power base of their own. Those that do are likely to attract the scorn of men (and of other women) due to the 'hardness' or unnatural competitiveness they have shown. Machismo is not seen as an appropriate female characteristic, even though the women who show it may be admired for their achievements. Women who fight rough are also not seen to make positive role models for other women, and they may pay an extreme cost in personal terms.

This is, of course, a stereotypically drawn culture which probably exists only at the margins of public sector organizations, being more developed among providers than purchasers, contractors than clients; though the margin is shifting as the core parts of organizations are themselves reorganized into 'business units'. However, no organization ever completely loses its traditional culture. It sits beneath the competitive culture and informs the hidden domain of gender relations. Women have to live out the contradictions between them, in a climate which is rife with mixed messages resulting from the interplay between old and new regimes, and between gender and racial stereotypes. At one moment they must be daughterly and decorous, at another pushy and tough. To succeed you have to join in the competitive ethos, but you have to retain your womanly characteristics and remain 'nice' while doing so. And the competitive, macho culture is not a nice place to be, and is certainly not a place where 'nice' women thrive.

Women in 'transformational' cultures

There is, however, an alternative vision of cultural change in the public sector, based around a different set of values. We can term this the 'heroic' or 'transformational' culture. Based on the new managerialist principles of culture, style, leadership, vision and empowerment (see Chapters 1, 7, 10, in this volume by Newman and Clarke, Cochrane, Flynn), it focuses not on cost cutting (though this remains important), but on working towards long-term competitive strength through building relationships with customers and through empowering staff. It is culture and value based; the leader's role is seen as that of communicating missions and visions, and building a 'strong' culture around a set of guiding principles through which those visions can be realized. This is a model which is developing greater salience in the public sector as organizations are moving beyond the impoverished efficiency frameworks of the Thatcher years and are attempting to rebuild cultures around delivering quality public services.

The emphasis on cultural change offers the possibility of new ways of doing things, and perhaps offers new organizational space for women. There is a recognition of the need to change the values and styles of management, with a greater emphasis on the 'soft skills' (communicating with staff and customers) at which women excel. There is even talk about organizations needing more 'feminine' management styles, or of a 'feminization' of management (for example, O'Brien, 1993), though this tends in practice to refer to the need for men to change rather than for women to be given new space and more power. At the same time, the emphasis on valuing human resources and 'empowering' lower-level staff requires that organizations address the barriers to women's effective contribution to the workplace at all levels.

The growth of service and quality orientations offers greater alignment between the values which women tend to emphasize and the organizational cultures within which they work. There are, of course, problems of identifying women with values based on sex role stereotypes, or with a distinctively 'women's way' of doing things. Nevertheless research on women managers (for example, LGTB, 1990; Allan et al., 1992; Davidson and Cooper, 1992) does tend to suggest that women often do not identify with cultures based on stereotypically male styles and values, and see these as one of the blocks to their own development as managers.

This optimistic reading of the implications of the 'transformational' regime, then, suggests that it may in part be good news for women in that it offers both more space (the possibility of more women in management and better training and development opportunities for female staff) and a more sympathetic climate for 'female' values and ways of working. Women can now perhaps become more active partners in the reshaping of cultures and the delivery of new styles of interface between the organization and its customers. Their communication and collaborative skills may become more valued as organizations recognize the need to build relationships with partners, stakeholders and communities. However, it is unclear how far those organizations which constantly rehearse the rhetoric of new values and styles are prepared to unlock the power bases in which 'old' ways of doing things are entrenched. To do things differently, women need a power base to work from. I will return to this point below.

The gender relationships of the transformational culture are encoded within the wider model of partnership. This is less familial than the 'traditional' culture, and less sexualized (within heterosexual bounds) than the macho culture. It is based on the establishment of horizontal patterns of working across partnerships and within teams, in which all are formally equal. Women are seen to have been 'liberated' from their traditional sex roles, and are no longer constrained by old-fashioned hierarchical patterns of power and authority. In the transformational culture, women must be 'free' to contribute on equal terms; their contribution is, moreover, an essential component of the building of happy, harmonious and therefore productive, teams and workplaces.

There are, however, specific sets of problems for women within this culture. First, the culture is gender (and racially) blind. Differences cannot be recognized and valued since this would undermine the consensual values which are an essential component of the transformational culture. The notion of equality (based on liberal notions of fair access) is illusory rather than real. The gender and racial inequalities of power operating beneath the surface of the seemingly consensual teams and workplaces remain. Women are, then, again operating within contradictory sets of meanings: contribute fully, but remember your real place. A further consequence of the ideology of equality in partnerships and teams is that women come to willingly take on much more responsibility than they are paid for: they may be the most junior member of the team, but are expected to make a full contribution. This may be good for the career development of some women, but can also be seen as exploitative of many.

But the most important problem lies in the model of leadership on which 'transformational' cultures are based. The emphasis is on the need for an inspirational and visionary leadership, which operates through affective (rather than cognitive) modes of interaction.[6] This has resonances with the older ideas of 'charismatic' leadership based on military or political models. It is represented through similar kinds of mythic or heroic imagery, though the new heroes are the business leaders who have become 'champions of change'. Some of these new leaders have entered popular culture in a way unprecedented in previous eras, with a rash of books on 'How I successfully turned around company x', popular stories and legends (for example, those of Richard Branson at Virgin) and even TV programmes (Charles Handy and John Harvey Jones).

Leadership of this type is seen as mysterious and elusive, based on the unique qualities of exceptional individuals. Leaders, we learn, are almost always born rather than made, and they are nearly always born male. Tom Peters suggests that leaders should be heroes, but there is little mention of heroines. Western popular culture in any case tells us that heroines give devoted and selfless service while heroes lead men into battle, and selfless service is unlikely to help women make it into the ranks of senior management.

There are, then, few points of identification for women in this imagery of heroic leadership (and even fewer for black women). This doesn't mean that women don't make effective leaders. The problem, however, is that women pioneers in the predominantly male cultures of senior management are both isolated and highly visible, and so have to make hard choices about whether to challenge or adapt to the norms of that culture. To join these all-male clubs it has usually been necessary to conform to the rules of who can join, and to learn male values, norms and ways of doing things. There will be little space or support for 'doing things differently' at the top until there are larger numbers of women in the senior ranks who can work together (rather than in isolated, token roles spread thinly across an organization) and provide different kinds of models for other women.

This is not, however, merely a question of numbers. Drawing on women's strengths to bring about organizational change is a project which will have very limited success unless organizations also address the issues which constrain women's power to make change. If the 'new managerialism' is concerned with transforming organizations around a different set of values and rebuilding their cultures, a key aspect of this must be to address the deficiencies of the gendered regimes of 'traditional' or 'macho' cultures which I have outlined above. This involves two related process. The first is to expose the invisible 'sexual regimes' of organizations. This means recognizing that sexuality and gender relations have important consequences in the workplace. It means addressing the treatment of female staff throughout the organization, not just that of women managers, legitimizing grievance procedures for harassment cases and supporting those women who try to use them. It also means acknowledging and respecting the diversity of women's responses to the informal sexual regime: women of different ages, classes and ethnicities, heterosexual and lesbian women, will experience it differently.

The second is to develop strategies of empowering women so that new values and ways of doing things can become represented within the process of cultural transformation. At a practical level, this means questioning the ethos, working styles and practices at senior management levels. Whilst change has made it possible for more women to take on jobs at these levels, they do so at an increasing cost as the expectations on senior managers have risen. You have to be tough, fit, able to work exceptionally long hours and be well supported in the domestic sphere if you want to survive. Some women I have worked with on development programmes, given the space to think about themselves and their lives, are choosing not to progress, or to move out altogether. The issue for the future may shift from getting women into management towards retaining those who get there by challenging some of the assumptions about how life at the top must be lived, for the benefit of men (and their families) as well as women.

In enhancing women's contribution to change, we also need to address how we can build on women's strengths in managing change. The skills of change management are central to the 'new managerialism', but are presented in rather different ways within the discourse. Rosabeth Moss Kanter has provided both a critique of, and a development from, the work of Tom Peters in her demand that we move beyond both the 'cowboy' and 'corpocrat' (traditional bureaucratic) styles of management (Kanter, 1989). Kanter sets out a 'post-entrepreneurial' strategy which emphasizes the need to develop value-creating synergy in the processes of restructuring, and to develop partnerships, alliances and links across and between organizations.[7] One recent study, reviewing the visions of change offered by Tom Peters (1989) and Kanter (1989), argues that: 'Paradoxically, the focus women bring to management is that cited as vital for the successful management of organisations of the future . . .' (Allan et al., 1992: 12). This study shows that women are aware of these strengths and of their value to their employers:

> A large majority of the women interviewed believed that there was a difference in male and female management styles. Women were seen as more supportive, caring, nurturing and better human resource managers than men. This supportiveness was often expressed as a means of getting the best out of staff, in the interests of the service. Men were perceived as less supportive and less interested in the feelings of their staff. Additionally, women were seen to have a more participative style of managing and men seen to be more directive, competitive and controlling. Some women talked of women explaining issues to their staff and trying to get them on board, even if the issue was unpopular or painful, whereas men would duck the debate and go into 'instruction mode'.

However the same study suggests that organizations were not prepared to draw on these strengths:

> In relation to change management, some women were convinced that women made better managers, because they more fully engaged their staff's commitment to achieve their tasks. Many felt that the management style developing in response to the new legislation and budgetary constraints undervalued the importance of human resource management and therefore the potential contribution of the skills women bring. (Allan et al., 1992: 38–9)

The tension between these different value orientations means that the development of new management cultures gives rise to different sets of responses for women considering becoming managers. In some ways, the new management addresses issues which have been of concern to women. It promises a regime which is less bureaucratic and paternalistic, which is more 'people-' and 'value-'centred. Against these potential attractions must be set the development of a more masculine imagery of 'becoming a manager', linked to the mastery of 'hard' competencies (financial, entrepreneurial and competitive abilities). Such imagery has consequences both for women's views of their own career prospects and for the visions of senior management of the qualities needed for success in the new managerial regimes.

There are, then, different versions of new managerial regimes, and the experience of women will differ depending on their interplay within specific organizations. And the discourse may be read in different ways. A positive reading suggests that its focus on the domains of culture, style and values may legitimate a new terrain in which women can mark out the need for change in the everyday assumptions and practices of their organizations.

But perhaps the most troubling aspect of the new managerialism is that it is underpinned by the idea of building organizations around a new consensus, implying the abandonment of traditional lines of struggle (most notably that between 'management' and trade unions). This has implications for all workers, and for other terrains of struggle (for example, around issues of race equality). But for women, whose areas of struggle have been rooted in demands for access to the workplace rather than the changing power relations within it, the implications are particularly important. It also has clear alignments with the imagery of a 'post-feminist' society in which the need for struggle on the terrain of gender relations is ended (Newman, 1991). It is to the politics of change that the final section is addressed.

The chance of change: political and managerial agendas

In this final section I explore some of the changing articulations between the equality agendas of political movements and the managerial and professional agendas of public sector organizations. In doing so I want to argue that equal opportunities is a historically and politically determined set of ideas, which has been articulated with different kinds of managerial and professional agendas. By 'articulation' I do not wish to suggest that managers have responded to equality agendas with a degree of comfort or acceptance; the norm has been one of either tacit resistance or open hostility. However, insofar as equality agendas have been built into policies and practices, this has happened within the framework of professional or managerial regimes current at particular historical moments.

The public sector has largely formed the seed-bed for the development of equal opportunity initiatives in Britain (Coyle, 1989). There have, in recent years, been a number of attempts to evaluate progress and review practice (for example, EOC, 1988) and in general these make depressing reading. It is widely acknowledged that real achievements have been limited, despite the widespread adoption of equal opportunity perspectives by public sector organizations. Some critiques have pointed to the conceptual limitations of policies (Aitkenhead and Liff, 1991); others to the micro-political dynamics surrounding policy development and adoption (Jones, 1988). Cockburn's work highlights the active strategies of resistance put 'in the way of women' by men (Cockburn, 1991).

Rather than evaluating progress, I want to focus on how the terms of the struggle itself have changed. Equal opportunity policies were formulated, and lines of action established, in a very different public sector climate from that which currently prevails. The original setting was a climate in which progressivism (gradual, incremental change towards a distant but desirable goal) formed a fundamental cornerstone of the belief systems of politicians, managers, staff and many activists. This belief system has been challenged and in many cases overthrown in the course of exposure to the radical, transformative changes of the Thatcher years. These destabilized taken-for-granted assumptions about what was desirable and achievable; and about the pace, nature and direction of change. For this reason, we need to conduct our assessments, and debate future courses of action in the light of the changing political and managerial regimes. We need to re-examine what 'equal opportunities' might mean, and how new policy agendas might be formed in the new realities of public sector organizations. But first I want to take a quick (and simplistic) journey through the history of equal opportunities and its articulation with public sector managerial regimes and concerns.

The history of equal opportunities in the British public sector is only partially written. Such a history is problematic for a number of reasons: the diversity of meanings attributed to notions of 'equality'; the diversity of belief structures, resources and political agendas of different organizations; the intersection of different equality struggles around different forms of discrimination and oppression; and, last but not least, the variations within any organization resulting from the changing commitments and energies of key individuals struggling with intractable structures and processes. Because of these factors, any attempt to write history will inevitably distort reality as experienced by those actively working for equality. Nevertheless, I want to distinguish between broad strands of ideology and action which can be traced in the post-war period in an attempt to understand changing definitions of 'equal opportunities' and shifting sets of policies and practices with which it has been associated. These shifting ideologies can be traced across different equality agendas (around race, disability, sexuality and so on) but take different forms and have rather different effects. While it is important to be sensitive to the significance of the interaction between these agendas, I want here to focus on gender.

The first ideological strand underpinning equal opportunities can be characterized as a *liberal model*, based on notions of citizenship. This can be linked to the social changes of the 1960s, which saw the struggle by political groups (women and black minorities) for civil rights and for individual rights of access to mainstream institutions and organizations. Equal opportunities meant 'fair access', and activity focused on the recruitment and selection policies and practices of organizations. This model has left a long-lasting legacy, and remains the dominant underpinning of many policy agendas (for example, in the creation of strong institutional links between equal opportunities officers or units and personnel departments). Its weakness lies in its individualism; its limited notions of justice and fairness; and its focus on access to organizations at the expense of what happens to groups within organizations once entry has been gained.

A second model can be characterized as a *social welfare model*. This developed out of the expansion of professionalized state welfare provision in the mid-1960s, which aimed to ameliorate residual social problems. A range of initiatives was developed to tackle the problems faced by particular groups so that all could have equality of access to the promised benefits of the affluent society – education, housing, employment and so on. The model entered the professional vocabularies of managers within the public sector and lingered long after the 'affluent society' was a thing of the past, receiving boosts as events (for example, the 'riots' of the early 1980s) moved particular problems up the political agenda and triggered new forms of action. One of the core discourses of Equal Opportunities remains that of overcoming disadvantage resulting from 'deficits', and is linked to the development of special provision (for example, training) for 'disadvantaged' groups. Such provision is often resisted by dominant groups (who see it as 'reverse discrimination') and may also be rejected by more privileged members of disadvantaged groups ('Don't link us with their problems'). The model takes us beyond the individualism of the liberal model, but it contains its own set of problems in the way in which race, gender, etc. are treated as universal categories and are linked to disadvantage, thus pathologizing and stigmatizing 'minorities' within a framework which attempts to bring them up to the 'norm' of society as a whole.

These first two models ('liberal' and 'social welfare') represented the dominant equality agendas of public sector organizations until the mid-1980s. Each interacts with managerial discourses: the first with the liberal discourse of 'fairness' and administrative justice built into public sector bureaucracies; the second with the welfare discourses of the public sector professions. However, it is important to acknowledge the development of political perspectives which entered managerial or professional vocabularies only at the margins, but which helped shape the political agendas of equalities activists. One development was the struggle within trade unions and within organizations for improved pay and employment entitlements for low-paid women workers; that is, the struggle for collective, rather than individual rights. A second set of developments stemmed from the 'new social movements' and radical politics which, throughout the 1970s and early 1980s, led to the recognition of multiple and interacting patterns of discrimination around gender, race and sexuality. This led to the establishment of new political agendas in some London and metropolitan local authorities, including, in some cases, policies on lesbian and gay rights, and the incorporation of such issues into organizational bureaucracies through the establishment of race equality units and/or women's units. More generally, the impact of feminism has led to dissatisfactions with the liberal and welfarist models of equality and a shift towards looking at the outcomes of public sector employment practices and of service provision – what some have termed a *radical model* of equal opportunities (Jewson and Mason, 1986.)[8] Women began to be concerned with how resources (jobs and services) were distributed, and to focus on the power structures and organizational cultures through which inequalities in outcome were reproduced. This operated alongside liberal or welfarist models and in tension with them, with equalities officers often negotiating the tensions between radical perspectives (held by parts of the workforce or by women's groups in the community) and the liberal or welfarist models acceptable to management.

The changing political and economic terrain of the 1980s has led to major shifts in the established patterns of articulation between equal opportunities and the managerial/professional regimes of public sector organizations. The political climate of liberal support for equal opportunities was radically curtailed. The institutional base for equality policies was eroded with government targeting of 'loony left' local authorities and abolition of the GLC and Metropolitan Counties. Particular policy areas which had incorporated elements of both welfarist and radical agendas ('multi-cultural' education and anti-racist policies) were attacked (Sondhi and Salmon, 1992); and in the case of policies on lesbian and gay rights, became the subject of legislation (Local Government Act 1988).

Economic factors also led to change, but this was more contradictory. The emphasis on cost constraints led many organizations to see equal opportunities as an 'expensive luxury', and to curtail previous initiatives. At the same time, other economic and demographic factors (potential skills shortages and cost of labour) led to a new focus on recruitment and retention issues. Many organizations began to set up women-returner schemes, and to offer better maternity leave provision, retraining and childcare support. There was a brief period of optimism in the late 1980s in which there was talk of demographic change leading to improvements in the employment prospects of women, and to better facilities and support for women staff as organizations adapted to their needs. Management was now going to have to address the issues which women had had on their political agenda for many years. However, the changes which followed did not fulfil their promise for two reasons. First, demographic change was accompanied by recession which meant that labour was not as scarce as had been anticipated, so changes were of smaller scale and less radical. Secondly, the new provisions for women with young children often resulted in the establishment of a 'mummy track' running alongside, but not integrated with, the mainstream career tracks of an organization (Hall, 1989).

There are, however, some linkages between these improvements and developments within management in the 1980s. We can identify a new equal opportunity model emerging in this period – *maximizing human resources* – which is articulated with the growing organizational salience of Human Resource Management. This differs from the older personnel management articulation which focused on recruitment and selection and the fair administration of equal opportunity systems, rules and procedures. HRM is concerned with maximizing the contribution of all categories of staff, and thus has to address the factors which might inhibit or block the release of the energies and talents of women staff. As well as childcare and maternity or parental leave, questions of training, development, appraisal, promotion and status are raised; and some (admittedly few) organizations have begun to look at issues of culture and management style in order to maximize the strengths of a diverse workforce. And women may be seen as having particular contributions to make to the project of rebuilding more people-based organizational cultures. Linking the rise of HRM to the new focus on business efficiency, Everitt comments: 'The new wave of enterprise incorporates women more firmly into management; after all, interpersonal skills are their very *raison d'être*. At the same time, equal opportunities requirements appear to be met' (Everitt, 1990: 144).

There are clear links, then, between the HRM approach and the *business efficiency* model of management increasingly being adopted within the public sector. Here, equality issues are dependent on the labour market needs and profiles of organizations and their sub-units. In some they will be ignored. Others may adopt positive recruitment or retention policies to overcome skills shortages. Yet others may adopt high-profile equality policies to raise their public profile and image. This model is perhaps the dominant model at the time of writing. It underpins the Opportunity 2000 initiative, which was launched in 1991 to encourage British business to take full advantage of the economic potential of women in the workforce. Its philosophy is spelled out in its publicity materials: 'Campaign members accept that in the long term their companies will be best served by a balance of women and men in their workforce in all areas and at all levels, especially in management, that reflects the abilities of the labour force as a whole.'

One of the interesting features of the HRM and business efficiency models is the often explicit contrast with earlier equality discourses. For example, in an interview, Caroline Langridge, head of the NHS Women's Unit, identified the meaning of the success for the Opportunity 2000 initiative in the health service as follows: 'We are not saying we've cracked the problem, but we're getting there. This is not just some woolly, liberal, social justice campaign. One of the real driving forces is *the need to make the best use of resources and avoid wastage*' (*Guardian* 21 October 1992: 35, my emphasis).

The earlier liberal or 'rights'/justice models are rejected and the new efficiency arguments are stripped of any political inflection. The articulation with equality discourses is one in which managerialism is clearly dominant. These perspectives, then, do not grapple with the deeper lines of inequality which stem from the realities of the gender dynamics of organizational power. In providing a legitimating framework for the reworking of equality goals, the goals are stripped of their politics.

But the new business language and managerial agendas can nevertheless provide different points of articulation with more politically based equality perspectives. There are (at least) three potential lines of articulation. First, the new managerialism, with its focus on outcomes, can provide a set of techniques (the setting of goals and performance targets, the developments of indicators of progress, the monitoring of performance) which can be used to support the implementation of policies designed to foster women's development. Organizations can move from a policy agenda oriented towards 'how things should be done' (for example, the procedural basis of recruitment policies) to an agenda which sets out what should be achieved. They can set targets and evaluate results (an approach promoted by the Opportunity 2000 initiative designed to increase the numbers of women in management posts). They can use the frameworks offered by contract, inspection and audit to monitor the progress and achievements of different units within an organization and its partners, and to help them identify blocks to progress. (A number of organizations are beginning to hold 'equality audits'.) They can begin collecting data to monitor and evaluate the distribution of internal resources such as training.

Secondly, the significance of culture in the managerial literature can be used to raise questions about how organizations can build cultures which sustain women who take on managerial roles. Policies (and government-led initiatives such as Opportunity 2000) are important; but so are the more intangible dimensions of culture, symbolism and values. The history of equal opportunities has demonstrated that rational plans (however well intentioned) are not enough to bring about change. It is the values, culture and informal messages that run around and through the plans that make or break the initiatives. However, the current popularity of 'culture' as a management concept will by no means automatically lead organizations to address the cultural barriers to women. The homogeneous and consensual model of culture which pervades the managerial literature is profoundly flawed (Newman, 1992a, 1992b). And although culture may have become an important concern of women managers, it remains a marginal concern for many equalities activists in the light of the erosion of jobs, pay and entitlements of the female workforce as a whole.

Thirdly, the new discourses of quality can be used to help take equal opportunities beyond the workplace. There is an emerging model of *quality/equality* which redirects attention towards equality issues in the design and delivery of services (for example, LGTB, 1990; LGIU, 1991). This model sees quality as more than setting standards for existing services. Quality is recognized as a contested issue, with diverse definitions and criteria resulting from the interests, priorities or needs of different groups of users or consumers. To deliver quality, it is argued, we need to take account of the diversity of needs in the community. Equality considerations must be addressed in taking decisions at a strategic level (what services and for whom; how scarce resources are to allocated) as well as in decisions about service design and delivery.

There are some limitations to this model. One is the rather unfocused and all-encompassing perspective on equality on which it sometimes seems to be based. In talking about 'diversity' an equivalence between different inequalities (of gender, age, disability, ethnicity) may be assumed. The model has resonances with the earlier 'social welfare' model – the talk is of 'needs' and 'disadvantage'. Questions of power are still not fully addressed, although there is some talk of the need to involve and 'empower' users. the model does, however, draw attention to the inadequacies in the kinds of information which is gathered about communities and service users, and on which the quality and performance of services is evaluated. The collection of such information must be understood as a political as well as technical activity, reflecting the interests and concerns of dominant groups. Lupton (1992: 97) notes that women tend to be absent as a category of knowledge, and so their experience is hidden from the policy process:

> As the role of local authority social service departments changes, their knowledge infrastructures will become more critical in affecting the distribution of resources in a more diversified care market. In this context it is essential that the

androcentric and ethnocentric nature of much organisational 'knowledge' is identified, and confronted with more methodologically rigorous data which reveal the particular experiences and needs of black and white female clients.

The quality/equality approach has resonances with the social welfare underpinnings of professional practices. In the 1970s and 1980s issues of gender and ethnicity were incorporated within professional discourse (for example through training) and aligned to new welfare practices. Within these professional discourses gender and ethnicity became represented in the form of new sets of 'needs' to be acknowledged alongside the class-based needs of poverty, housing and health which dominated the post-war welfare orientations. There was some acknowledgement of issues of diversity (for example shown in the growth of 'multi-cultural' education). However, the structural inequalities between men and women, between black and white, largely remained invisible: the problem was constructed as that of bringing disadvantaged groups up to the standard of the 'norm'.

We can perhaps, then, trace two divergent lines along which political equalities agendas have become incorporated into organizational regimes: one through professional and welfare practices; the second through managerial discourses and practices, based on notions of HRM and of business efficiency. These two streams have followed different trajectories. Although there have been many points of overlap, the key difference is between the external focus of professional discourses (inequality operates somehow 'out there' and does not touch us personally) and the internal focus of HRM. I want to suggest the possibility that these two streams are being rearticulated around the new discourses of quality which are becoming increasingly significant within public sector organizations in the 1990s. Quality offers a new point of energy and excitement for professionals, since it provides a new focus on the services which they deliver, and for managers, since it seemingly offers a source of positive change (in contrast to the value for money ideology of the 1980s) and a means by which their skills can be seen to 'add value' to the organization. The appearance of the term 'quality and equality' signifies a concern with issues of access, of user involvement in the design and delivery of services, and the recognition of a diversity of perspectives on what quality might mean. It has occurred mainly in local authorities where it provides a new focus for those of a left/liberal persuasion who might earlier have been involved in community development (in the 1970s) or decentralization to neighbourhood offices (in the 1980s). And it suffers from a similar set of problems: in the same way that concepts of community and neighbourhood were weak and often untheorized, so too is the concept of inequality here.

In this final section I have traced a number of strands in the articulation between equalities agendas and the new managerialism. The 'organizational effectiveness' arguments for equality can be seen as a new phase of equal opportunities ideology which, while legitimizing the equalities terrain, robs it of any political inflection. It can be seen as the latest in a series of equality ideologies (justice, fairness, social welfare, recognizing diversity, etc.), which have gained greater or lesser prominence as the history of the last thirty years has unfolded. Today equality has been dressed in management garb, is articulated through the language of effectiveness, performance, human resource management and competitive success.

I have suggested that there may be a number of limitations inherent in managerialism as a means of delivering equality goals. Each of these is based on the fundamental problem concerning the ability of managerialism to deliver any change which presents challenges to established sources of power. A number of issues emerge for those concerned with bringing about change aiming to benefit women, or to achieve a greater recognition of the value of women's work. One issue concerns how far a political, rather than managerial, agenda for change can be seen as legitimate in the political climate of Britain in the mid-1990s. If there is acknowledgement of a need for a continued or re-energized political agenda, a second issue arises: this concerns how far the current patterns of organizational change might help or hinder women as agents of change, rather than just the recipients of managerially approved amendments to the status quo. A critical factor here is how women (and others) are treated when they stick their heads above the consensual parapet of the new managerialism and argue for change which is perceived as inconvenient, uncomfortable or threatening. The third, and perhaps most important, set of issues concerns how far change which is bounded within organizations, and which does not address the material factors which affect women's lives as service users and as members of families and communities can be effective.

As we move towards the second half of the 1990s, it is likely that the pace of public sector change will decrease and that a new orthodoxy about what public sector organizations should be like and how they should be managed will emerge from the ruins of the old. The present period of shifting and uncertain cultural patterns is a transitional moment between the old fixed bureaucratic and professional cultures in which women knew their place (but at least their place was relatively secure) and the new cultural forms presently taking shape. It is important that the future is shaped in a way which does not merely reconstitute the problems of the past in new guises. How far women can do so within the efficiency frameworks and consensual bias of the new managerialism remains a key question for the 1990s and beyond.

Notes

I would like to thank Gail Lewis for her detailed and helpful comments on a draft of this chapter.

1. These and subsequent comments are based on discussions with personnel officers in local government, with equality officers in trade unions and my own research with women leaders across the public sector.

2. Quality is a more ambiguous terrain, with men tending to dominate the technocratic and bureaucratic quality assurance approaches linked to BS 5750, but greater female involvement in (and leadership of) the 'softer' approaches to quality management based on customer care and user involvement. These patterns are not yet fixed, however, as the field is still emerging and developing, and many exceptions to this general pattern occur.

3. Restructuring is also shifting this kind of labour out into the 'community' to be handled by domestic labour and voluntary work.

4. These comments are drawn from emerging evidence from interviews with women managers and leaders across the public sector.

5. Cultures are of course racialized as well as organized around gender divisions, but this has not been the prime focus of my study. It is likely, however, that the three cultural forms I identify will have different kinds of implication for black managers. For example, 'traditional' cultures are essentially white, with little tolerance of difference and diversity. The shift to 'competitive' cultures may open up some space for entrepreneurial black managers, but only at the margins. Transformational cultures are based on an essentially white imagery of the charismatic leader, and are built around profoundly ethnocentric models of leadership.

6. See Hunt (1991) for a summary of the literature on 'transformational' leadership.

7. These ideas are of crucial importance for the new public sector. They signal the need to go beyond functional rationality and cost criteria in the restructuring processes which beset public sector organizations. They suggest a need to devote energy and resources to building successful partnerships in the new 'mixed economy' of provision – working with other organizations in the public, private and voluntary sectors requires more than the technical skills of sewing up a technical specification or writing a loophole-free contract.

8. The distinction between 'liberal' and 'radical' models is widespread in the literature, and is based on Jewson and Mason (1986). Cockburn (1991) prefers a rather different formulation which distinguishes between different lengths of equality agenda rather than a binary division between liberal and radical models.

References

Aitkenhead, M. and Liff, S. (1991) 'The effectiveness of equal opportunity policies', in J. Firth-Cozens and M. West (eds), *Women at Work: Psychological and Organisational Perspectives*. Milton Keynes: Open University Press.

Allan, M., Bhavnani, R. and French, K. (1992) *Promoting Women: Management Development and Training for Women in Social Services Departments*. London: HMSO (Social Security Inspectorate).

Clarke, J. and Newman, J. (1993) 'The right to manage: a second managerial revolution?' *Cultural Studies*, 7(3): 427–41.

Cockburn, C. (1991) *In the Way of Women: Men's Resistance to Sex Equality in Organisations*. London: Macmillan.

Coyle, A. (1989) 'The limits of change: local government and equal opportunities for women', *Public Administration*, Spring, 67(1): 39–50.

Davidson, M.J. and Cooper, C.L. (1992) *Shattering the Glass Ceiling: The Woman Manager*. London: Paul Chapmen.

du Gay, P. (1990) 'Enterprise culture and the "search for excellence"', paper presented (with G. Salaman) to conference on 'Employee Relations in the Enterprise Culture', Cardiff Business School, September.

Equal Opportunities Commission (1988) *Local Authority Equal Opportunity Policies: Report of a Survey by the EOC*. Manchester: EOC.

Everitt, A. (1990) 'Will women managers save social work?' in P. Carter, T. Jeffs and M. Smith (eds), *Social Work and Social Welfare Yearbook, 1990*. Milton Keynes: Open University Press.

Foster, J. (1987) 'Women on the wane', *Insight* 2(50): 14–15.

Foster, J. (1988a) 'On the hop', *Insight* 3(21): 20–1.

Foster, J. (1988b) 'Girls on top', *Insight* 3(22): 12–13.

Hall, D.T. (1989) 'An organisational change approach: moving beyond the "Mommy Track"', *Personnel* (December): 23–9.

Handy, C. (1989) *The Age of Unreason*. London: Hutchinson.

Hansard Society (1990) *Women at the Top*. London: Hansard Society.

Hunt, J.G. (1991) *Leadership: a New Synthesis*. London: Sage.

Institute of Management (1992) *The Key to the Men's Club*. Bristol: IM Books.

Jewson, N. and Mason, D. (1986) 'The theory and practice of equal opportunities', *Sociological Review*, 34(2): 307–34.

Jones, P. (1988) 'Policy and praxis: local government, a case for treatment?' in A. Coyle and J. Skinner (eds), *Women and Work: Positive Action for Change*. London: Macmillan Education.

Kanter, R.M. (1989) *When Giants Learn to Dance: Mastering the Challenges of Strategy, Management and Careers in the 1990s*. London: Simon & Schuster.

Local Government Information Unit (1991) *New Directions in Local Government 3: Quality and Equality*. London: LGIU.

Local Government Training Board (1990) *Breaking Down the Barriers: Woman Managers in Local Government*. Luton: LGTB.

Lupton, C. (1992) 'Feminism, managerialism and performance measurement', in M. Langan and L. Day (eds), *Women, Oppression and Social Work*. London: Routledge.

Nevill, G., Pennicott, A., Williams, J. and Worrall, A. (1991) *Women in the Workforce: The Effect of Demographic Changes in the 1990s*. London: The Industrial Society.

Newman, J. (1991) 'Enterprising women: images of success', in S. Franklin, C. Lury and J. Stacey (eds), *Off Centre: Feminism and Cultural Studies*. London: Harper Collins.

Newman, J. (1992a) 'Beyond the visions: linking strategy, culture and change', paper presented to the British Academy of Management Conference, September.

Newman, J. (1992b) 'Language, culture and change', paper presented to the International Organisational Development Association conference, December.

O'Brien, P. (1993) *Taking the Macho out of Management*. London: Sheldon Business Books.

Peters, T. (1989) *Thriving on Chaos*. London: Pan.

Pinch, S. (1992) 'Labour flexibility and the public sector', paper presented at the conference 'Towards a Post-Fordist Welfare State?', University of Teesside.

Social Services Inspectorate (1991) *Women in Social Services: A Neglected Resource*. London: Department of Health, SSI.

Sondhi, R. and Salmon, H. (1992) 'Race, racism and local authorities', *Local Government Policy Making*, 18(5): 3–10.

Walby, S. (1992) 'Professionals and post-Fordism: the NHS in transition?' paper presented at the conference 'Towards a Post-Fordist Welfare State?', University of Teesside.

Wood, S. (1989) 'New wave management', *Work, Employment and Society*, 3(3): 379–402.

10

Control, Commitment and Contracts

Norman Flynn

Metaphors and the reforms in the public sector

Morgan (1986) argued that there is a variety of metaphors which managers use to make sense of the organizations in which they work. For example, some use the metaphor of the machine, in which the parts of the organization relate to each other according to pre-designed mechanical routines. Others see the organization as a brain learning about its environment, or as an organism which develops to fit well with its environment. The organizations which make up the welfare state in the United Kingdom are in the process of being reformed and redesigned by a series of structural and procedural changes. We can deduce the dominant metaphors from the actions which the government has taken and the behaviour of the managers in the new structures and systems.

The major changes have been:

1 Organizations have been divided into 'buyers' and 'sellers'. This has been done very starkly in the NHS, Units, whether directly managed or organized as NHS Trusts being clearly the providers and the Districts acting as service purchasers. While there is some ambiguity about GPs, who are both services providers and purchasers, the roles are relatively clear. In local authorities the division is happening at varying speeds. Some authorities have enthusiastically embraced the idea of a division into the two activities, while others are trying to preserve the integration of service specification and service delivery. In the civil service there are agreements between the executive agencies and the parent departments which in some cases look the same as a contract to provide services, but it is not clear that the specification of the work is equivalent to the activity of purchasing in the NHS.

2 There has been an increase in competition, both within and between organizations. Compulsory competitive tendering in local authorities has been in force for some activities since 1981 and has been spreading to all the activities done by manual workers and more recently to activities carried out by white-collar and professional workers. Market testing has been introduced in the civil service, which is a similar process. There has been a great deal of 'externalization' or contracting out of activities which is also now spreading to professional and

technical activities and not just ancillary functions such as building cleaning and catering.

3   There have been moves towards the devolution of responsibility and accountability, but uneven devolution of authority and control. Parallel with the introduction of competition, the institutions are being broken up into cost or profit centres which have increased accountability for the way they use money and for the services which they perform. Sometimes this is accompanied by increased managerial authority, but sometimes the increased accountability does not bring with it the 'right to manage' or the control over resources which would be necessary to meet the accountability targets.

4   There are gradual moves away from national pay bargaining, which is allowing managers of departments or units to include wage bargaining in their managerial set of tools. This is often accompanied by increased flexibility in pay and conditions, with local and skill supplements, upwards and downwards flexibility as a result of competition.

5   At the same time there are increasing differentials, especially between the extremes of top and bottom. Competition on price for the work done by manual workers has tended to reduce the total remuneration of, especially, women manual workers. The introduction of general management at unit level, whether hospitals or schools, has produced higher management salaries.

Scientific management in the machine bureaucracies of the market

The basic idea underlying these changes is superficially that of a market with trading, competition and bargaining among purchasers and relatively autonomous sellers. Within the seller organizations the emphasis is on performance against the prices set and delivery to the specification. This idea of the organization is likely to produce an approach to management within the provider organizations which follows the machine metaphor and the principles of 'scientific management'. The purchaser parts of the organizations specify what is required of the providers, mainly through a description of the work processes which they are expected to perform. In the case of education the National Curriculum and the use of Standard Attainment Tests were two attempts to define in the 'contract' between the Department for Education and the schools what the schools are expected to do. The use of independent inspectors to make sure that they do follow the rules is the main control mechanism between the government and the schools. The standardization of work processes in health care is similar. Contracts in many cases are very specific about the way in which work is to be done, rather than what the result of the work is expected to be.

The use of standardized work processes as the main co-ordination and control mechanism is the major feature of organizations which Mintzberg (1983) characterizes as 'machine bureaucracies'. The market which the reforms have established contains a machine metaphor within the organizations, and in the relationships between the purchasers and providers in practice. In these systems, it appears that managers are using some of the techniques of scientific management as a way of controlling the labour process.

Braverman (1974) says that there are three principles in scientific management as expounded by Taylor. The first is 'the dissociation of the labour process from the skills of the workers'. The way in which work is carried out depends not on the skills of the workforce but on the design of the work processes by the management. The second is 'the separation of conception from execution'. This is not just the separation of mental from manual labour, but also the separation of conception from execution even within mental labour: 'mental labour is first separated from manual labour and . . . is then itself subdivided rigorously according to the same rule'. The third principle is that management develops a monopoly of knowledge and uses that monopoly to control the labour process.

Management within a contract environment has a tendency to follow these principles. The separation of the conception from the execution occurs within the contract which defines how the work is to be done. An example of scientific management in practice is the increasing use of performance measurement and performance-related pay in the provider organizations. These efforts increase the individualization of work and the division of labour, since individual performance has to be related to individual rather than group or team tasks. By definition, control is exercised by a superior through the use of the performance-related pay system, rather than being self-imposed by the worker. Later we shall see that this is not a necessary consequence of the contracting process, as contracts could be written in a way which allows workers, both manual and mental, more control over the labour process.

From control to commitment: the 'new human resource management'

Meanwhile there is a counter-tendency in management thought and practice. Many organizations in the private and public sectors have been trying to find an alternative way of managing workers which does not involve the principles of scientific management. One such alternative is the attempt to control labour and the labour process by developing commitment among the workforce. Rather than measuring performance and managing through a process of direct supervision, more emphasis is placed on self-control and the development of the skills and contribution of the workforce. The elements of such an approach to managing people have been termed the 'New Human Resources Management' by people in the human resource management field or 'New Management Techniques' by the left. The overall approach stresses the importance of getting away from the minute division of labour and the 'separation of conception from execution'.

Let us consider which of these paradigms, scientific management and management through commitment, is likely to dominate the future of management in the public sector. While the two approaches are clearly contradictory, it may well be the case that they will develop simultaneously within organizations, causing anxiety for the workforce and confusion among managers. These ideas about managing people appear unevenly in the UK private sector but many have been adopted, in principle at least, by managers in the public sector. For each feature there is likely to be a counter-tendency pushing in the opposite direction.

The features of the commitment approach include:

- flexible job descriptions;
- an emphasis on team-working and team-building;
- an emphasis on commitment and trainability as criteria for selection and promotion;
- personnel functions and human resource management are devolved 'down the line';
- assessment used as a way of stretching and developing people;
- harmonization of conditions of service.

Its introduction in the UK has been patchy, especially compared with the UK's competitors. There have been many managers in the public sector who recognize the value of these approaches. However, there are many contextual factors in the 'new public management' which push them in the opposite directions.

There has been much rhetoric about 'close to the customer', 'value management', 'delayering' and other catchphrases in the public sector in the last decade. For example, the Benefits Agency has adopted four core values as the basis for the Board's management approach. These include 'closeness to the customer' and 'a bias for action' as value principles which should be enacted by a different approach to the control of the work process. Many local authorities have adopted an approach to quality management which emphasizes more self-control by workers and a team-based approach to service delivery.

In this section we look at the elements of the new approach to human resource management and ask whether they are likely to be implemented in the new frameworks which have been established by the recent reforms.

Flexible job descriptions

If the division of labour is to be made less fine, then people's job descriptions need to be broader and the tasks specified in the production process need to be more flexible. For example, the flexibility of the workforce on the Nissan production line allows management to move workers from task to task as required, subject to their having the relevant skills.

The stated reasons for such an approach are not only that the absence of demarcation creates fewer productivity problems, but also enables people to change, learn and develop. The tendency is partly a result of the speed of technology change: as the life-cycle of machines shortens, so the possibility of a worker acquiring and using one set of skills for a lifetime reduces. Flexibility and continual retraining are one solution to the problem of technology change: the other is a continuous replacement of the workforce by new people with new skills. The other reason for having flexible job descriptions is that it enables the plant to work with fewer workers: people can be moved to another task if they have no work at their original work station. The total amount of unproductive time can be reduced.

There is some evidence of this tendency in the public sector: in some manual trades in building maintenance, there are now tradespeople who will do work previously only done by other trades, for example plumbers carrying out plastering or carpenters painting their own repairs. Teachers' duties are more wide-ranging in their new contracts. Care workers in social service departments are expected to be flexible about the locations in which they work and the tasks they perform. Rather than being employed at one location, people are increasingly employed by the department and expected to travel to wherever the clients are.

The counter-tendency arises from the use of service contracts which are highly specific about work practices. If a contract specifies in detail the duties to be carried out and the qualifications of the service providers, there is less room for flexibility. For example, contracts for home-care services can be very specific about the exact individual services which the care worker is expected to perform and how long each should take.

An emphasis on team-working and team-building

If the labour process is not to be determined by scientific management techniques and individual tasks and jobs designed in great detail, one option is to encourage teams to develop, on the assumption that teams are more productive and creative than fragmented individuals. This approach challenges the scientific management assumption that managers can design every aspect of the work process. There are some efforts in this direction. Sometimes temporary teams are established to work on quality problems, for example. Such quality circles have been fashionable in parts of the civil service. There is a tradition in social work of team-working which still persists in some departments. There are experiments in Northern Ireland in which a team-based approach to care, based on GPs' surgeries, brings together professionals from a number of disciplines in a patient-centred service. The teams collaborate to provide a range of services.

However, many forces pull in the opposite direction. For example, performance-related pay in the public sector is more often individually rather than team based. This places the emphasis on individual rather than team contribution. The buyer–seller divide in social services tends to split teams and establish new forms of relationship based on quasi-contracts rather than collaborative working. As services are contractualized, the elements of service which an individual receives are defined in detail and a package of individual services is created.

*An emphasis on commitment and trainability as criteria for
selection and promotion*

Trainability is really an aspect of flexibility and is based on the idea that the organization's employees must develop or the company will stagnate. Again, Nissan use willingness to train as a criterion for selection of employees. Commitment to the company is clearly not an inherent characteristic, rather something which is engendered by other elements of the employment bargain. There are some signs of this in the public sector, although recruitment is still largely based on existing qualities, skills and qualifications rather than the potential for development, except on special training programmes. It may be that if the use of the National Vocational Qualifications develops, that the willingness to move through the NVQ levels will become a selection criterion.

*Personnel functions and human resource management are devolved
'down the line'*

The separation of personnel functions from general management implies that managers' work is about organizing and directing the work process, not recruiting, training and motivating the people who are carrying out the processes. The integration of the personnel functions with general management assumes that managers need to include the process of developing people in their work. In the Executive Agencies, personnel matters are normally transferred with the agency functions, but still operated in a relatively centralized way within them. There are exceptions, such as in the Employment Service, where many of the functions of personnel are devolved to line management. In the NHS, the Trusts have to take on the personnel tasks previously carried out by the District Health Authorities, since trust employees are now the responsibility of the Trusts. As national wage bargaining breaks down because of the splitting up of the public sector into relatively autonomous units, more human resource management matters are dealt with at local level. In the education service, teachers are recruited at school level although technically they are still employed by the education authorities. School governing bodies now have to deal with questions of pay, promotion and dismissal.

There is some evidence that the devolution of personnel responsibilities causes problems for managers who have not necessarily acquired the skills required for these functions. This is probably a transitional problem which will be overcome by training and development of managers at local level. Currently, however, problems are arising through lack of basic knowledge about employment law and rights and lack of basic skills of supervision and disciplinary procedures.

The counter-tendency comes from the assumptions about pay levels which are included in the pricing policy of purchasers. The flexibility to change pay and pay regimes is circumscribed by the available money. In the NHS for example, there is still a strong tendency to use the national pay scales as a basis for pricing.

Assessment used as a way of stretching and developing people

Appraisal schemes are more based on performance than attributes, and the assessment process is more used as a way of finding out how people can improve their skills than as a way of judging their previous performance. Performance appraisal and assessment are areas in which the division between scientific management and more modern approaches are most clear: the processes can be used either to judge retrospectively performance against a target which has been imposed by the hierarchy, or to help people develop more of their potential in the interests of the performance of the organization.

There is little sign of this tendency in the public sector because the appraisal schemes are having to cope with the task of assessing individual performance against targets set for the previous year.

Harmonization of conditions of service

Many Japanese, North American and European companies have harmonized their conditions of service to remove the differences between the condition of manual, clerical and managerial labour. Unified eating and parking arrangements, hours of work, holiday entitlements and so on are supposed to create a spirit of unity which increases commitment to the company. There are not many signs of this tendency, except in some parts of local government. 'Industrial civil servants' are a surviving category who have different conditions from other civil servants. Within the white-collar civil service, the idea of a unified service with equal conditions is breaking down as the executive agencies slowly develop their own personnel policies.

Greater differentials between the top and the bottom of the organizations are arising in the NHS, and especially the NHS Trusts, with managers getting higher rewards and many fringe benefits. Short-term contracts are in fact turning out to be very lucrative for those whose contracts are terminated early. The first Director of Finance for the Guy's and Lewisham Hospital Trust, for example, lasted less than a year and was entitled to a large compensatory payment because of his fixed-term contract. Meanwhile, ancillary workers are increasingly being employed by contracting companies on terms and conditions which do not match those of the direct employees and certainly not those of the managers. Short-term contracts and part-time work for the manual workers are far away from the contractual positions and performance-related pay arrangements for trust managers.

What is the likely future for human resource management in the public sector?

There are many managers in the public sector who realize that management through the development of commitment can be more effective than management through work study and the detailed design of jobs. While they will not be fooled into trying to adopt practices which are clearly well out of line with their actual context, they still like the idea of managing through commitment and the development of the values of the organization rather than through the mechanistic approach implied by scientific management. In any case, as Mintzberg argues, it is difficult to manage professional work, in which the work processes derive from long training and custom and practice, through scientific management and the definition by managers of the individual elements of the work process.

There is pressure to introduce individual performance-related pay schemes. The Treasury and the Citizen's Charters promote individual performance measurement and individual performance-related pay. The evidence from both the private and public sectors indicates that performance-related pay works well in a limited range of circumstances: where individual contribution can easily be identified; when the amounts of money involved are substantial and when the workers can see a clear relationship between their effort and their reward. There are schemes in the public sector in which most of these conditions apply. However, there are others in which small amounts are paid for performance which in fact depends on a group effort.

Competitive tendering or 'market testing' leads to job insecurity and a concentration on short-term considerations. This makes managers feel that a developmental approach to managing people is a long-term luxury which reduces competitiveness. In a sense this is correct: allowing people to grow into jobs which may exist only until the next tendering round brings an unreality to the process. Meanwhile, allowing groups to redesign the way they work is contrary to a contract culture in which work processes are part of the contractual agreement.

What is likely to happen is something much closer to Charles Handy's 'shamrock organisation' (described in *The Age of Unreason*, 1989: 75–81) in which there is a core of relatively secure, professional workers. There will be a 'flexible' (that is, short-term contract) workforce and a series of contractors and subcontractors, which Handy calls the 'contractual fringe'. It is difficult to predict the functions of the 'core' or how big it will be. The contracting process fragments the public services: organizations which were previously vertically integrated fragment into independent service delivery parts, purchasing parts and policy-making parts.

As local authorities approach the task of preparing their professional services for competitive tendering, it is less easy to identify the core of the organizations. There is a debate about how much of the local authorities' workforce is there to help the process of democratic representation and how much is actually concerned with either direct or indirect service delivery. Those tasks which are concerned with helping to articulate and implement political choices about how money is spent and what services are provided are distinct both from the tasks which are about specifying and commissioning services, and distinct again from those which are about providing services. If the core consists only of the first of these three categories, then it is likely to be very small indeed. Even if it includes the second, that of specifying and commissioning services and organizing the rationing process, it excludes the bulk of the workforce.

If we look at the service delivery side of the organization, this too may be divided into Handy's three categories. For example, a school has a permanent staff of teachers, some of whose jobs are also managerial. It also has a small core whose task is to look after the buildings and the administration. It then has series of people on different sorts of contracts: teachers hired on a sessional contract; classroom assistants who may be hired on annual contracts. Then there are people who work for firms which have contracts with the school: building maintenance and grounds people and, increasingly, professionals previously employed by the local education authority. As the education authorities break up and become much smaller, many services such as staff and curriculum development become 'contractorized' and are sold and provided to schools by units whose existence depends on them being able to win contracts with the schools.

If we look at the case of home care in social services we see a slightly different pattern. Once the social services department are divided into purchasers and providers, as many are already, the service delivery part of the home-care service consists of a core of managers and organizers and a series of workers with varying degrees of attachment to the core: some may be permanently employed, others temporarily employed and there is a growing number of independent contractors. In turn, the contractors have employees, mainly organizers and a series of self-employed home carers who contract with the contractor for access to clients.

How this model applies will depend in part on the degree of competition and the way in which that competition is conducted. If contractors are hired on relatively short contracts, then the job security of the employees will be low. Contractors, whether in the public or private sector, will only be able to survive by expanding and shrinking the workforce in line with their workload.

If there is a relatively stable competitive environment and some degree of predictability about workload, modern ideas about human resource management may be able to develop. Even then, employers will be subject to the impact of variable budgets and changing competitive conditions. We have seen that companies that had a relatively modern approach to personnel management, such as IBM and SAS, make redundancies and therefore create uncertainty when the recession or competitive pressures mean that costs have to be cut to ensure survival. If there is any stability, it is most likely to occur in the 'core' areas, rather than those which are subject to competition. The way in which people are able to manage in other parts of the organizations, whether they are private or public sector contractors, will depend to a large degree on how the competition and contracting process is itself managed.

The impact of contracting on the management process

The relationship between purchasing strategy and human resource strategy is crucial: modern purchasing behaviour involves long-term contracts and interlocking relationships between purchasers and sellers. In the case of the Japanese car industry, for example, component supplies are organized through long-term agreements which involve not only supply of the parts but, in many cases, a profit-sharing arrangement between the component maker and the final producer, agreements on the development of the product and a high degree of co-ordination of the production processes to ensure delivery. Oakland describes the process in *Total Quality Management* (1989): 'The development of long-term relationships with fewer suppliers, rather than short-term ones with many, leads to the concept of co-producers in networks of trust providing dependable quality and delivery of goods and services.'

He goes on to say that such methods are more common in assembly-line operations, but: 'Nevertheless, there must be a recognition of the need to develop closer relationships and begin the dialogue – sharing of information and problems – which leads to the product or service of the right time' (Oakland, 1989: 99–100).

This degree of interdependence would produce an unsatisfactory outcome if components were purchased through a series of competitive bids. If such arrangements were made with price the main criterion for choice of supplier, quality would also suffer. Deming (1986) argues that purchasing mainly on price has a detrimental effect on quality. Long-term relationships produce greater stability and allow a way of managing people which emphasizes commitment and development. Short contracts, and contracts which result from a sudden-death competition based on price, make such an approach to HRM less likely.

Most of the recent reforms involve the establishment of contractual relationships, either within the public sector institutions or between them and the private and voluntary sectors. The introduction of competitive tendering in local government, the division of the NHS into purchasers and providers, 'market testing' of civil service functions, the competitions for prison management, the move towards a division between purchasers and providers in the personal social services, all involve new relationships. Potentially, such developments substitute contractual methods of control over services and service delivery for the previous hierarchical methods. Far from introducing the above ideas of management through the development of commitment, this set of relationships requires the development of different techniques to achieve control through contracts.

There are two related sets of problems: how the purchasers control the delivery of services by the providers; and how the provider organizations manage themselves within the contractual framework. There are many different combinations of the ways in which the solutions to those problems produce new management practices. There are various options for the way in which purchasers can operate.

What to purchase

The first option is that the purchasers can choose to *take detailed instructions from politicians*: they represent the electors and taxpayers and they alone should decide what service is provided. This choice is partly a constitutional one: if local authority elected members or ministers have a constitutional right, then, of course, managers have to obey instructions. If purchasers follow this option, they orient their effort towards understanding the politicians' interpretations of what is required and the management of the political process to ensure that the instructions of what to purchase are delivered in a way which can be operationalized through their purchasing behaviour.

The second option for the purchasers is to *ask the users of the services what they want* and then, subject to budgetary and political constraints, use professional judgement and purchase services accordingly. Under this option, purchasers have to conduct market research under the assumption that services are provided according to an individualistic notion of consumer rights.

The third option is to *consult the service providers*, who are most in touch with the service users, and have greatest professional expertise, and ask them what they would like to sell. This option recognizes the value of 'closeness to the customer' and that people delivering services are more likely to receive messages about users' preferences. The providers become the main source of feedback from the users of services and have an ambiguous relationship with them: while they are responsible for finding out what service users prefer, they then have to persuade the purchasers about what they should fund.

Where to purchase and from whom

Here the purchasers may decide to *get the cheapest possible*, subject to a minimum quality standard. Only purchase from people who can provide to the quality required but then organize the purchasing process in such a way that the price is pushed down as far as possible. There is some evidence that the way in which the NHS market has developed is that purchasers concentrate mainly on volume and price.

Secondly, the purchasers may *make a trade-off between price and quality*. This puts a great deal of discretion and judgement in the hands of the purchaser and implies that they should know a lot about how the services are delivered by the service providers.

A third option is to *fix the price in advance and organize the competition process on the quality of services to be provided* at that price. The development of standard prices for services, such as residential care for older people, implies that the only variable to be used in judging from whom to purchase is the quality of the services available for that price.

Managing or controlling the providers

The third set of choices for the purchasers is how to control what the providers do. Here the options are parallel with the choices of how to control the work processes within the organization. Contracts can be written in a way which reproduces the Taylorist approach of breaking the services down into their component parts, specifying what those elements are and then supervising the contract to ensure that each operation is carried out as specified. On the other hand, it could be that the purchaser believes in the development of commitment among the supplier's workforce, the development of new services and new ways of delivering them. The purchasers' answer to this question can have a large impact on the way in which the providers run their organizations.

First they can *control the providers through a detailed specification* of the inputs to be used and the process of producing the service. This reproduces a Taylorist method of control within the previous directly managed supplier.

Secondly, they can *manage the providers by defining very clearly what outcomes are expected* from the service. This approach allows the providers to manage in a way which emphasizes the results of the work and not the elements of work involved in service delivery. Here team-working, flexible job descriptions, personal and service development in response to the preferences and wishes of the service users can all be used as ways of allowing services to develop and allowing the workforce to expand its skills.

Thirdly, purchasers may *control the providers by a process of close and detailed monitoring and inspection*, preferably by independent inspectors. The use of inspection reproduces direct supervision as a management control technique. This method of control could allow the use of commitment as a control mechanism, if the inspection is concerned with the management processes, rather than the detail of service design and delivery.

Fourthly, they may *manage the providers by becoming closely involved in their management and quality assurance procedures*. This approach to service providers has precedents in industrial purchasing, where companies require high-quality components and manage their relationship with their dependent suppliers in such a way as to extend their management processes into those of the suppliers. Just-in-time production, for example, requires suppliers' scheduling of production to fit exactly the final assembly production schedules. The interlocking relationship between companies can even extend to collaborative research and development programmes to ensure compatibility of the new products as product ranges change.

Supplier behaviour

Suppliers in the markets may also choose how to behave, subject to the regulatory framework in which they find themselves. The degree of freedom to manage may vary widely. The managers of the Executive Agencies have found themselves very constrained (see Common et al., 1992). Managers of private and voluntary agencies in the social welfare field still have a degree of independence of action. They can choose their overall strategy, can enter competition if they wish and can decide on the kinds of relationships they wish to have with their staff and the people who use their services.

With regard to the *overall purpose* of the supplier organization, this may be, first, *to make as much money as possible*. While this may be achieved by providing quality services, management effort will be directed towards making sure costs are kept down and revenues are kept up. Secondly, the overall purpose may be to *provide as high a quality of service as possible*, subject to the resources available. If this means making losses on some activities at some times, this will be less important than the quality of the service. Finally, the overall purpose of the supplier organization may be to *grow as big as possible*, not necessarily because big is profitable, but because status and job satisfaction come from organization size. In this case, market share would become the main criterion for judging the success of the organization. Saltman and Von Otter (1992) have suggested that in markets for health care, providers should be allowed to grow as big as possible, as their size will demonstrate their success in meeting the preferences of purchasers and service users.

So far as the *freedom to compete* is concerned, *managers may be allowed to compete for their own work* with outside suppliers but not to go outside and find customers elsewhere. (There are extreme cases in which managers are not even allowed to do this. For example, British Rail maintenance engineering is being contracted out without the in-house teams being allowed to put in a bid.) Secondly, *managers may be allowed to go and find customers* anywhere as long as they make money. For example, in some cases, charities have decided to enter fields of activity in which they previously had no experience. Thirdly, *managers can change their strategy*, including their service portfolio to make themselves more competitive.

Regarding the *freedom to mange*, there are two options: *managers may have a great deal of discretion* to recruit, reward, retain and drain the people who work for them; or *managers may have to work within a framework* set down by an external, controlling body (such as Treasury, Office for the Management of the Civil Service (OMCS), personnel department).

Finally, there is the question of how managers handle the *relationship with service users*. There are a variety of ways in which they can interact with the users of services, according to the way in which the markets are constructed. First, *managers may have to ration services* within criteria laid down by the purchasers and deliver the services according to the specification given by them. Secondly, *managers are responsible for promoting the service*, finding out about customers and their requirements and designing and delivering the services to meet those requirements.

The future

The future of public sector management, from the providers' point of view, depends largely on the nature of the relationship between the state and the users of the services. The entitlement which service users have can range from having a right, either as a citizen or an insured person, to some form of service as long as they meet predetermined criteria of need, to having no pre-set entitlement other than those which come from satisfying locally determined criteria.

Once people have a right to the service, they may then have a variety of rights within it, whether to service standards or to control over the manner of service delivery. The exercise of rights has an impact both on the behaviour of the purchasers and rationers and on the service providers. A move towards rights within services, exercised through the right to choose, would require the implementation of a consumer-based model of service delivery with an emphasis on individual preferences and the design and delivery of services with their consumers. The provider organizations would here take their lead from the consumers, rather than the purchasers. As consumers exercise their power or influence over the services, the provider organizations also have to empower their workers to enable them to respond to the consumers. Detailed control of the work processes through scientific management and through the contracting process denies such empowerment.

The other scenario is that services become increasingly subject to rationing, with few rights exercisable without detailed control through state employees. The division of service delivery between service purchasing and service providing then implies that the purchasers are engaged in a rationing process and determine the volume, shape and standards of services to be provided. The service users then have to accept whatever is offered as a result of the contractual relationships which have been established between the purchasers and providers.

Within the next few years, there will be a continuing emphasis on saving money, to reduce the pressure on spending in the public sector as a whole. This implies stricter rationing, the withdrawal of the state from those responsibilities which it can place on individuals and insurance schemes. It also implies a style of management which emphasizes price and volume control, rather than quality and service development. This control implies detailed control over work process, not least to ensure that the volume and nature of the services is contained within the budgetary and contract constraints.

Rather than entering a period of freedom of choice for service users and post-Taylorist management for the state workers, we are more likely to see a period of strict rationing, price competition and managerial efforts to reduce cost. Management which emphasizes commitment and the development of the workforce implies that service quality can be improved and that workers and service users can enhance the value of services together. It is the opposite of an approach which implies that management designs services, instructs workers how to perform them and then delivers them to the users.

Deming warned that organizations which purchase components and services on the basis of price will never achieve quality products. He argued that people and organizations which need to purchase components and services ought to develop a relationship with their suppliers which allows those products and services to develop in line with the improvement of the final product. Recent experience in both health purchasing and community care purchasing does not seem to be following that advice. In both sectors the emphasis in the purchasing process is on volume and cost.

The new human resource management argues that people should be helped to grow into their jobs rather than be constrained into strictly defined parts of the labour process if organizations are to produce quality services and products. However, the more likely approach is that the emphasis of management will be on control rather than growth of quality and innovation. The consequences for the users of services would be that they will have less control and the services will be less responsive. For the workers in most of the fields of the welfare state there will be strictly defined tasks, control through detailed monitoring and an emphasis on individual performance.

Placing a strong emphasis on the development of people and their commitment requires a different approach. If we assume that markets (or quasi-markets to use the term of Le Grand in *Quasi-markets and Social Policy* (1990) and elsewhere) are to be an essential feature of the welfare state in future, then the approach to management depends on how those markets are operated.

The first requirement is for collaborative arrangements between purchasers and providers. The idea that the purchasers can determine not only what is to be purchased but also the details of the service process reduces the likelihood of flexibility and of service development. Collaboration, recognizing the contribution of the providers to service development and the close relationship between the providers and the service users is more likely to lead to innovation.

The second requirement is an emphasis on outcomes rather than process within the contracts. Especially in those cases where the services are provided by professionals, the purchasers only need to be able to specify the outcomes which are required. The idea, for example, that the Secretary of State for Education, acting through a series of quangos, can determine in detail what will happen in every classroom in the country, implies a view of the education process in which schools are machines, teachers are components and the pupils are raw materials which will respond to the education process in a predictable and uniform way.

The third requirement is the development of trust between purchasers and providers and between provider organizations' managers and their workers. Contracts based on outcomes imply that the people providing the services have skills and experience which enable them to adjust the service process to produce the required outcomes. Such adjustments cannot be subject to detailed and frequent scrutiny other than at great cost.

The final requirement is a definition and recognition of the rights of service users to and within services. Only when these are available to service users will they be able to exercise some control over the services. Only then can public sector managers pursue an approach to quality which is based on what service users prefer.

Unfortunately, the over-riding objective of the current government is to save money. Only when the pressure to reduce or contain spending is eased will it be possible to operate markets in a way which emphasizes quality and service user control.

References

Braverman, H. (1974) *Labour and Monopoly Capitalism*. New York: Monthly Review Press.

Common, R., Flynn, N. and Mellon, E.O. (1992) *Managing Public Services: Competition and Decentralisation*. Oxford: Butterworth-Heinemann.

Deming, W.E. (1986) *Out of the Crisis*. Cambridge MA: MIT.

Handy, C. (1989) *The Age of Unreason*. London: Business Books.

Le Grand, J. (1990) *Quasi-markets and Social Policy*. Bristol: School for Advanced Urban Studies.

Mintzberg, H. (1983) *Structure in Fives: Designing Effective Organisations*. New Jersey: Prentice-Hall.

Morgan, G. (1986) *Images of Organisation*. Beverly Hills: Sage.

Oakland, J.S. (1989) *Total Quality Management*. Oxford: Heinemann.

Saltman, R. and Von Otter, C. (1992) *Planned Markets and Public Competition*. Buckingham: Open University Press.

11

Mission Accomplished or Unfinished Business? The Impact of Managerialization

John Clarke, Allan Cochrane and Eugene McLaughlin

In this book we have made strenuous efforts to avoid a simple or one-dimensional evaluation of the progress and impact of managerialism. There is, therefore, an understandable temptation to make the concluding chapter a definitive audit or 'executive summary' for the reader which states categorically that managerialism represents the rescue of the public sector from its past troubles and will ensure that it never 'reinfects' itself with inefficiency, apathy and waste; or that it is little more than an ideological con trick – a superficial gloss painted over the decaying structures of an under-funded set of public services; or, worse still, that it represents the fifth horseman of the apocalypse, let loose by Thatcherism to lay waste Britain's welfare state. There is evidence to support all these story lines. Our problem is that we believe none of them. While it is possible to indicate what managerialization was supposed to achieve, it is more difficult to determine whether these have been the outcomes in practice. In trying to understand the meaning of the extensive changes that the government (and its opponents) believe they have effected it is easy to confuse intent and accomplishment. With these caveats in mind, this final chapter explores the overall impact of managerialization in the field of social policy.

The politics of change?

Throughout, we have focused on the processes of managerialization and their role in reshaping the core activities of the British welfare state. Each of the chapters has stressed the importance of understanding the politics of these processes, highlighting the crucial role played by post-1979 Conservative governments in framing the wider politics of welfare and providing a context for the new managerialist agenda. It is not possible to avoid discussing the economic, political and ideological conditions in which the micro-processes of organizational change have occurred. In the search for the three 'E's, 'economy' has consistently been given priority over 'efficiency' and 'effectiveness' in the attempt to contain and reduce public spending. These overarching political objectives have also pushed other concerns – questions of equity or social justice, for example – off the social policy agenda. Despite some of the grander claims, therefore, fiscal considerations have placed budgetary control at the core of managerial discipline at the expense of more expansive or radical concerns. Nationally, too, the concern to reform delivery systems has gone hand in hand with a commitment to deliver specific political goals, such as redefining the relationship between the state and the family – with all that that implies in terms of reviving and restoring patriarchal structures of gender relationships and sexuality.

It would, therefore, be tempting to simply place managerialism solely in relation to some 'Thatcherite', neo-liberal or neo-conservative political project which was intent on resolving the fiscal crisis and the ills of British society by replacing the social democratic state with a new market-based managerial regime.

However, we think that such a conclusion represents a partial and incomplete reading of the changes that have occurred in the 1980s and 1990s. It carries with it the danger of leaving critics with nothing more than a politics of nostalgia for the 'old' welfare state. As we have seen throughout this book, one of the effects of managerialism has been to leave opponents and sceptics in the fall-back position of defending the old paternalistic professional bureaucracies as the only, or only 'politically correct', way of co-ordinating the provision of public services. This is clearly not a sustainable position for a variety of reasons. First, the 1980s produced a reworking of party political positions on the provision of public goods, with an increasing degree of consensus about the need for, and irreversibility of, organizational reform, whether in the form of internal markets, mixed economies or welfare pluralism. Of course, each of these reforms may be given different political inflections but all presume that there can be 'no going back'. Secondly, it should never be forgotten that the critics of the old settlements and the practices of the professional bureaucracies were not only to be found in neo-conservative think tanks (indeed they came rather late to the scene). State services, and the value systems underpinning them, had been the object of wide-ranging and fundamental critiques from a variety of positions – feminists, anti-racists and 'user' movements – long before 1979 (Taylor, 1993; Williams, 1993). The new urban left council administrations of the early 1980s also stressed the importance of user involvement, empowerment and decentralization, as well as the need to break down traditional (male-dominated) professional hierarchies within local welfare states (Gyford, 1985; Blunkett and Jackson, 1987). Despite the official government denunciations of the time, some aspects of the new managerialism in practice can be understood as a reworking of these ambitions to fit with a period of fiscal austerity and apparently permanent Conservative Party rule at national level.

There is a danger of seeing too close a fit between the political objectives of the Conservative governments of the 1980s and 1990s and the character of managerialism itself. The rise of managerialism across the public sector is *not* just a product of changes initiated by those governments. On the contrary, while their policies may have helped to shape what is (and is not) possible – for example, as Norman Flynn argues in Chapter 10, by effectively narrowing the managerial choices which are available – managerialism has its own independent significance. As earlier chapters have indicated, the interaction between political programme and managerial agenda has been crucial in determining outcomes and both may also be seen as implicated in wider processes of social, economic and political restructuring (such as the move towards a Schumpeterian workforce state which is discussed by Tom Ling in Chapter 2). A conclusion which centres solely on the dimension of national politics would misread the nature of the changes.

An ideological success?

We have no doubt that the ideology of new managerialism has helped to unlock the 'old settlements' of the social democratic state and is part of a strategy to move beyond the resultant 'gridlock'. Our view of ideology is not one which sees it as a 'smokescreen' separate from or a disguise for 'real changes' taking place. 'Taking managerialism seriously' as an ideology means looking at the way in which it reshapes or recasts the contexts and the frames of reference – indeed the very language – within which decisions about public services are made. It has destabilized and reorganized the complex balance of powers and interests which characterized the old regimes by, at one and the same time, providing a prescriptive explanation of what was wrong and highlighting what could be done to make things right. Earlier chapters have analysed specific dimensions of the processes of destabilization and reorganization across a range of policy sectors. Here we return to some of the broader patterns of change, focusing on the role of the managerial discourses in the move to mixed economies of provision and the disciplines of quasi-markets.

Although the provision of key social and welfare services in Britain has never been, as is sometimes assumed, a state monopoly (since there have always been mixed economies involving distribution of tasks and responsibilities between different sectors) the policy shifts of the 1980s and 1990s have changed the nature of the prevailing mix and blurred the boundaries between sectors (Pinker, 1992; Clarke and Langan, 1993). The new relationships between statutory, private, voluntary and informal provision have changed both organizational boundaries (through joint working, 'strategic' partnership and contracting) and undermined distinctions between previously differentiated workforces. Perhaps the clearest example of this is to be found in the growing 'professionalism' of the voluntary sector – where moves towards paid volunteering have been accompanied by increased investment in training and certification, quasi-contractual employment relationships and greater managerial supervision and direction (see, for example, Gutch and Young, 1992). All organizations – not just the public sector ones – are now striving to become 'more business-like' which implies the development of managerial competencies and capacities such as contracting and marketing skills, financial management and performance assessment systems.

The development of this cluster of orientations reflects the permeation of managerialism throughout the field of public provision (no matter what the status of the provider organization). The motivations are complex, ranging from the necessity to develop such capacities to survive in the new mixed economy (by winning contracts and obtaining grants), through to perceived opportunities for advancing both interests (servicing a specific need) and principles (community self-government). All of these can be mobilized through managerialism, even though the organizations may not be committed to managerialism itself other than as a tactical necessity. But in the process they become available for 're-presentation' as the successful embodiments of a common principle, as for example in the subsumption of diverse and often conflicting initiatives under the umbrella of the 'entrepreneurial spirit' by Osborne and Gaebler (1992). In this sense, managerialism has been a profound ideological success. The fundamental logic of 'economy, efficiency and effectiveness' (and 'value for money') is now widely accepted, providing the frame of reference within which decisions must be justified. In the process, alternative forms of legitimation and justification (such as those concerned with equity, which Alan Clarke stresses in Chapter 8) have been marginalized.

Embracing managerialism has real consequences. It is not simply a matter of learning to speak the language or adjusting to new rules of the game – because both the language and the rules have material effects. Which targets or performance indicators are chosen may reflect the politics of organizational power and compromise, but in turn they shape the flow of power, resources, organizational attention and rewards. Contracting for services puts a premium on delivering those parts of the organization's service specified in contract no matter how valued other activities might be. The choice of which powers and resources to devolve (and to whom) is not just a central issue: it helps to determine the lines of future power relations (and conflicts) within organizations.

Just as managerialization has spread through the cluster of organizations involved in the provision and regulation of public goods, so too has it influenced the internal lives of those organizations. While most organizations are becoming 'business-like', so, too, everybody within them has to come to terms with managerialization. The impact of the new managerialism, with its stress on devolution, decentralization and organizational cultures in which 'we all take responsibility', has brought the proliferation of managerialization deep within organizations. In the process, increasing numbers of people at different layers in a range of organizational settings have had to consciously reimagine themselves and their roles within the framework of managerialism. Whether this be the setting of objectives or targets, preparing business plans or managing limited resources, there has been a dispersal of 'managerial consciousness' beyond the higher echelons. This aspect of managerialism is profoundly populist, stressing the capacity of everyone to take responsibility and make decisions rather than identifying 'management' with a distinctive cadre or organizational élite. In the process members of the organizational elite are reinvented as 'leaders' or 'strategists', but in the context of shifting intra-organizational balances of power. Again, this multiplication of management is not all pointing in the same direction: as the chapters by Norman Flynn and by Sylvia Walby and June Greenwell indicate, 'Taylorism' is alive and well in many of the 'new' arrangements. But it does reframe where and how decisions can be made and justified.

The new managerialism presents itself as an agency of revolutionary change within organizations, often utilizing the language of paradox to emphasize its claims. Organizational pyramids are to be inverted, impossible thoughts thought, chaos thrived on and unreason embraced. Management (not the proletariat) is to be the agent of permanent revolution. These are powerful and exciting claims for those used to the stifling conservatism of public bureaucracies. And, in principle at least, they appear to offer new hope to groups that have been systematically marginalized and controlled within those bureaucracies. In particular one might expect them to open up new opportunities for women who have been sidelined by the old professional structures. In practice, however, matters have been rather different, so that for example – as Sylvia Walby and June Greenwell note – in the NHS is those areas (like nursing) with large female workforces which have been most clearly subjected to neo-Taylorist approaches, while – as Janet Newman powerfully argues – even women within the managerial strata find significant new obstacles to their progression and their ability to influence managerial practices. Ironically (although perhaps not surprisingly) it is – as Mary Langan and John Clarke note – precisely in those areas of welfare professionalism (such as social work) where women have tended to dominate that the managerial challenges have been most extensively developed.

The proliferation of managerialism is one of the clearest indications of the processes of restructuring in state organizations. It marks a significant shift away from the old assumptions which dominated the cultures of professional bureaucracies. However, it is less clear that a 'new regime' has been created in the form of a restabilized balance of power and interests. The remodelling of the public sector remains 'unfinished business' rather than 'mission accomplished'. Despite appearances to the contrary, managerialism has not placed an 'unbreakable seal' over British society. In the remainder of this chapter we will discuss how managerialism, in its attempt to deliver depoliticization and the 'right to manage' through empowerment and customer choice, is also generating new alliances and new sites of conflict.

Depoliticization?

There are a number of ways in which it is possible to see managerialism as part of an attempt to 'depoliticize' social policy provision. In the context of competing objectives, multiple demands and limited resources, there is no doubt that part of the appeal of managerialism lies in its promise to go beyond politics (whether party, interest group or organizational micro-politics) and produce rational and efficient decisions about the deployment of resources. As we have argued at the beginning of this chapter, managerialism has helped to shift the public political discourse about social policy away from traditional concerns with inputs and outputs towards an overarching concern with efficiency and the organizational means of service delivery. In the neo-conservative vision managers take on the responsibility for the delivery of services while the government prioritizes, funds and evaluates. This reconceptualization involves a double paradox. On the one hand, the 'apolitical' character of management replaces the 'apolitical' bureau-professionalism which had previously exemplified the technicist and depoliticized response to social problems in social democratic states. Both bureaucracy and professionalism were 'sold' to the public in the 1960s and 1970s as representing transcendent sets of rules and knowledges (expertise) which supposedly guaranteed the neutrality of state intervention. By comparison, in the 1980s and 1990s bureaucracy and professionalism have been identified as partisan interests which require the creation of new 'apolitical' disciplines (the market place, management and the evaluative state) to check their powers. In part, this paradox is an outcome of the second one. The 'depoliticization' associated with managerialism is being driven by one of the most politicized restructurings of the core of the British state during this century. In the process, as was outlined by Janet Newman and John Clarke in Chapter 1, the various powerholders within the old regime were identified as problems or potential blockages to the reform programme.

The restructuring around managerialism, as many of the chapters have noted, has involved a double movement, with a highly visible devolution of responsibilities taking place at the same time as less visible centralization of power to ministers. In effect this has ensured that the devolved responsi-bilities and powers have been tightly framed both in terms of policy and in terms of financial control. As a result, attempts to 'depoliticize' social policy by stressing the apparently superordinate, and neutral, criteria of 'economy, efficiency and effectiveness' that are to be achieved by the new manage-ment, have only been partially successful. In a variety of areas – the NHS, the introduction of Community Care, the Poll Tax, education, law and order – the government has failed to devolve responsibility (and blame), being publicly and politically identified with (and blamed for) the new policies.

This has been exacerbated by the political problems of governing these semi-devolved state regimes. Attempts to maintain 'arm's-length' or 'hands-off' governance of agencies have been undermined by the constant temptation and, in certain instances, political necessity to intervene in order to reaffirm policy directions, reconsider the direction of reform or to deal with emergent problems of process and practice. Thus, when the NHS's internal market produced (economically rational) patterns of spending whereby hospitals had met their contractual quotas in the first nine months of a twelve-month period (in 1992–3), ministers were obliged to intervene to reset the rules of the contracting 'game' to ensure that other objectives were included in the calculations.

With such interventions a variety of dissatisfactions with the new regimes and new tensions within the regimes have become visible. Government unpopularity increased as their policies were held responsible by customers (for example, in their role as voters in by-elections) for producing irrationalities in the first place. The government publicly castigated managers for failing to manage effectively. Managers became disenchanted and angry as the 'market' no longer resembled a market but was apparently subject to political whim and diktat. Disgruntled professionals used the irrational outcomes to demonstrate that the reforms were flawed in the first place, and to remind the public that they, rather than the managers, were the guardians of a 'quality' public service. These tensions serve as a reminder that, while managerialization played a central role in destabilizing the power bases and relationships of the old regime, the new regime remains contested *and* contestable at a variety of levels. As a consequence, in certain instances, it may be more accurate to argue that managerialism precisely because it has dislocated the old regime, has in certain instances, *politicized* rather than depoliticized public service issues, even if the form of politics has begun to change.

The old in the new?

There is little doubt that in the 1980s whole groups of state bureau-professionals were on the defensive in the face of a concerted managerialist onslaught. Previously taken-for-granted professional powers, discretion, roles and values were constantly challenged and frequently displaced. The chapters in this book demonstrate just how widespread and thoroughgoing that dislocation has been in education (Chapter 5), criminal justice (Chapter 6) and leisure services (Chapter 8) as well as social services (Chapter 4) and the NHS (Chapter 3), central government (Chapter 1) as well as local government (Chapter 7). However, the operative words here are 'challenge', 'displacement' and 'dislocation' – not 'abolition' and 'overthrow'. As managerialist gurus constantly stress, redefining the balance of power within an organization is different from removing power.

There are a number of different reasons why bureau-professionalism has survived within the new regimes as a troubling presence. First, established professional power and status provided an important basis from which managerialization could be resisted and/or negotiated. The differences are significant: the medical and legal professions have fared better in their ability to negotiate change than have teachers and social workers, for example. Their ability to resist owes much to the degree of traditional professional independence from the state they enjoy in comparison to the dependent 'semi-professions' of teaching and social work (Johnson, 1973). But even they have not been immune from an approach which identified all professions as monopolies, even those who might have seen themselves as 'natural' conservative constituencies, as problems to be overcome. Thus, as Brazier et al. (1993: 199) argue, even the medical and legal professions at the end of the 1980s 'were more tightly controlled by the state than at the start of the Thatcher era, and were also more exposed to competitive forces'. More and more GPs have had to adjust to the uncomfortable disciplines (as well as the incentives) imposed by being partners in fund-holding practices while law firms are having to come to terms with the consequences of the recent overhaul of the legal aid scheme. In addition, barristers have had to remain ever vigilant to the possibility of the government breaking their monopoly over high court business.

Secondly, it has become increasingly apparent that within the restructuring of the state, bureau-professionalism cannot simply be dispensed with. Even reorganized departments and agencies require service deliverers with particular skills, service orientations and commitments. Thus, we would argue that the survival of bureau-professionalism in a variety of organizational settings is not just an idiosyncratic hangover from the old regime; nor does it always constitute residual pockets of countervailing power. It is a *necessary* component of the new: what is at stake is not the eradication of bureau-professionalism but the degree to which *relevant* clusters of skills and values can be subordinated to and accommodated within the new political and organizational logics embodied in managerialism. The chapters in this book identify a variety of ground rules for this accommodation and subordination: the exposure to market-testing and alternative delivery systems; the removal of discretionary powers; the positioning of management over professionals; the conversion of bureau-professionals to managers and the creation of localized settlements. All of these have sought to constrain professional autonomy within new and tighter forms of organizational discipline but their overall success is contingent on the nature of the organization and the power base of particular professions.

The result is the creation of highly unstable balances of power and 'dangerous liaisons' in which a multiplicity of both public and private struggles persist. These have ranged from periodic confrontations between the government and professionals (for example, the BMA over the consequences of the government's health reforms and the teaching unions over testing) to intra-organizational skirmishes about the boundaries of professional and managerial power and control. What these conflicts demonstrate is the ongoing potential for managerialist discourses and practices to be ruptured by bureau-professionals and allied occupational groupings who are still capable of exercising control over work situations and wresting concessions and legitimacy from management.

Dependency culture?

There is a fundamental paradox at the heart of managerialism. It presents itself as a strong and authoritative discourse: it speaks of leadership and strategies for the future; of rational and effective use of resources and of vigorous pursuit of goals, missions and targets. Yet management is a profoundly dependent relationship in two senses. As Newman and Clarke argue in Chapter 1, it is a mode of power which is essentially devolved and is thus *dependent* on both the direction set from above and the degree of power devolved from above. One recurrent complaint from managers in the public sector is that for the most part they are not allowed to be 'real' managers (that is, like those in the private sector) because they are still ring-fenced by the limitations of political direction. They are not, as yet, allowed sufficient autonomy to exploit the 'right to manage': a concern exemplified in the reaction of health trust managers to the Secretary of State for Health's decision in 1993 to retain Regional Health Authorities to oversee the internal market. In the same period there have been similar complaints from those in charge of government departments that have moved to agency status. Ministers hoped that agencies would opt for fully private status but the necessary environment was not forthcoming. Managers found that the overall policy parameters were tighter and that the freedom to manage had only been made secure in relation to staffing issues. Therefore, there was no incentive to move fully into the private sector.

Managers are also dependent on those who constitute their human resources. Employees form the core resource through which missions may be accomplished, targets met and long-term cultural shifts achieved. One view of the history of managerialism places this issue at its centre – the problem of how to co-ordinate and control the potentially recalcitrant workforces which it seeks to direct (Rose, 1975). Managerialism is marked by a sequence of promises that a given approach will overcome this fundamental issue – the 'people problem' of the 'people business'. While the policy, organizational and industrial relations changes of the 1980s un-questionably tilted the balance of structural power towards managers, they did not resolve the problems of directing and motivating the remaining workforce in an environment of performance-related pay, radically altered working conditions and the ever-present threat of outsourcing. The role of management in the public sector and the lessons drawn from the private sector remain uncertain. Some organizations (and some parts of some organizations) explicitly set out to pursue straightforward Taylorist attempts to impose increased labour discipline at the same time as others (and even other parts of the same organization) set out to pursue a more conscious policy of devolved and collaborative working, in which discipline is largely self-imposed.

Within the new balance of power, management must still strive to win the 'hearts and minds' of the managed rather than be satisfied with mere grudging acquiescence. As Norman Flynn's chapter demonstrates, manage-ment within public services may choose to adopt different strategies for 'human resource management' (although financial constraints limit even these). But the motivation problem will always be just beyond resolution by these strategies and it is in the complex of motivational issues within public services that management will remain vulnerable. These issues are usually addressed in terms of 'values' – corporate values, professional values, vocational values or the ethos of public service. And it is on this uncomfortably transparent normative terrain that management is exposed because the value systems which managerialism promotes, as they are constructed within managerialism, are limited, being viewed as functional, shared and essentially integrative (Painter, 1992; Willmott, 1993). The resultant 'commitment' to agreement and consensus paradoxically provides a space for dispute and contestation. It is no coincidence that professional and occupational resistances to managerial authority and managerial changes continue to question fundamentally management's commitment to the 'real' values of public service as opposed to the cost-effective values of the market. Thus there is considerable scope for interrogating managerialism on its own terms by pointing to the inconsistencies and contradictions of and deviations from its stated value systems.

The outcome is complex patterns of intra-organizational conflict, co-option and compromise as management seeks both to bring professionals 'on board' (through the promise of a 'people-centred' environment) and haul them 'into line' (through the threat of compulsory competitive tendering and neo-Taylorist strategies). As a consequence, public sector organizations have taken on the character of unstable alliances and oppositions – producing peculiar hybrids either as professionals become managers or as managers and professionals produce uneasily balanced missions, visions and objectives which try to reconcile and articulate 'business', 'professional', 'corporate' and 'bureaucratic' cultures. We have suggested that these are unstable because the patterns of restructuring have created a variety of inconsistencies and fields of conflict around managerialization. These might be seen as ranging from an attempt to specify 'what business we are in' in broad terms, to the minutiae of what aspects of the organization should be reflected in targets, objectives or performance indicators. 'Quality', for example, has become a point of reference to which all parties are formally dedicated. However, they may well take it to mean profoundly different things, with managerial visions of quality assurance or TQM jostling uncomfortably alongside professional visions of quality as the attainment of professional standards, while both have an uneasy relationship with the hopes, needs and ambitions of 'users'.

Reconciling multiple interests?

The tensions between professionalism and managerialism are only one subset of a wider cluster of processes associated with managerial restructuring. In public service settings, managerialism is exposed to the demands of competing interests (or, in its own terms, multiple stakeholders) which identify themselves as having a legitimate voice in the creation of objectives, standards and agendas. Such interests include different occupational groups within service organizations, the varieties of national and local political representatives, 'partner' organizations in the statutory, voluntary and private sectors, 'community' representatives, service users and tax payers.

The language of managerialism, with its stress on responsiveness, implies a degree of openness to the interests of these multiple constituencies, and such orientations are further strengthened by the salience of ideas of collaboration, strategic partnership and customer-centredness. An optimistic reading of such developments suggests that they have created a greater degree of accountability in public service organizations as managers have had to respond to the expressed concerns and needs of diverse 'stakeholders' and consumers. In the process, old-fashioned and moribund democratic processes of legitimation and representation linking the agency to the public have been transcended by more dynamic, multi-faceted, transparent and therefore 'real' forms of accountability to 'customers'.

A less optimistic reading would see such changes as creating a significantly enhanced flexibility for management. They create a field of competing demands and multiple interests within which managers assess, negotiate and trade off between the different interests, calculating where power, interest and advantage lie. In such a scenario, responsiveness is likely to follow well-worn channels associated with social, economic and political power. However, even within this more pessimistic reading, there remain questions about both the degree to which management has been empowered in the process of restructuring and how far its capacity to define directions and set agendas has been enhanced. The existence of differential sources of power which work themselves through the managerial decision-making process means that the freedom of managers to manoeuvre in their 'task environment' may be profoundly constrained, not least by the increased capacity of the state to define both policy and resourcing. Thus, as management is finding out, its 'right to manage' is, in practice, very tightly framed.

In part, the complexity of this situation is illustrative of the argument made by Newman and Clarke in Chapter 1 that management itself has no 'superordinate' goals, only those devolved to it and to which it dedicates itself in pursuit of efficiency. This exposes the 'superordinate goals' – the missions – of public services to a high degree of contestation as different coalitions of politicians, professionals and users attempt to inflect those goals in particular directions. One certain effect of managerialism is this increased exposure to conflict over what 'superordinate goals' should be.

Empowerment?

One particular site of these complex conflicts is the increasingly widespread enthusiasm for 'empowerment' in a period of de-democratization. We can identify a multiplicity of empowerments which are current in the contemporary world of public services. One, as we have already discussed, is the empowerment of managers themselves in the creation of greater autonomy and the enhanced 'right to manage' services. A second is the commitment of the new managerialism to empower employees as participants in the process of change, to devolve greater autonomy and responsibility within organizations to, or at least towards, the 'front line' in the search for more responsive working practices. A third is the empowerment of the service user in relation to public organizations, most characteristically in the form of increased 'choice' or personalized attention and the establishment of limited quasi-contractual rights concerning service delivery (for example, the citizen's charter and its variants). A fourth is the empowerment of communities, sometimes defined in terms of their geographical basis but more often as 'communities of interest' which involves more or less expansive views of redressing imbalance of power between the state and particular social groups or within the broader social structure (these debates are discussed by Allan Cochrane in the local government context in Chapter 7). In their most developed form, these arguments about empowerment are the expression of demands from and responses to social movements 'beyond' the state, for example, feminism, anti-racism and disability (see, for example, Croft and Beresford, 1992).

Empowerment thus has a place at the intersection of a variety of interests and appears to connect very different discourses – political, professional and managerial. But the objectives and processes at stake in these different approaches to empowerment suggest that their intersection is more apparent than real. Empowerment as devolved responsibility, empowerment as customer rights and empowerment as redistribution of power constitute very different processes and very different definitions of power. As a consequence, empowerment functions as a focal point for both potential consensus and potential conflict. In this sense empowerment is a 'loose cannon'. Its ambiguity allows the possibility of consensus which 'takes account of', even if it does not satisfy, different interests – and, like efficiency, its desirability seems self-evident.

However, each of the variants mentioned above carries, in practice, the potential for further conflict. Thus devolved responsibility creates organizational disturbances where real or effective power is not seen to be accompanying ever-increasing responsibility (and becomes perceived as dumping the dirty work on those at the bottom) or where such empowerment occurs in an environment of service rationing, cutbacks and closures. Customer – or market – empowerment creates frustrations where promises are qualified by arbitrarily imposed contractual limitations or where, as in the case of British Rail, contractual redress substitutes for effective service delivery. It may also cause problems where customers take their 'promised' empowerment too seriously and become only too aware of the fact that there has been a clear cutback on rights in the gradual demise of universalism. Community empowerment is potentially the most fraught version. It invokes both the need and demand for an effective redistribution of power, and is thus the object of considerable resistance from existing power holders. However, it can also be conceptualized as the transfer of responsibilities such that communities (of interest or geography) find themselves encouraged to 'take the lead' or 'provide for their own' without the transfer of power or resources to achieve effective results. The government's public sector housing 'right to manage' scheme is a classic example of the problems surrounding community empowerment. Tenant groups can choose to take over the client function from local authority housing departments but at present they are excluded from taking responsibility for the capital programme and rent and repair policies. This leaves participating groups with considerable responsibilities but little real power.

Customer choice?

The issues surrounding empowerment raise more general questions about the meaningfulness of the customer revolution. The ideological figure of the sovereign customer – the rechristened citizen – is one of the points of connection between neo-conservative social policy and the new managerialism. Both are committed to the centrality of the customer in the re-making of organizations. But, as many of the chapters in this book have detailed, the customer of public services is a much more ambiguous figure than the one celebrated in classical economics and management texts. The conventional market relationship is neither so simple nor so transparent in the public realm. Public customers include those who pay for services but do not consume them (streetlighting on a dual carriageway); those who are forced to consume them but may not have to pay for them (prison sentences); those who benefit inadvertently (visitors using services in a local authority area) and those where the exercise of choice is either undesirable or unimaginable (policing). Thus, in the case of the public realm, 'the customer' is constructed at a distance with complexly delineated rights and interests.

Of all the problems that have emerged, by design or default, out of the empowerment and consumerization process, none is so potent as the issue of competition between customers for access to public services. In a resource-limited environment, there is an emerging 'politics of difference' as increasing stress is laid on setting priorities for services. This evokes a variety of special pleading based on the worth or value of different and competing needs – ranging from health priorities to library services – and runs the risk of prioritizing different groups of need as more or less worthy. Such competition takes place in a field of conflicting criteria for judgement, with conflicting ideologies underlying those criteria. In such situations, concerns for cost effectiveness – and what effectiveness should mean – coexist uneasily alongside criteria of social justice, individual rights, professional evaluations of merit and desert. Status, in the sense of social evaluation of worthiness, and wealth muddy the waters of priority setting further in an overall context where payment for certain public services has become an increasingly significant issue. There is little reason to believe that managerial judgements and criteria will resolve, rather than further complicate, the tensions embedded in the relationship between need and resources. Such tensions are endemic to the public sector and while empowerment and customer rights are presented as solutions they should be seen as no more than 'magical solutions' – rhetorically powerful, but leaving the underlying tensions unaltered. What they do change is the way that these tensions are conceptualized, discussed and evaluated.

The politics of policy

As we have seen, managerialism has helped to shift the public political discourse about social policy away from the traditional concerns with inputs and outputs into an overarching concern with efficiency – the organizational means of service delivery. But as the chapters in this book have demonstrated, there is a wide variety of politics which now contest managerialized social provision. One dimension is the complex of intra-organizational struggles for power and authority. A second is the cluster of struggles around the boundaries of state and non-state agencies concerning the balance of different components of the mixed economies of provision. A third dimension concerns the efforts to shape different versions of 'accountability' and 'representation' within a state system which has seen both the multiplication of diverse forms of accountability and the multiplication of non-elected forms of government. A fourth concerns the struggles to articulate and prioritize 'needs' and interests of different kinds and to connect them to power and resources. Finally, as Norman Flynn's chapter demonstrated, there are conflicts between different versions of 'how to manage'. None of these conflicts maps coherently on to another – professionals may ally with user groups in the name of self-determination against the exercise of managerial control; the efforts of marginalized social groups to gain access to managerial positions do not always sit easily with struggles of such groups as service users; the advocates of radical decentralization and empowerment find themselves aligned with advocates of minimally resourced 'self-help'.

In these complex realignments there is the possibility of a new 'consensus' which could be built around managerialized social provision. It would rest on the fundamental commitment to be 'business-like'; a recognition on all parts that managerial authority and disciplines are necessary to create efficient services. Around that core, though, it is possible to see a variety of concessions which address some of the interests of different groups as part of a settlement. So, service users are promised a degree of empowerment/choice/personalized attention in return for taking 'greater responsibility' for themselves. Professionals are promised a stake in redefining the culture or public service ethos of the organization in return for subjecting themselves to managerial authority. Employees are promised a more 'people-centred' working environment (or the chance to keep their jobs) in return for doing 'more for less'. Local political representatives are offered a 'strategic role' in exchange for conceding to managers the 'right to manage'. Voluntary organizations are promised an expanded role and continuing funding if they turn themselves into well-run (business-like) enterprises. There is a sense in which managerialism has opened up the possibility that 'everyone can be a winner' – the claim that organizational reform created the conditions of getting 'more for less' underpins these multiple promises. It is no longer a zero-sum game in which any new win is achieved at someone else's expense. We are sceptical about whether the conditions underlying these changes can in fact deliver on these multiple promises. But at present, these seem to us to be the dominant trends in the way managerial authority is reshaping social provisions and constitute the skeletal form of a new consensus.

In this context of multiple and fragmented conflicts and diverse possibilities, it is difficult to write a simple, singular conclusion about the managerialization of social provision. Too much is still at stake, and there are too many stakeholders, for us to be prescriptive at this point. What we see, and what we hope this book had made clear, is that the transformative power of managerialism has been profoundly effective in unlocking the old structures of provision and considerably less effective in producing a new settlement. Such destabilization has created a new and complex politics which includes possibilities for radical changes in favour of service users, in the direction of more decentralized systems, towards more 'empowerment' of individuals and communities. But such an optimistic reading of the possibilities needs to be set against a more pessimistic reading of the conditions under which these changes are developing.

The continuing 'fiscal crisis of the state' and government solutions which have prioritized the containment or reduction of public spending have necessitated the search for 'alternative approaches' to service delivery but simultaneously constrain the resources within which such alternatives may operate. For both state and non-state agencies, the themes of economy and efficiency have predominated over effectiveness – or any other objectives such as equity. Such fiscal conditions have placed a premium on budgetary control as a core of managerial disciplines at the expense of more expansive or radical concerns. In national terms, too, social policies have tended to be framed by overarching neo-conservative commitments to shifting the relationship between the state and the family. It is, perhaps, too easy to forget these macro-dimensions of economics, politics and ideology when examining the micro-politics of organizational change. As the chapters of this book have shown, however, the two are interlinked. Organizational reforms have not gone on separate from policy changes: rather, the concern to reform 'delivery systems' has gone hand in hand with viewing those systems as delivering particular policies – whether it be the shift of responsibility to carers in community care or the delivery of more targeted benefits through new agencies.

These dimensions of national policy coincide with a further cluster of concerns about the politics of organizational change, which have to do with the capacity of forms of power to resist and redefine themselves in the face of change. Within this, we might refer to both occupational groupings as power bases and to the intersection of organizational authority with wider social dimensions of power. In the former, we might consider the ability of both managerial and professional groupings to re-legitimate themselves by 'speaking for' the service user (the one by virtue of customer surveys; the other by virtue of by 'close to the customer'). In the latter, particularly in the light of Janet Newman's chapter, we might consider the recuperative capacity of male power within organizations in the face of demands for greater access for women to managerial positions (see also Cockburn, 1991).

These pessimistic observations are intended as a reminder that 'playing fields' are never level and that the 'rules of the game' always represent somebody's rules rather than an abstract or disinterested set of principles. In the language of management itself, there may be 'multiple stakeholders' but there are profound differences in the power, authority or influence which different stakeholders can bring to bear. There are diverse possibilities associated with the process of managerialization but there are also clear indications of the ways in which some of these possibilities are likely to be accentuated or foreclosed in the 1990s. That likely pattern of development may be less than a fully blown 'business plan' but it certainly prioritizes some 'visions' over others.

But alternative visions *are* possible. It is still feasible to imagine 'blue skies' possibilities for radical changes in favour of service users, in the direction of more decentralized systems, improved service delivery, towards a greater empowerment of individuals and communities in ways that were not imaginable under the old social democratic settlement and are not realizable under the new managerialism. If managerialism, with all its limitations, can envision a post-capitalist world shaped in its own image (as Drucker, 1993, does) it must also be possible to conceive of a 'post-capitalist' world constituted around principles of citizenship and social justice. Reinventing democratic citizenship, where power rather than responsibility is shared, would bring users and citizens into political decision-making processes about the shaping and provision of services. This would imply a real cultural change with the negative contractual rights accorded by the market place replaced by the positive social, political and economic rights conferred by participatory citizenship. More important, as we have tried to indicate throughout the book, there are already tensions and pressures at the heart of this new world which are likely to generate forms of oppositional politics that continue to suggest different possibilities and cannot just be 'managed' away.

References

Blunkett, D. and Jackson, K. (1987) *Democracy in Crisis. The Town Halls Respond*. London: Hogarth Press.

Brazier, M., Lovecy, J., Moran, M. and Potton, M. (1993) 'Falling from a tightrope: doctors and lawyers between the market and the State'. *Political Studies*, 41(2): 197–213.

Clarke, J. and Langan, M. (1993) 'Restructuring welfare: the British welfare regime in the 1980s', in A. Cochrane and J. Clarke (eds), *Comparing Welfare States*. London: Sage.

Cockburn, C. (1991) *In the Way of Women: Men's Resistance to Sex Equality in Organizations*. Basingstoke: Macmillan.

Croft, S. and Beresford, P. (1992) 'The politics of participation', *Critical Social Policy*, 35: 20–44.

Drucker, P. (1993) *Post-capitalist Society*. London: Harper Collins.

Gutch, R. and Young, K. (1992) *Partners or Rivals? A Discussion Paper on the Relationship between Local Government and the Voluntary Sector*. Luton: Local Government Training Board.

Gyford, J. (1985) *The Politics of Local Socialism*. London: Allen & Unwin.

Johnson, T. (1973) *Professions and Power*. London: Macmillan.

Osborne, D. and Gaebler, T. (1992) *Reinventing Government: How the Entrepreneurial Spirit is Transforming the Public Sector*. Reading, MA: Addison Wesley.

Painter, C. (1992) 'The public sector and current orthodoxies: revitalization or decay?' *Political Quarterly*, 62(1): 75–89.

Pinker, R. (1992) 'Making sense of the mixed economy of welfare', *Social Policy and Administration*, 26(4): 273–85.

Rose, M. (1975) *Industrial Behaviour*. London: Allen Lane.

Taylor, G. (1993) 'Challenges from the margins', in J. Clarke (ed.), *A Crisis in Care?* London: Sage.

Williams, F. (1993) 'Gender, "race" and class in British welfare policy', in A. Cochrane and J. Clarke (eds), *Comparing Welfare States*. London: Sage.

Willmott, H. (1993) 'Strength is ignorance; slavery is freedom: managing culture in modern organisations', *Journal of Management Studies*, 30(4): 515–52.

Index